SOPHIE
SCHOLL

THE REAL STORY OF
THE WOMAN
WHO DEFIED
HITLER

FRANK McDONOUGH

For Cecile Lowenthal Hensel
who also opposed Hitler's Nazi regime

Cover illustrations: (front) Sophie Scholl as a teenager, 1938 © Manuel
Aicher; (back) Sophie Scholl at home in Münsterplatz, 1942 © Manuel
Aicher

First published 2009
This edition 2010

The History Press
The Mill, Brimscombe Port
Stroud, Gloucestershire, GL5 2QG
www.thehistorypress.co.uk

British Library Cataloguing in Publication Data.
A catalogue record for this book is available from the British Library.

ISBN 978 0 7524 5511 2

Typesetting and origination by The History Press
Printed in Great Britain

CONTENTS

The political history of all nations has hardly ever produced anything greater and nobler than the opposition which existed in Germany. These people fought without any help, whether from within or from without, driven only by the uneasiness of their consciences. As long as they were alive, they were invisible to us, because they had to put on masks. But their deaths brought their resistance to light.

SIR WINSTON CHURCHILL

I know that life is a doorway to eternity, and yet my heart so often gets lost in petty anxieties. It forgets the great way home that lies before it.

SOPHIE SCHOLL

INTRODUCTION

On 22 February 1943, three Munich University students belonging to a non-violent resistance group called 'the White Rose' were executed by the Nazi regime. One of them was a twenty-one-year-old woman called Sophie Scholl. Her youthful defiance against a monstrous tyranny has made her a legendary figure. There are countless schools, streets and squares named in her honour. In 1999, the popular German women's magazine *Brigitte* voted her 'Woman of the Twentieth Century'. In a major German TV series in 2003, called *Greatest Germans*, Sophie Scholl was the highest-ranked German woman of all time. In 2005, a German film called *Sophie Scholl: The Final Days* became a major box-office hit.

In this book I provide the first full-scale biography of this truly iconic figure, which draws on a wide variety of original documents, including her letters and diaries, key Gestapo interrogation documents, court files and interviews with important survivors. The problem in dealing with the life of such a saint-like figure is the easy temptation to ignore evidence or gloss over incidents that render the image more complex. I have decided to present what I have discovered in full. I know every biographer claims they are about to relate an incredible story, but what is so fascinating about this biography is that I take you not only inside Sophie Scholl's inner thoughts and feelings, but also on a journey inside Nazi Germany to the life of an ordinary family living in a small city.

What emerges is the story of an ordinary person who chose to make a courageous stand against Hitler's regime, not with bombs, but with words, expressed in leaflets, that proclaim a moral and religious opposition to

Nazism and a passionate desire to live in a free society. This is a heart-rending tale of a principled, free-spirited, fascinating and life-affirming young woman living in the wrong place at the wrong time. Let's go in search of Sophie Scholl.

ONE

GROWING UP

Sophie Magdalena Scholl was born in Forchtenberg on 9 May 1921. This small, provincial, scenic rural village had a population of 900 people at the time of Sophie's birth. It is located on the Hochstrasse, in the district of Hohenlohekreis, in the south German state of Baden-Württemberg. It lies on the site of a partly fortified north-facing hill, overlooking the rich vineyards and farmland of the picturesque Kocher valley, at the point where the Kupfer River flows into the Kocher River. Sophie's earliest memories were of playing in the beautiful countryside surrounding the picture-postcard village and swimming in the river. Wine-producing has always been a central aspect of the area. Vineyards enclosed by stone walls litter the terrain.

Forchtenberg was originally established as an overspill from the nearby town of Wülfingham, which lies directly on the opposite side of the river. The two large cities closest to Forchtenberg are Stuttgart and Nuremberg. It lies on the 'barbarian' side of the famous Roman Limes Wall, which stood at the edge of the Catholic Holy Roman Empire. The original Christian church dates back to 536 and the centre of the village can trace its history back to the Middle Ages.

The local residents of the region are known as 'Swabians'. They do not regard themselves as full-blown Bavarians, retaining a distinct history, identity, a recognisable dialect, a well-known reputation for non-conformity and a healthy disrespect for authority. The most well-known Swabian saying is 'Kiss my Ass'. Swabia was once part of Bavaria, but it is now in the state of Baden-Württemberg, in the administrative region of Stuttgart.

9

Outside of Germany, many Swabians settled in Hungary, Romania, Turkey, Serbia and Kazakhstan. In 1814, Ludwig Uhland, a leading figure in the German Romantic movement, wrote a poem called 'Swabian Intelligence' (*Schwäbische Kunde*), which recounts the story of a brave Swabian soldier, serving in the army of Frederick Barbarossa, who remains cool and calm during a ferocious battle, enduring constant attacks by the Turks with enormous restraint, until quite suddenly and unexpectedly he fights back, killing all his opponents.

In Germany, Swabians are often depicted in jokes as stingy, prudish and overly serious. In the famous fairytale 'The Seven Swabians' (*Die Sieben Schwaben*) they are portrayed as stupid. A famous Swabian homily is: 'A man saves the most if he buys nothing at all.' It is difficult to fathom these unfair images of Swabians when it is realised that among those born in this region of Germany were Friedrich Schiller, the poet; Friedrich Hegel, the philosopher; Rudolf Diesel, inventor of the diesel engine; Karl Benz, inventor of the first petrol powered motor car; and the world-renowned physicist, Albert Einstein. These days, Swabians are still viewed as frugal and hard-working, but also now as clever and entrepreneurial. Baden-Württemberg is the most economically successful state in modern Germany.

But at the time of Sophie Scholl's birth Germany was in the grip of a deep political and economic crisis, brought about by military defeat in the First World War. There were riots, assassinations and gun battles in all the major cities. In November 1918, Adolf Hitler, then just a lowly corporal in the German army, was recovering from a mustard gas attack in a military hospital when he heard news of the German defeat. 'Everything went black again before my eyes', he later recalled, 'I tottered and groped my way back to the dormitory, threw myself on the bunk, and dug my burning head into my blanket and pillow ... So it had all been in vain.'[1]

Then came the 'hated' Treaty of Versailles, imposed on Germany by the victorious Western Allies.[2] Under its terms, Germany lost 13 per cent of its territory, the army was reduced to 100,000 men and the navy whittled down to a small coastal force. Even worse, Germany was ordered to pay massive financial compensation to the victorious Allies – known as reparations – set at the seemingly impossible figure of 6.6 billion marks and payable until the 1980s. Finally, under Article 231 Germany had to accept 'sole guilt' for the outbreak of the war.[3] For Germans this was a crippling humiliation.

Germany was also suffering terrible economic problems. Between 1919 and 1923 inflation rose to astronomical levels. A single US dollar in January 1923 was worth 17,000 marks, by July 353,000 marks and by

December 4.2 billion marks. On 29 July 1923, the *Daily Mail* reported: 'In the shops the prices are typewritten and posted hourly. For instance, a gramophone at 10 a.m. was 5 million marks but by 3 p.m. it was 12 million marks.'[4]

Yet in the sheltered idyllic surroundings of Forchtenberg all these problems seemed a very long way away. Sophie, the fourth child of the Scholl family, was born in the local town hall. Her father Robert Scholl was the mayor.[5] The family lived during her early childhood in a palatial and roomy apartment located inside the town hall building.

Robert Scholl was born on 13 April 1891 in Steinbrück, then a poverty-stricken area, north of Forchtenberg, known as the Mainhardter woods. At secondary school he made a very good impression on a local Protestant pastor, who encouraged him, after he left school, to attend a highly reputed college for management professionals and lawyers in Stuttgart. He emerged with very useful qualifications in taxation and law.

During the First World War, with German nationalist feelings running high, Robert Scholl adopted a highly unusual pacifist stance. He refused to serve in the military or even carry a gun and he was deeply opposed to Germany's militaristic and expansionist war aims.[6] After this non-conformist protest, he was assigned to a post in the ambulance corps of the Red Cross and served in a military hospital in Ludwigsburg, a suburb of Stuttgart.

One of the people he met everyday at the hospital was Magdalene Müller, a polite, sensible, softly spoken nursing sister, who was born on 5 May 1881. She was a devoted Lutheran lay preacher. Her Lutheranism was rooted in a diligent and frequent reading of the Bible and she was attracted to biblical passages about love, salvation and moral principles. She felt great sympathy for children without shoes on their feet, the infirm, the sick and the bereaved. She was patient, kept her opinions to herself and her gentle benevolence shone through to everyone she met. Inge Scholl remembered that:

> She was a cheerful woman, open to people and to life. Later, as the mayor's wife, she fulfilled social obligations, not because that was what a mayor's wife was supposed to do but because she genuinely felt compassion for the sick and the poor. As for us children, she was deeply interested in everything we experienced. She lived with us totally.[7]

Magdalene was obviously impressed by Robert Scholl's drive and easy-going nature. He was nine years her junior, but in spite of the wide age gap they got on very well. Long talks in the hospital led to social outings, which grew into friendship, then romance and marriage in 1916. Their union produced six children: Inge was born 1917, Hans arrived in 1918, followed by Elisabeth, 1920, Sophie, 1921, Werner, 1922, and Thilde, 1925, but the latter child died only a year later. The couple lived at first in Ingersheim in Crailsheim, before moving to Forchtenberg in 1919.

In the 1920s, Robert Scholl was a tall, confident, non-conformist; liberal, strong willed and very independently minded. He was a believer in Christianity, attended church regularly, but he was not deeply troubled by questions of deep religious doctrine. He sported a then fashionable moustache, regularly smoked cigars, but rarely drank alcohol or visited the local taverns, which were a social focal point for the local farmers, peasants and shopkeepers who made up the bulk of the townspeople and his voting constituency. He had an open and lively disposition, was often opinionated, sometimes emotional. At heart, Robert Scholl, although from a humble background and living in a small village, was forward-thinking and free-spirited. A provincial village was not the ideal place for his talents. He looked at the bigger picture. He kept in touch with the latest local and national news stories and subscribed to a number of periodicals on current affairs and financial matters.

As mayor, he tackled the problems of the village with a bold programme of modernising policies. When he arrived, the only link between Forchtenberg and the outside world was by a single-track road. The only transport to the nearest railway station in the Kocher Valley was a horse-drawn mail coach. One of his major achievements was to establish a rail link between Forchtenberg and the rest of Germany. He also commissioned important road and building works and his financial skills allowed him to put the finances of the village in good order. But Robert Scholl's desire to modernise the village was often greeted with suspicion by some of the local rural population. A local pastor once noticed him reading a periodical in a cafe, written by the social liberal Friedrich Förster, and said in a critical voice: 'You really read that stuff?'

At home, the structure of the Scholl family appeared patriarchal, with Magdalene Scholl playing the role of reliable housewife. She kept the house clean, supervised the kitchen and tended to the needs of the children. But Robert Scholl ensured that discussions around the dinner table were democratic and he sought his wife's advice on every major issue. For her part, Magdalene Scholl stressed the importance of religion to her children and urged them to have a strong moral and social conscience. The Scholl children had a home life that was comfortable and lacking in material deprivation during a time when most people in Germany were enduring major financial difficulties. It was a household that encouraged education and bred self-confidence.

Sophie Scholl's early childhood and character can only be described in glimpses. According to Otl Aicher, a family friend, 'Physically and mentally, Sophie resembled her mother. Look at the physical similarity: the dark eyes … her face almost boyish – she was the quiet one and, like her mother, she really didn't talk much.'[8] She suffered – like many children in the time before the advent of modern antibiotic drugs – from frequent bouts of ill health, enduring mumps, measles, colds, bouts of flu and bronchitis.

Books played a very important role in the Scholl household. There were hundreds on the bookshelves at home. Sophie was a sensible and intelligent child who read widely and liberally. Some of her favourite books, such as *Slovenly Peter* by Sibylle van Olfer, the charming fairy tales of the legendary Brothers Grimm and Wilhelm Hauff and Schnorr von Carolsfeld's *Illustrated Bible* were read over and over again. She also loved to read and recite poetry, and her favourites were Goethe and Schiller.[9]

Sophie's education began at the age of seven at the tiny village school, which only had room for three classes. Sophie particularly liked to hear the teacher read out the story of *Robinson Crusoe* by the English satirist Daniel Defoe. The story of a sailor trapped on a desert island delighted her. She identified greatly with Crusoe's character. Other great childhood favourites were the Rulaman stories of cavemen and bears that offered vivid descriptions of the beautiful Swabian countryside.

'Sophie liked to play with dolls', recalls Inge Scholl, 'My mother being a great believer in this children's hobby.' Every Christmas Eve the dolls' house was redecorated and the dolls were given new clothes. Music was a family pastime which came easily to Sophie, and she became a good pianist who would play for family and friends. She wrote lovely stories and poems, and was good at freehand drawing and painting. She was very athletic and sport. She became very close to her younger brother Werner. 'They were like twins', Inge recalled, 'I can see them hand in hand, tripping along barefoot.'[10]

But Sophie's greatest passion was nature. All youngsters in Germany tended to idolise nature, especially in this period. It was widely believed in Germany that close proximity to mountains, trees, rivers, flowers and wildlife placed a person in close harmony with God. As Inge Scholl puts it: 'We loved our land dearly – the woods, the river, the old grey stone fences running along the steep slopes between orchards and vineyards. We sniffed the odour of moss, damp earth, and sweet apples whenever we thought of our homeland.'[11]

Wherever Sophie went she drank in her surroundings using all of her senses:

> I can never look at a limpid stream without at least dangling my feet in it. I cannot walk past a meadow in May. There is nothing more enticing than a fragrant piece of land … Luxuriant in its flowers, and I am knee-deep amid luscious grass and flowers … I press my face to the tree's dusky, warm bark and think 'My homeland', and I am so inexplicably grateful.[12]

Sophie's rhapsodic passion towards nature remained with for the rest of her life. She loved everything God-given with an incredible, almost indescribable passion. This is why she loved outdoor pursuits, most notably swimming, going for nature walks, climbing very tall trees and alpine sports.

Of all her siblings, Sophie's eldest brother, Hans, increasingly came to occupy the first place in her heart. She admired him, respected him and loved him unconditionally. To understand Sophie Scholl you must also understand the important place her brother occupied in her life. Hans Fritz Scholl was born in Ingersheim, on 22 September 1918, at the foot of the Alps. Hans, the eldest son, was very much the 'family favourite' – not just of his parents, but also his brothers and sisters.[13] Hans was tall, athletic and extremely handsome, with dark brooding eyes. He had a very strong personality and could be charming, impulsive, volatile, sullen and outspoken, depending on the company and his mood. If there is such a thing as a natural leader, then Hans Scholl fitted the bill. He was also an avid reader of the Bible, one of his favourite passages being:

> And though I have the gift of Prophecy, and understand all mysteries, and all knowledge, and though I have all faith, so that I could move mountains, and have not charity, I am nothing.[14]

As a child, Sophie was short in stature, slender, with brown eyes, and she liked her dark brown hair cut into a boyish short bob. Her face often had a very serious expression upon it, as if she was deep in thought, troubled or worried. Throughout her life she wrote numerous letters and kept a daily diary. It is through these sources – especially as she gets older – that we are able to glimpse her personality more fully and to understand her better.

She was cool-headed and sensible, with a steady character, and her parents thought she was a very patient child. She was more of a listener than a talker, who liked to develop her ideas after very careful consideration. But Sophie had a great strength of character and confidence in her abilities that could not be glimpsed in her shy outward expression.

At school she excelled in a wide range of subjects. In the view of Inge Scholl, Sophie 'didn't view herself as anything special – quite the contrary. She was endowed with an acute unpretentiousness and with a remarkable irony that must have served as a kind of self-protection'. Robert Scholl felt Sophie was 'the wisest of my women'. He especially admired her humility and her incredible calmness under pressure. Nothing seemed to faze her. She could quickly brush away incredible disappointment. 'I realise that one can wallow in the mind', she once told a friend, 'while one's soul starves to death.'[15] She was not a person who blurted out what she thought on every issue. She took her time to think things over before offering an opinion.

Even before Hitler came to power, German schools had a reputation for their strong devotion to strict discipline. Teachers inculcated pupils with a strong sense of patriotism, encouraged conformity and offered a largely bourgeois view of the world. Authority was something to be obeyed at all times. Students were discouraged from asking questions. Corporal punishment was used with regularity to supplement this strong disciplinarian environment and German schoolchildren were always told to love the Fatherland. There were few chances to write essays containing opinions on current affairs.

Sophie was a quiet pupil, who was only caned once during her school education in Forchtenberg. In those days the academic status of each pupil was measured by the seating position in the classroom. The best pupils were placed at the front, the average in the middle and weakest and most ill-disciplined at the back. One early instance of Sophie's willingness to take a strong stand against rigid authority came when her younger sister Elisabeth was demoted by her teacher to the second row on the same day as her birthday. Sophie was extremely angry about the thoughtless timing of this demotion and said to her teacher as she escorted her sister back to the front row: 'Today is my sister Elisabeth's birthday. I'm promoting her back.' Even at this early age, Sophie was unafraid to act in a bold manner in the face of what she felt was injustice.[16]

The calm life of the Scholl family suffered a severe upheaval in the spring of 1930 when Robert Scholl was voted out of office.[17] He was replaced by Friedrich Kramer, who only stayed in office until 1933 when the Nazis came to power. It seems his defeat was due to several factors. The local villagers were becoming much less tolerant of Robert Scholl's 'liberal views' as Germany moved sharply to the right. A new bylaw had been introduced which meant that local taxes would have to increase substantially to pay Robert Scholl's salary as he was entitled to large family allowances. His electoral opponent was a bachelor and less costly to the local taxpayers. But there was also some gossip going around prior to the election which alleged that Robert Scholl was having an affair with a local woman. It was something he denied, but many voters thought the story was true.[18]

But the resourceful Robert Scholl was not out of work for very long, even during the period after the Wall Street Crash of October 1929, which plunged Germany into economic chaos. He worked for a trust company in Stuttgart and quickly became the leader of the local Chamber of Commerce. In the summer of 1930, the Scholl family moved to the small town of Ludwigburg, seven miles north of Stuttgart.[19] The family rented a large apartment in a house at 7 Schillerplatz. 'My father always rented big apartments', Inge Scholl later recalled, 'no matter how badly off we were. He felt everyone should be able to move around freely and be able to get out of everyone's way once in a while.'[20] The Ludwigsburg apartment was very close to a local castle with a beautiful park attached to it. Sophie greatly enjoyed the idyllic rural surroundings of this park and she spent two years at the local girls' public school, today called the Anton Bruckner School.[21]

In the spring of 1932 the family moved to the small city of Ulm, which then had a population of 60,000 people. They lived briefly in an apartment located at 29 Kernerstrasse, but later in the year relocated to a larger apartment at 81 Olgastrasse, and in 1939 they moved to an even more spacious apartment at 33 Münsterplatz, located in the fashionable cathedral square.

Robert Scholl became a partner in a company that specialised in financial services and tax consultancy.[22] Ulm lies at the point where the Blau and Iller rivers join the Danube. It is surrounded by lovely forests and hills. It became an important trading area from the fifteenth century onwards, noted for the export of high-quality textiles. During the Reformation Ulm was a Protestant stronghold. In 1891, Ulm Cathedral (*Ulmer Münster*) – which boasts the world's highest church steeple at 161.5 metres – was finally completed. The city was also important in the industrial development of Germany, beginning with the establishment of a train station in 1850. The most important industries in Ulm were motor vehicles, electronics and pharmaceuticals.

Ulm was the place where Sophie Scholl lived for the rest of her life. The hills, the caves, the green fields and the verdant woods surrounding the city provided a wonderful playground for a young outdoor girl. One day Sophie went on a school hiking trip into the hills and mountains surrounding the city. She climbed to the top of the highest tree. She was in a world of her own, completely oblivious to the fact her teacher and fellow pupils were frantically signalling her to come down, and when she finally did her teacher told her not do such a thing again without her permission. Sophie promised not to do it again, but with a glint in her eye, which said she would make up her own mind.[23]

TWO

HITLER YOUTH

Shortly after noon on 30 January 1933, German national radio interrupted its normal programmes. A serious-sounding newsreader read the following message: 'Adolf Hitler has been appointed by President Hindenburg as the new German Chancellor.'[1] A few minutes later, ecstatic Nazi supporters poured onto the streets, embraced each other and asked complete strangers whether they had heard the news. Soon newspaper vendors were shouting: 'Get your special edition: Hitler is Chancellor'. Nazi flags were hung from the windows of houses and public buildings throughout the country. Young people everywhere in Germany wanted to join what seemed like a great joyful party.[2] In Ulm, a classmate told Sophie's sister Inge: 'Hitler has taken over the government. Now there will be better times in Germany.'[3]

During the evening, a torchlight procession in Berlin – composed of an estimated 700,000 loyal Nazi Party supporters – marched triumphantly down the tree-lined Unter den Linden,[4] through the impressive Brandenburg Gate, to celebrate the victory of their beloved Führer.[5] They finally congregated outside the Reichstag (the German Parliament building), chanting their leader's name over and over again. Suddenly, Adolf Hitler, dressed in an everyday pinstriped suit, came to the open window and waved to the massive crowd below. Joseph Goebbels, his 'spin doctor', described the moment in his diary:

> Hitler is in raptures. His people are cheering him … Wild frenzy of enthusiasm. Prepare the election campaign. The last. We'll win it hands down.[6]

The last democratic elections in Germany were held on 5 March 1933. Just a week before polling day, the Reichstag building had been burned to the ground in a huge fire. The Nazis claimed it was the work of a twenty-four-year-old 'lone nut' Dutch communist, Marius van der Lubbe. To this day, it has not been fully resolved whether van der Lubbe acted alone or was a Nazi stooge. Either way, once the fire started, the fire brigade was in no hurry to put it out.

The Reichstag fire allowed the Nazis to crush all communist opposition, to win the election, then to push through parliament on 23 March 1933 – with the help of the conservative nationalists – 'The Law for the Alleviation of the Distress of People and Reich' (known as 'The Enabling Act'). The significance of this act must be appreciated by anyone wishing to understand the legal basis of Hitler's dictatorship and the events which follow here. The Enabling Act allowed Hitler to issue his own laws and decrees without the need of endorsement from parliament. In effect, Adolf Hitler's wishes became the law of the land.

The Nazi criminal justice system forms a key part of this story from this point onwards, and it is important to understand how it worked in order to put what happened to Sophie Scholl and her brother Hans into context. The existing German legal system continued in the Nazi era, but incorporated within it and acting alongside it were the newly created 'Special Courts' – set up in 1933 in the local regions to deal with 'political crimes' – and, from July 1934, the highest Nazi 'political' court of all, 'The People's Court', whose all-consuming aim was to 'exterminate enemies of the Third Reich' in a fast-track justice system.[7] Most trials in these courts were dealt with in a single day – sometimes a single morning or afternoon.

To deal with 'political crimes' the regime created its own secret state police: the *Geheime Staatspolizei* – more famously known as the Gestapo. It worked closely with the ordinary judicial system and the German police force. It was the Gestapo's task to find and arrest 'enemies of the people', interrogate them, interview witnesses, collect evidence and then decide whether the accused person should be charged and face trial, be released or sent to a concentration camp. The judges decided the appropriate level of sentence in each case. This gave judges great leeway, resulting in widely differing sentences for the same crime.

The Nazi regime criminalised all kinds of 'normal' activities. Telling anti-Nazi jokes with friends, listening to foreign radio broadcasts, forming a youth group outside the Hitler Youth, making critical comments about the regime in bars, at work and even at home, were all offences and often resulted in arrest, interrogation, prosecution and even imprisonment. In terms of valid law, most Nazi 'political' and 'racial' laws were false and technically illegal.[8] Hence, when looking at any matters that are related to the Nazi terror organisations – the Gestapo, the Special Courts and the People's Courts – it is important to appreciate that these organisations were instruments of Nazi criminality – not upholding valid law, but using a veneer of legality to punish people illegally. At the same time, it must also be understood that not every law in Germany between 1933 and 1945 was illegal. Most of the cases dealt with by the ordinary criminal police contained 'valid cases', involving recognisable crimes such as theft, rape and murder.

If the autobiographies and eyewitness accounts of people who lived in Nazi Germany are to be taken at face value, it seems that this was a place in which no one felt safe. But is this really true? It would be very foolish to question that many people in Nazi Germany did live in constant fear. But we should not take a lot of what was said in the post-war era for granted. Most 'ordinary' Germans wanted to give the impression that they lived in a terrifying and menacing society, in which they were just helpless victims 'taking orders'. In reality, most German people were very happy with their lives in this period. Hitler was one of the most popular leaders of any country at any time. The nightmare image of Nazi Germany as an all powerful 'Big Brother' police state, in which every citizen lived in everyday fear of imminent arrest, is largely a myth – popularised in British- and American-made films and television documentaries.

The Gestapo lacked the manpower and the resources to spy on everyone. There were only 30,000 employees of the Gestapo in the whole of Nazi Germany, including administrative staff. Many small towns in Germany did not have a single Gestapo officer. In many large cities there were often fewer than twenty officers dealing with all the 'political crime' in that area. In addition, there were just 50,000 ordinary policemen to deal with the usual criminal casebook of a modern industrial society. As the German population in the Nazi era was 66 million, it can be seen that the Gestapo and the police were incredibly over-worked, under-resourced and over-stretched. The Gestapo files show they rarely instigated any major surveillance operations – even of political opponents. It was really – like most police forces in democratic societies today – a 'reactive force', relying on tip offs from the public. Only 1 per cent of the German population was ever arrested by the Gestapo during the era of the Third Reich for 'political crimes', but 3 per cent of the population were arrested for what we would describe as the usual crimes dealt with in democratic societies today.

Nazi terror was heavily targeted. It was directed with great ruthlessness at clearly defined groups who fell outside the 'national community' or were opposed it: Jews, communists, Jehovah's Witnesses, Sinti and Roma people, foreign 'slave' labourers, habitual criminals, religious and political dissidents, homosexuals, prostitutes and the mentally and physically handicapped. These were the 'targeted groups' in Hitler's Germany. 'National comrades' – which meant anyone German in the eyes of the Gestapo – had very little to fear and could conduct their lives, with a few modifications, pretty normally.[9]

Now imagine a small city that was not very enthusiastic about the Nazi Party before 1933. Welcome to Ulm – where Sophie Scholl lived at 81 Olgastrasse from 1932 to 1939. Hitler only gave one major speech there in 1933, but a brave local anti-Nazi cut the cable to his microphone. Hitler was suitably outraged and he reportedly never gave another speech there.[10] After 1933, the Nazi Party took over in Ulm and attempted to implement the nationwide policy of *Gleichschaltung* (co-ordination), designed to indoctrinate the nation with Nazi ideas and to remove all organised political opposition.

In Ulm, the process towards converting the entire population towards Nazism resembled a slow evolution rather than a revolution. Of course, many cosmetic things happened quickly. A framed picture of Adolf Hitler was soon hanging on the wall of every school classroom. The libraries were cleared of 'subversive literature' and filled with books glorifying Hitler and the Nazi Party. Political opponents were taken off to a hastily created local concentration camp in an old castle on the edge of the city.[11] On 30 July 1933, a government decree spelt out 'Guidelines for History Textbooks', which were rewritten to conform to the ideals of National Socialism. Most teachers joined the National Socialist Teachers' League and the Nazi Party. School students were soon writing essays on 'Hitler as Leader'.

The Nazis made great efforts to win over young people. Adolf Hitler was only forty-three years old when he was made German chancellor, which was exceptionally youthful for a major world leader. Most of the leading figures in his Nazi elite were under forty. The average age of Nazi Party members was below thirty.[12] Baldur von Schirach, the leader of the Hitler Youth and a member of the Cabinet, was just twenty-five years old. He said the Nazi Party was 'the party of youth'.[13] 'A violently active, dominating, brutal youth – that is what I am after', said Hitler in one of his speeches.[14] In a speech to the 1935 Nuremberg rally he said:

In our eyes the German boys of the future must be slender and supple, swift as greyhounds, tough as leather and hard as Krupp steel. We must bring up a new type of human being, men and girls who are disciplined and healthy to the core.[15]

Inge Scholl recalled that:

for the first time in our lives, politics came into our lives ... We heard much oratory about the Fatherland, comradeship, unity of the *Volk*, and love of country. This was impressive, and we listened closely when we heard such talk in school and on the street ... Adolf Hitler – so we heard on all sides ... would help this Fatherland to achieve greatness, fortune and prosperity ... He would not rest until every German was independent, free, and happy in his Fatherland.[16]

All the Scholl children were initially attracted by the Nazi youth organisations. 'You have to remember', Elisabeth Hartnagel recalls, 'there was great excitement when Hitler came to power. All the school books, newspapers, films and radio were all putting out Nazi ideas. It was very difficult for young people not to want to be part of such excitement.'[17]

Robert Scholl was definitely not in tune with the prevailing mood of most of his fellow Germans. He retained his liberal and pacifist attitudes during the entire Nazi period. He hated Hitler and everything he stood for. He disliked the Nazi torchlight parades he often saw in the streets, led by flag-carrying and violent-looking Nazi storm troopers. He did not like the old black-red-gold flag of the democratic Weimar Republic being hauled down from all the public buildings in the city, then replaced by the black-red-white of the imperial Hohenzollern banner, accompanied by the swastika – which started to appear everywhere. Robert Scholl was a pacifist and one of his favourite books was *All Quiet on the Western Front* by Erich Remarque.[18] 'We children felt', says Elisabeth Hartnagel, 'that our father was out of touch with the new times and a generation gap grew in the those early years of Hitler's rule.'[19]

At home, Robert Scholl was not afraid to tell his children that the Nazis were 'beasts and wolves'. Hitler was little more than 'the Pied Piper of Hamelin', luring youths to follow him by playing 'pretty tunes on the flute'.[20] Robert Scholl thought that Hitler had only come to power because of Germany's economic problems:

Once people lose their bare subsistence, once the future looks like nothing but a grey wall to them, they will listen all the more to promises without wondering who makes them.[21]

The dilemma of the Scholl children and their father in this period found an echo in the extraordinarily popular 1933 Nazi propaganda film *Hitlerjunge Quex* ('The Hitler Youth Called Quex').[22] It was one of the Nazis' most convincing and successful propaganda films. It tells the story of a young boy with middle-aged communist parents who are bitterly opposed to Nazism. But the young hero of the film 'Quex' is portrayed as a very engaging boy who is greatly attracted by the Hitler Youth and wants to join, in spite of the vociferous opposition of his parents. In the end, he bravely defies his father and joins.[23]

In the Scholl household, Hans and his father had very similar arguments. When Hans told his father that Hitler was putting people back to work and dragging Germany out of the depression, he was told all this was being done to aid rearmament and to prepare Germany for war. 'Can't you see where it will all end?' Robert Scholl pleaded with him.[24] In many families, rifts over National Socialism between parents and children went far deeper than the tolerant and free-spirited Scholl household. One old soldier said of his son – who became active in the Hitler Youth:

The lad had already been completely alienated from us … I'm against war, and this lad is just mad about war and nothing else. It's awful, sometimes I feel as if my lad is a spy in the family.[25]

Luckily for Robert Scholl, his children loved him and never reported his anti-Nazi views to their teachers or to the Gestapo. 'The Scholls' spirit was very open', remembers Franz Müller, who knew the family in the period they lived in Ulm.

In March 1933, Hans Scholl joined the Hitler Youth.[26] At the time, membership was only voluntary. It became compulsory following the Hitler Youth Law of 1 December 1936, which incorporated all German youth between the ages of ten and eighteen into the organisation. Before 1933, there were hundreds of German youth organisations; many were religious, with over 3 million youngsters in Protestant and Catholic groups. Some were political – the nationalist, communist and socialist parties all had youth associations – and various independent so-called *Bündische* youth groups also existed.

When Hitler became chancellor, the Hitler Youth had only about 55,000 members. The Catholic groups were tolerated until the late 1930s, then closed down. The vast majority of German youth joined the Hitler Youth. By the end of 1933, the Hitler Youth had 2 million members. By the end of 1934, 50 per cent of all children had joined. In the end, every young German was compelled to do so. Between the ages of ten and fourteen boys joined a feeder youth organisation called the German Young People (DJ) and girls joined the Young Girls League (JM). Between the ages of fourteen and eighteen boys entered the Hitler Youth (*Hitler Jugend* – HJ) and girls joined the League of German Girls (*Bund Deutscher Mädel* – BDM).

Hans, Sophie, Inge, Elisabeth and Werner joined the Hitler youth organisations of their own free will. In the view of Inge Scholl: 'We all entered into it with body and soul and we could not understand why our father did not approve.'[27] It seems the children enjoyed the sporting and leisure activities and the camping trips organised by the Hitler Youth rather than the ideological aspects. In any case, the military and ideological emphases in the Hitler Youth – especially the Ulm branch – were played down. Many girls like Inge, Sophie and Elisabeth Scholl found joining the German girls' league a surprisingly liberating experience. It allowed them to escape from assisting their mother in domestic duties and offered opportunities to organise and lead outdoor activities.[28]

Hans Scholl was outwardly the very model – in the Nazi way of thinking – of a perfect Aryan member of the Hitler Youth. He was tall, exceptionally good looking, athletic, with strong leadership qualities. He excelled in the long marches and lung-busting gymnastic exercises. Within a few months, Hans was promoted in the Hitler Youth to the rank of *Fähnleinführer* (squad leader), and put in charge of about 150 boys.[29] He was very enthusiastic about his role. The only youth group he ever joined before 1933 was the YMCA.

Hans wore his Hitler Youth uniform – brown shirt with a swastika armband, black shorts and grey knee-length stockings – with great pride. He learned to give a perfect Hitler salute and he impressed his superiors. He was put in charge of the physical training regime of new recruits and made sure fellow members listened to the weekly Hitler Youth programme on the radio. He knew the black swastika was a symbol of Aryan racial superiority. When Hans' Hitler Youth squad paraded through the streets of Ulm in torchlight processions, led by the drummer boys beating out their insistent Nazi backbeat, Hans was watched and admired by his school friends and his three sisters. No one denies that Hans Scholl threw himself, body and soul, into the Hitler Youth.

All the Scholl girls joined – in defiance of their father's wishes – the female equivalents of the Hitler Youth. Sophie started in the Young Girls League, then at fourteen entered the German Girls League. 'BDM girls' were expected to eventually get married and have children, but high importance was also attached to job training and education. The BDM uniform consisted of a brown coat, a white blouse, a black tie with a swastika pin, a black scarf, a navy blue skirt and white stockings. Hitler stated in *Mein Kampf* that 'The one goal always to be kept in mind when educating girls is that someday they are to be mothers', and outwardly the BDM encouraged the limited boundaries of the ideal German woman: *Kinder, Küche und Kirche* (children, kitchen and church).[30]

But it was the traditional 'boyish' independent activities, such as camping, hiking and playing sport, which attracted Sophie Scholl to the BDM. She tended to be much less enthusiastic about Nazi ideals than Hans and especially Inge Scholl. Sophie was also impressed by the attempt of the BDM to mix all the social classes together, which had not happened in the more middle-class orientated youth groups of the pre-1933 period. Sophie – like Hans and Inge – was promoted to the rank of squad leader in 1935.[31] She later admitted that she threw herself into all the activities of the BDM with 'girlish enthusiasm'.[32] Inge Scholl remembered her sister's attitude to the BDM:

> As I recall it, Sophie was less carried away than Hans and I by the excitement of 1933–34. True, she cheerfully took part in the hustle and bustle of her *Jungmädel* group, in their hiking, camping and scouting. The solemn speeches by the bonfire, the torchlight songs must have impressed her. But they never took complete possession of her.[33]

The experiences of twelve girls who went to school in Ulm with Sophie Scholl between 1933 and 1936 is brilliantly recounted in the documentary film *Kinderland ist abgebrannt* ('The Land of Children has Burned Down'), directed by Sibylle Tiedemann. The film contains interviews with six Jewish and six non-Jewish women, all over seventy years old, who were schoolchildren in Sophie's class in Ulm. Five of the non-Jewish pupils recalled the very strong early enthusiasm they had for Hitler, but one pupil said she was singled out for punishment by a teacher because her Social Democrat father had been imprisoned in Dachau concentration camp as he had warned that Hitler's rule would lead to war. One woman called Marianne remembered that it was said in Ulm that: 'Those who can't shut up will end up in a concentration camp.' All the non-Jewish pupils said Sophie and her classmates really enjoyed the marching, the music and the leisure activities organised by the Nazi youth organisations.[34]

The Jewish pupils in the class said that the process of isolation in Ulm from their non-Jewish school friends was quite slow. They all said they did not notice any immediate change of attitude in Ulm in the early years of Nazi rule. Sophie Scholl had two very close Jewish friends in her class, Anneliese Wallersteiner and Luise Nathan, who were the daughters of solid middle-class parents. Both of these Jewish girls were refused entry into the BDM, prompting Sophie to comment: 'Why can't Luise, with her blonde hair and blue eyes [not] be a member, while I with my dark hair and dark eyes am a member?' Such outbursts show that Sophie was never in tune with Nazi racial doctrines, in spite of the all-pervasive nature of them. Sophie maintained her friendship with the Jewish girls in her class and often invited them to her home.[35]

The Jewish pupils at Sophie's school remember that it was the introduction of the Nuremberg Laws in September 1935 that really brought a major change of attitudes in Ulm. These anti-Jewish laws were presented by Hitler as a 'stabilising measure' that would help to define the role of Jews in German society. Any Jewish person with at least three grandparents who were Jewish had their German citizenship withdrawn. People with only one Jewish grandparent were defined as 'mixed race' and also became second-class citizens. After the introduction of the Nuremberg Laws, all the Jewish girls at Sophie Scholl's school in Ulm said their lives and their friendships changed quite dramatically. Sophie's friend, Anneliese Wallersteiner, remembers that one fellow pupil in her class spat in her face as she came out of school and denounced her for being a Jew. The Jewish girls in Sophie's class were soon forbidden from going to swimming baths, movie theatres, sports centres and even parks. They were soon going to a separate school. They said it just became much too risky for any German – no matter how sympathetic they were to their plight – to maintain open friendships with Jewish people.[36]

The BDM was supposed to prepare young German girls for their later roles as mother and housewife, but the non-Jewish girls in Sophie's BDM group found the hiking, the sporting activities and the singing of songs with a guitar around the bonfire very liberating. Sophie and most of the other girls cut their hair short in order to be 'like the boys'. One of Sophie's class mates recalled:

Almost all [German] women get excited when they think of their time as BDM leaders … For us, it was a kind of emancipation, even if nobody today wants to believe us. As a leader I received an instruction booklet every two to four weeks ... and even if they were a little oversimplified, I relayed them to the younger girls. There were tales in the booklets about the German farmer who lives in the east, motherhood, the brave mother who makes sacrifices for Germany and other sentimental stuff.

At the same time, the pupils admitted that the discipline and hierarchical structures of the BDM were often excessive and group leaders like Sophie were expected to administer strong reprimands if a member even failed to turn up for a meeting.[37] Some leading Nazis soon recognised that some of the activities of the BDM were actually being viewed by many girls as a form of liberation. Heinrich Himmler, the leader of the SS, once said: 'When I see these girls marching around with their nicely packed backpacks, it makes me sick.'[38]

The Hitler Youth in Ulm undertook activities that were identical to the non-ideological activities of long-standing German *Bündische* youth organisations.[39] A secret Social Democratic report on Hitler Youth activities recorded that older boys (of Hans' age and above) tended to retain many of the non-Nazi beliefs of their parents much more strongly than younger children, who seemed more easily attracted by 'the National Socialist spirit'.[40] It seems the 'classless' claims of Nazi propaganda about the Hitler Youth were a myth. Camping trips proved much more attractive to poor working-class boys as they had not had the chance to go on such heavily subsidised holidays before. For a solid and affluent middle-class family like the Scholls – who had many holidays throughout the year – camping trips alone had little chance of maintaining their interest for too long. This explains why many highly educated and affluent members of the middle class who displayed an initial enthusiasm for the Hitler Youth became gradually disillusioned as they got older. The Hitler Youth did not break down traditional class divisions. Class-based patterns of friendship were largely untouched. The Scholl family had hardly any friends who were the sons or daughters of the unskilled or skilled members of the working class or even the lower middle class. They were more likely to look up the social scale than down when seeking friends.

Hitler Youth organisations were very top-down and hierarchical organisations, governed by strict leadership principles and guidelines laid down by the Reich Youth leadership. Every member was told what to do by their superior leader. Everyone who joined swore an oath to the Führer – similar to the one taken by the German army. Each Hitler Youth group was supposed to follow a set syllabus and could not decide their own activities. The only songs they could sing were official and rather boring Nazi songs of the 'We All Love the Führer' variety. The leaders read out orders from specially prepared information packs and factsheets.

It is pretty clear that most members of the Hitler Youth in Ulm did not have a very firm grasp of the ideas of National Socialism at all. The vast majority had been members of Weimar youth groups, most notably the boys-only German Boys League, of 1 November 1929 (*the Deutsche Jungenschaft vom 1 November 1929* or 'd.j.1.11' for short). It was a radical non-conformist German youth group, set up in 1929, as a breakaway group from the more formally organised and pro-nationalist Volunteer Corps of the Young Nation.[41] It was originally led by Eberhard Köbel – known as 'Tusk' – who had been a member of the Communist Party (KPD). He introduced a strong pro-Soviet tinge to the organisation by promoting the singing of Russian folk songs on camping trips. In 1933, Köbel was put in a concentration camp – classed as a 'political dissident'. After his release he fled into exile in Britain, but he kept in correspondence with his followers and he remained their guru and undoubted spiritual leader. After 1945, he chose to live in communist East Germany.[42]

The d.j.1.11 group harked back to the open and liberated ideals of the progressive forces of Weimar. Their distinctive style was comparable to the trendy Bauhaus movement, which gave new directions to Weimar art and architectural style. The followers of d.j.1.11 – like the adherents to Bauhaus – did not use capital letters in their correspondence. They loved to recite lyrical poetry to each other, read banned books, staged impromptu plays and sang mostly Balkan, Russian or Scandinavian songs.

These young boys had a very distinctive and independent fashion style – they wore smart 'sailor'-style shirts, distinctive cord trousers, and their favoured musical instrument was the triange-shaped Russian balalaika. On camping trips, they stayed in Lapland-style black *kothe* tents in wooded and mountainous areas.[43] They even developed a distinctive slang language, using nicknames and catchphrases. One of their favourite jokes was to ask each other while sitting together around the camp fire: 'What is an Aryan?' To which they would all reply: 'Blond like Hitler. Tall like Goebbels. Slender like Göring.'[44]

They also liked to hitchhike in a free-wheeling style across the country, not to the Rhineland or the Bavarian mountains, the favourite haunts of their Hitler Youth friends, but outside Germany to Sweden, Finland and Sicily. The members of d.j.1.11, according to Otl Aicher, were very 'cosmopolitan' in outlook and they encouraged a distinctive form of dress. 'Books played an important part', recalled Otl Aicher. 'The boys discovered literature and got involved in what was called degenerate art ... They would read to each other into the night, discuss what they heard and plan the next meeting.'[45] The members of d.j.1.11 did not have 'leaders'. There were no set rules; the key aim was free expression.

Before 1933 Hans Scholl had not been a member of d.j.1.11, but in November 1933, Hans was 'ordered' by a local senior Hitler Youth leader in Ulm to form an autonomous elite 'A Squad' based not on Hitler Youth ideals, but on the independent traditions of d.j.1.11. The original mission – defined for Hans by his HJ leader – was to use this 'approved d.j.1.11 style group' to train future Hitler Youth leaders. In effect, Hans was being given permission by the Hitler Youth to engage in non-conformist activities. The reason was because the local Youth leader felt most of the Ulm Hitler branch had not yet grasped their 'ideological mission' in the service of the Führer.

But what started out as a mission to help the Ulm Hitler Youth develop better leaders had a major impact on Hans' own thinking. Hans became increasingly attracted to the d.j.1.11 ideology and way of life, in particular its carefree and independent approach. What the local Hitler Youth leader did not seem to appreciate was that there was a fundamental difference between the free-spirited ideals of d.j.1.11 and the rigid conformity of the Hitler Youth. What followed was an inevitable conflict between Hans and the local Ulm branch of the HJ. It was a conflict that would ultimately have disastrous consequences for him and affect the whole Scholl family.

In the spring of 1935 Hans was ordered to disband his individualistic 'A squad' by his local Hitler Youth superior, who felt enough young boys had been recruited from it as Hitler Youth leaders. Hans was bitterly disappointed with this decision and – according to Hans – 'strained relations' now developed between him and the local Hitler Youth squad leader.[46] Hans refused to accept the order and he went on meeting with his d.j.1.11-style group in secret. In May 1936, Hans was removed from his role as a Hitler Youth leader for his insubordination and he was only restored when he promised finally to disband the group.[47] Franz Müller recalled that:

Hans Scholl was a very complicated person, very special, different from other guys. He was highly educated and had leadership qualities. He was not so orthodox ... Hans had no fear. He had no sense of danger. That was very bad. It sounds terrible, but it is a fact. If you have no fear you can have a clear vision. But it is dangerous.[48]

By this stage, Hans Scholl was leading a double life: he was simultaneously a highly regarded Hitler Youth leader, but his spirit was really in tune with the ideals of d.j.1.11. He was crossing back and forth between conformity and non-conformity. The pressure was mounting on this young, edgy teenager. He was becoming increasingly miserable and bad tempered. In the summer of 1935, the Ulm Hitler Youth leadership, in a move designed to bring him back into the fold, selected Hans as the major-flag bearer of the Ulm Hitler Youth group at the upcoming Nuremberg rally in September. Inge Scholl later recalled that when Hans was selected it was viewed by locals and the family as a 'great honour' and one of her friends said to her: 'Your Hans is so handsome. He is the right boy to carry the flag of his *Stamm* [600-member group].'⁴⁹

When Hans left for Nuremberg on a special train in September 1935 he seemed relaxed and happy. On arrival, the city was crowded with Nazi fanatics. The rally was held on the outskirts of the medieval town centre in the huge Zeppelin field. A vast tented city was constructed outside the main arena for the week-long event. There were speeches, march-pasts and evening torchlight processions. Surrounding the arena were huge flood-lights, which cast vertical beams around the Zeppelin field to symbolise vast classical Roman pillars. These floodlights picked out the dramatic 'entrance of the Führer' and the endless march of the Nazi flag bearers into the arena. The 1935 event was called the 'Rally of Freedom', which is deeply ironic when it is realised that it was at this event that the anti-Semitic Nuremberg Laws were announced.

Outside, local street traders were selling postcards, posters and other Hitler merchandise in the manner of vendors at a modern rock concert. Hans Scholl and his Ulm troop spent their week in the tented village surrounding the massive arena. In Ulm, Hans had attended Hitler Youth events and many of the marches, parades and sports activities. But at Nuremberg he was mixing not just with the members of his own Hitler Youth group – most of whom were similarly well-brought-up members of the middle class – but with the more rowdy, brutal and anti-intellectual brown-shirted storm troopers, mostly of lower middle-class or 'rough' working-class origin. For Hans, these were the lager louts from hell. This was no place for a high-minded teenager who liked art, novels, poetry and folk songs.

It is not difficult to imagine why this graphic glimpse into the mass conformity of the true Nazi believer was, for Hans, very depressing. When he arrived back home he was exhausted, distraught and demoralised, and according to Inge Scholl 'completely changed: tired, depressed and taciturn.

He didn't say anything, but we could all tell that something had happened between him and the HJ.' Hans later admitted to his sister that the drills, the constant marching, the roll calls, the vulgar jokes and the lack of a 'sensible conversation' turned him right off – if not yet against – the Hitler Youth.[50] Hans told Sophie that he was greatly disillusioned with Nazism after spending a full week with 'real' Nazi activists.[51] Sophie could also sense that something 'was wrong' with her elder brother after he returned from Nuremberg, but she did not know what it was.[52] What Hans Scholl said to his family about his experience at Nuremberg was no doubt true, but not the whole truth. What can now be revealed is that Hans was in the midst of a deeply personal relationship at this time, which he had kept secret from his family, but one that was causing him uninterrupted strain and would soon come out into the open and have enormous ramifications.

THREE

SOWING THE SEEDS OF DOUBT

On 7 March 1936 German troops marched into the demilitarised Rhineland. William Shirer, the famous American journalist, recorded in his diary what happened when Hitler announced the news to a Reichstag packed with fanatical Nazis:

> They spring yelling and crying to their feet ... Their hands are raised in slavish salute, their faces now contorted with hysteria, their mouths wide open, shouting, shouting, their eyes, burning with fanaticism, glued to the new god, the messiah.[1]

Here was an opportunity for the Scholl children to rejoice in the success of their beloved Führer. But Sophie, only fourteen, was already having doubts about the total submission and conformity being demanded by the Nazi regime. When a popular young male teacher was suddenly dismissed Sophie commented: 'What did he do? Nothing ... He just wasn't a Nazi, so it was impossible for him to belong. *That* was his crime.' Sophie once asked her father if Adolf Hitler knew about the concentration camps:

> How could he not know? They've existed for years and were set up by his friends. And why didn't he use his power to do away with them at once? Why are those who are released from them forbidden on pain of death to tell anything about what they went through?[2]

Yet the Scholl family had no material reason for being unhappy. Robert Scholl was a very successful self-made businessman in financial services, earning the very healthy income of 1,500 marks a month.[3] All the family possessed the *Ahnenpass*, a special hereditary passport which documented the ancestry of every German citizen. The Scholls had impeccable 'Aryan pure blooded' German credentials.[4] This meant they were classed as 'national comrades'. For such solid German citizens there was considerable space to grumble and even vent minor frustrations. To a large degree, such Germans had a great deal more latitude to act independently than is often appreciated. Those 'racially pure' Germans who were dissatisfied could retreat into the home – known as 'internal emigration' – or go on holidays and hiking trips to the countryside or rent remote ski lodges with like-minded friends. In these places trusted friends could talk openly.

The Scholl children were now at that teenage period when they quite naturally wanted to experiment sexually and socially, but they were forced to endure the rigid conformity of school and the increasingly militaristic Hitler Youth organisations. The Scholl apartment at 81 Olgastrasse was slowly becoming a magnet for kindred spirits who felt disillusioned or alienated. Most of the circle of friends around the Scholl family were free-spirited in outlook.[5] As Elisabeth Hartnagel puts it:

> In the home or with the family you could talk openly, but outside the safety of the home you had to be very careful about making any critical comments about the regime, because you did not know whether a person was a Nazi or not.[6]

By now, Sophie Scholl was a budding artist who admired modern artists considered 'degenerate' by the Nazi regime. 'If you admired such artists', says Franz Muller, 'you were considered an outsider.'[7] Otl Aicher – a very talented young modern artist – now became a close friend of the Scholl children. He was admired because he bravely refused to join the Hitler Youth and was punished by the school, which would not allow him to take his *Abitur* – school-leaving examinations, the essential qualification for university entry.

A much older person became a friend of Hans Scholl just before Christmas in 1935: Otto 'Ernst' Reden, a twenty-one-year-old soldier completing his compulsory military training in the Wehrmacht's 56th Infantry Regiment, stationed in Ulm. He was born on 10 June 1914 and came from a solid middle-class family in Cologne. Before 1933 he was an active member of a number of youth groups, including d.j.1.11. In May 1933 he joined the Hitler Youth, rising to the rank of leader of a *Jungvolk* squad. He passed his *Abitur* in the spring of 1934. After completing his compulsory labour service he studied philosophy at college in Cologne.[8] By the time he was discharged from military service, in September 1937, he had attained the rank of non-commissioned officer.[9]

Ernst Reden was dark-haired, handsome and he was viewed as very attractive by many females, including Sophie and Inge Scholl. It seems he was regarded as a 'very special person' by some of his friends, but others thought he was manipulative.[10] Hans Scholl admitted that Reden had exerted a 'certain influence' over him. He read books and he sang songs Reden recommended to him.[11] Reden encouraged Hans to continue with his separate dissident *Bündische* youth group and he participated in camping trips and club meetings of his d.j.1.11 group.[12]

It is pretty clear Reden saw himself as a real risk-taking bohemian living in a conformist society. He wrote poetry, spoke with great emotion on every subject, and generally viewed himself as something of a budding intellectual. In other words, just the type of person the Nazis despised. What Hans Scholl did not know was that Reden liked to live on the very edge of society and he liked to have company there. With hindsight, it can be seen that there was a certain amount of premeditation in the way the much older Reden swiftly ingratiated himself with the Scholl family and their teenage friends. He would often read poems by banned Jewish writers and poets. He told Hans about a brilliant lecture he had heard by Ernst Wiechert, the playwright, at Munich University, entitled *The Author and His Time*, in which he had attacked the treatment of the arts and literature in the Third Reich and in which he had said 'Youth must not be seduced into silence when conscience demands it must speak.'[13]

Reden was an enthusiastic adherent to the spirit and philosophy of d.j.1.11. He even went to London to meet 'Tusk', the exiled leader of the group.[14] But a local Hitler Youth squad leader in Ulm, when he heard Reden was there, warned Hans Scholl he would be well advised not to have any involvement with him, without giving any reasons for his objections. Hans decided to ignore this advice from a Hitler Youth superior on the grounds that a *Jungvolk* leader had the right to speak with any other Hitler Youth leader he wished.[15]

By this time, Hans was finding himself at odds with superior officers on Hitler Youth camping trips. He was relieved of his Hitler Youth leadership duties on more than one occasion for not following the orders of his superiors, but he used his considerable charm to gain reinstatement after a suitable period of *purdah*. One time Hans was discovered by a Hitler Youth commander reading a book by the Jewish writer Stefan Zweig called *Sternstunde der Menscheit* ('Mankind's Stellar Hours'), which concentrated not on rigid totalitarian discipline but on individuals following their own conscience. It also stressed that many great achievements had been by people born outside of Germany, many of whom were Jewish. Zweig was a 'non-Aryan writer' and his books firmly on banned lists. Hans was told that he could not read such 'Jewish filth' on Hitler Youth trips and the book was confiscated.[16] But Hans just obtained another copy. During the camping trips Hans would sometimes sit around with a group of friends, openly playing Russian, Swedish and Norwegian folk songs – not the prescribed Nazi songs.

Hans was even determined to bring some individuality to his leadership of the Hitler Youth in Ulm. To this end, he decided his group should design and produce a distinctive flag, without the usual swastika emblazoned upon it. Hans suggested they decorate their flag with a griffin. His troop designed and embroidered the new flag. It was proudly mounted on a huge flagstaff. One evening, an important adult Hitler Youth leader came along a line to inspect a number of newly created Hitler Youth flags. He then looked at the flag made by Hans' troop with an angry expression on his face. 'Hand it over', he said to a twelve-year-old boy holding it, 'Let him keep the flag', Hans protested. 'You people have no right to make a flag of your own', the Hitler Youth leader shouted. 'You are to keep strictly to the flags prescribed in the [Hitler Youth] manuals.' Hans told him this flag meant a great deal to his boys. The Hitler Youth leader then tried to pull it out of the young boy's hand. 'Leave him alone. Stop bullying him', Hans shouted. A fierce struggle ensued, ending with Hans landing a punch on the chin of the outraged Hitler Youth leader.[17] According to Elisabeth Hartnagel, this incident was one of the first signs of Hans' growing disenchantment with the rigidity of the Hitler Youth.[18]

During this period Sophie was enjoying the ups and down of being a teenager. The Nazi regime did not ban music and dancing to approved traditional tunes was permitted. Sophie loved to visit dance halls in Ulm with her sisters and her friends. As Inge Scholl recalls:

> We went together to carnival balls and artists' balls. The tango, fox-trot and English waltz were fashionable at the time … Sophie was an excellent dancer. She danced with great abandon, she let the music carry her away, oblivious to her surroundings, truly going along with her partner.

One of Sophie's schoolmates objected to her 'indecent way of dancing'. But Sophie ignored her, and danced on. She felt energetic; uninhibited dancing was liberation from the rigid conformity of Nazi society. Sophie had full knowledge – in a more innocent age – of 'the facts of life'. After a sex education class at her school, she said to Inge, who shared a room with her: 'Listen, today we had a terrific lesson. I want to explain it to you.' She slid under the blanket, took a pad and a drawing pencil and in great detail drew what the biology teacher had taught them. They then laughed hysterically at her graphic drawing.[19]

Meanwhile, the youthful discontent and nonconformity of her brother Hans was intensifying. In the summer of 1936, Hans decided to organise a three-week camping trip with his 'A Squad' of d.j.1.11 friends. He sought permission from the Reich Youth Ministry for the trip, but just two days before departure this permission was suddenly withdrawn.[20] The increasingly rebellious Hans chose to ignore this order and he went ahead. There were ten participants on the three-week camping trip, including his younger brother Werner. The group even visited a number of places outside Germany, including Copenhagen and Stockholm – which was very unusual for young Germans to do at the time. While they were away Hans took charge of the money of the group. At this time there were very strict foreign currency rules, which severely limited the amount of money any German could take on increasingly rare trips abroad. The limit was 10 marks per person, but when the group crossed the Swedish border Hans had approximately 180 marks (18 marks each). Hans doled out ten marks to everyone, so they could get through the border patrol, but he decided to hide the rest in an empty Nivea hand cream tin. Hans knew he was breaking the currency law, but he felt such a small breach would not 'harm the Reich'. He never thought it would ever come to light.[21] On the trip, the group read books to each other, gave lectures, sang songs and engaged in discussions, which were mostly philosophical and non-political in nature. Hans was keen to stress that his group was influenced by some of the rituals of d.j.1.11, but was a distinct group in its own right of like-minded friends. It was primarily an outlet from the Hitler Youth.[22]

In the spring of 1937, Hans gained the coveted *Abitur* and won a place to study medicine at Munich University. But all young Germans who wanted to go on to college had to first undertake a spell of compulsory service in the *Reicharbeitsdienst* (National Labour Service – RAD), followed by two years compulsory military service in the German armed forces. When Hans volunteered for labour service in spring 1937 he was no longer required to be a member of the Hitler Youth.[23] The primary aim of the labour service scheme was to keep young teenagers off the street and give them useful employment. But the scheme applied to everyone, irrespective of social background, in keeping with the Nazi desire to create a classless folk community.[24] In April 1937, Hans was sent to Göttingen camp to undertake his labour service. The road-building work he endured in the Swabian countryside at the labour service camp did not produce the type of negative reaction he exhibited at Nuremberg. Hans was helping to build Hitler's motorways (*Autobahns*). He told his mother:

> I've changed a little bit I suppose. This does not mean I've renounced my old principles and perceptions. I've just taken another step up the ladder … It's good for young people like us to get away from home for once … We're always singing with all our hearts, though, and it's a comfort to be able to vent your innermost feelings, if only in song.[25]

In reality, Hans was still going on – by now – illegal trips with his *Bündische* youth group.

In the summer of 1937, Hans visited the House of German Art in Munich with his sister Inge.[26] The exhibition was billed as a celebration of National Socialist art. Adolf Hitler, who opened it, warned those who still had sympathy with radical modern art:

> From now on we shall wage a remorseless war of cleansing against the last elements of subversion in our culture … I will assure you here – all those cliques of chatterers, dilettantes and art-frauds who puff each other up and so keep each other going, will be caught and removed.[27]

The Nazi paintings in the main exhibition displayed medieval Teutonic knights, idyllic rural scenes, muscular storm troopers and German maidens.[28] Because the Nazis thought their art was so genuinely superior to modern art, they decided to include a separate collection as part of the exhibition, calling it 'Degenerative Art'. The intention was to show how poor the work of such artists looked in comparison with new 'Nazi art'. This exhibition opened on 19 July 1937. The 650 paintings on show in the 'Degenerate Art' exhibition had special Nazi-penned captions beside them such as 'Farmers – as seen by Jews' and 'Insult to German womanhood'. But all the most world-famous modern German artists were displayed. Hans found the so-called 'degenerate' paintings of the Dada movement, Bauhaus artists and the cubists far more intellectually stimulating and sophisticated than dull and lifeless 'Nazi Art'. In fact, the exhibition on 'Degenerate Art' attracted well over 2 million visitors. Joseph Goebbels, the Nazi Propaganda Minister, who had organised the exhibition, quickly realised he had made a major mistake and closed it.[29]

Sophie was also showing signs of early doubts about Nazi conformity. One example occurred when she was reading poems at a BDM meeting from a book called *Buch der Lieder* (Book of Songs) by Heinrich Heine, whose most famous statement on Nazi intolerance was 'Where books are burned, they will ultimately also burn human beings.'[30] Sophie was overheard reading out a poem by Heine enthusiastically to her troop by a BDM group leader. Heine was a Jewish writer. All his books and poems were banned by the Nazi Ministry of Propaganda. The irate BDM leader who warned her never to read out such a poem again was told by Sophie that 'whoever did not know Heine did not know German literature'.[31] At school, Fräulein Kretschmer, one of Sophie's teachers at the Ulm Gymnasium, recalled that in classes Sophie grew increasingly fond of airing 'startling opinions'.[32]

At home, Sophie was reading numerous books by many other banned authors, including Paul Claudel and Thomas Mann. She was also mixing with talented painters and sculptors; most notably, Bertyl Kley and Wilhelm Geyer. Kley often invited the teenage Sophie to his house and, according to Inge Scholl, who accompanied her younger sister on many of these visits:

> For hours on end he would let us gaze at his paintings at his home and discuss colours and plain surfaces with us. On one such occasion he told us how a certain green had almost struck him dead. I can still hear that sentence. Good lord, I thought at the time, can a colour strike one dead? And then I saw that blazing green and was convinced that green could truly do it.

Sophie particularly loved drawing and sketching children and she started to sculpt using modelling clay. 'At first', recalls Inge Scholl, 'she did not think highly of modern art, but under the guidance of another friend of the family, the Ulm painter Wilhelm Geyer, she revised her attitude about expressionism and became an ardent admirer of modern art.'[33]

Sophie was also exhibiting the natural yearnings of youth. She increasingly visited the house of a close school friend, Annelies Kammerer, who had a phonograph and a large collection of 78 r.p.m. records. It was at Annelies' house, in the summer of 1937, when sixteen-year-old Sophie first met Fritz Hartnagel. He was four years older, a graduate of the prestigious Potsdam Military Academy, the elite training centre for officers of the Wehrmacht. When Sophie first met Fritz he was serving in Augsburg, about 50 miles to the south of Ulm. Fritz believed the army was still a non-Nazi organisation, with some independence from Hitler's regime – which at this time was partially true. Fritz had been a member of the Hitler Youth, but he also joined a d.j.1.11 group.

Fritz Hartnagel was Sophie's most profound 'romantic friend' and a deeply significant character in her life from this moment on. She kept up an extensive and truly fascinating personal correspondence with Fritz for the rest of her life. They actually spent more time writing to each other than in each other's company. It is through Sophie's letters with Fritz Hartnagel that we can discover Sophie's innermost thoughts and feelings. Fritz noted that:

> we shouldn't make Sophie into a saint. She was a girl like other girls ... Sophie was not a coldly calculating women and could be very emotional ... she thought things through with acute intelligence and logical consistency ... At first, we did not agree on anything ... only after much hesitation and reluctance did I find myself ready to follow her ideas.[34]

Sophie's many letters to Fritz Hartnagel between 1937 and 1943 exhibit a wide range of emotions and opinions. Some are very warm, others flippant and self-pitying, a great many more are serious and deeply perceptive. The vast majority of Fritz's replies to Sophie are judicious, balanced and reasonable. Sophie is initially very flattered that such an older, charming and worldly-wise young officer is deeply attracted to her. She often craves more attention from her seemingly reluctant sweetheart than he appears able to satisfy. Many of Sophie's most impassioned letters bemoan the fact that Fritz does not reply often enough to her letters, even though he sent her about two letters each week. 'When I picture you at this time', writes the teenage Sophie in a typical early letter:

> I see you laughing, and that's why I'd like to slap you really hard ... Try to look serious. I think you are still laughing, but that would be horrible of you. I wouldn't want anything more to do with you. It's very silly, you are not answering me ... Get some time off. You can do, being a lieutenant and write to me. You can write anything you like, complete drivel and I'll read it.[35]

FOUR

THE TURNING POINT

The full story of the events which overtook the Scholl family at the hands of the Nazi criminal justice system between November 1937 and June 1938 has been either glossed over or simply ignored in most of the other published books on Sophie Scholl and the White Rose. But what happened to Hans Scholl for illegal activities associated with his d.j.1.11 group and other more serious charges profoundly affected the whole family. During this lengthy gut-wrenching ordeal at the hands of the Gestapo, Hans Scholl displayed honesty and courage, enduring weeks of solitary confinement, sleeping on a plank bed in a bleak prison. The bravery Hans Scholl displayed in his later resistance to the Nazi regime was forged during this crisis.[1] This crisis is the crucial missing personal ingredient and key turning point that propelled Hans and Sophie Scholl on the path towards their destiny.

To understand what happened, it is important to look at the context in which these events occurred. There is considerable evidence that a spirit of non-conformity started to develop among German youth in the late 1930s.[2] A great many young people were turned off by the increasingly militaristic nature of the Hitler Youth. Sitting around camp fires – often in the cold – singing endless dreary Nazi songs lost its initial novelty. One former member recalled:

> We had hardly any free time. Everything was done in a military way ... The camp leader was an older Hitler Youth functionary of the drill sergeant type. His entire education effort was barking out orders.[3]

The Hitler Youth tried to outlaw normal teenage desires such as dressing fashionably, growing distinctive hairstyles, smoking, drinking, partying, flirting and engaging in sexual experimentation. For teenagers going through the hormonal turmoil known as puberty, the sexual apartheid of Hitler Youth organisations made the sexual frustration much worse. Lengthy camping trips often added to this. Tension was increased for the 'elite' Hitler Youth squad leaders, such as Hans Scholl, as they were actively discouraged from having girlfriends. Even as adults, SS officers had to get permission to marry and this was only granted if the potential partner was deemed 'racially suitable'.[4] To try to prevent same-sex relationships developing, the Hitler Youth was organised to keep the boys constantly occupied with physical fitness drills. Young males were repeatedly told by Hitler Youth leaders that homosexuality was not just illegal, but a 'racial' and 'psychological' weakness. Even so, a growing number of incidents of homoeroticism and homosexuality were unearthed by Hitler Youth leaders during camping and hiking trips.[5]

Paragraph 175 of the German Criminal Code deemed 'sexual intercourse' between men aged twenty-one and over as punishable by a prison sentence. Those charged with male same-sex activity under twenty-one years of age were charged under 175a of the code. But to secure a conviction, proof was needed that 'penetration had occurred'. This clause made it difficult to gain a conviction in a great many cases. In June 1935, the Nazi regime decided to amend paragraph 175 to include any 'unnatural sexual act'.[6] This made it much easier to prosecute even very minor homoerotic incidents, which had previously not been illegal at all. Between 1933 and 1935 – using the old 175 law – 4,000 men were convicted of same-sex activity. From 1936 to 1938 – using the new law – 22,000 men were convicted. The overall number of arrests for homosexuality shot up to over 50,000 between 1937 and 1939.[7] Even these figures do not adequately convey how gays were increasingly becoming a key 'target' group of Nazi terror. Most gay people were now forced to lead a double life – many often maintained heterosexual relationships as a cover and had to engage in gay relationships under the very strictest secrecy. It made sense to have a well thought-out excuse for spending too much social time in the company of another single male.[8]

In same-sex male prosecutions the person defined as 'the seducer' was treated more harshly than the seduced, whom the Nazis felt could be 're-educated' by 'psychological therapy'. For this purpose, the regime established what it called 'Research Institutes' in which gays were re-educated to lead what the Nazis called 'normal lives'.[9] It had long been a rule in German penal institutions that those accused or convicted of homosexuality were kept in solitary confinement.[10] Many judges were reluctant to send first offenders to prison for 175 offences as it was felt that once inside they would be 'corrupted' by 'habitual offenders'. This was already a popular view in Germany before Hitler came to power. It was most dramatically presented in the 1928 popular German film *Sex in Chains*, which tells the story of an engineer convicted of killing a man who had tried to seduce his wife. Once 'inside' he starts a gay relationship with his cell-mate, and his wife begins a heterosexual affair while he is incarcerated. When the man is released early on his 'crime of passion' charge, the couple re-unite, but both are depicted as riddled with guilt. They end up committing suicide by gassing themselves, using a domestic oven.[11]

To deal specifically with same-sex activity in the Hitler Youth, a new law was introduced. Under paragraph 176 of the Criminal Code, sexual exploita-tion by superiors towards subordinates in the Hitler Youth or the League of German Girls was made a criminal offence. By and large, the Nazi regime wanted to keep homosexual cases involving members of Nazi organisations out of the courts.[12] But homosexual activity was widespread, not only within the Hitler Youth, but in the Nazi Party itself. A large number of incidents of homosexual behaviour by Hitler Youth leaders against younger mem-bers were hushed up. In 1935, there were a number of raids by the Gestapo on Hitler Youth leaders suspected of homosexual behaviour. Most of those arrested underwent brutal interrogations by the Gestapo until a full confes-sion – truthful or not – was extracted. In one notorious case in 1935 a young boy was sexually assaulted by several Hitler Youth leaders while on a camping trip. He was later stabbed to death when he threatened to report the matter to the police. When his distressed mother found out what had happened to her son she protested to Nazi officials, but she was promptly arrested by the Gestapo and sent to a concentration camp in order to keep her quiet.[13]

The Nazi regime was not averse to using false accusations of homosexu-ality to discredit all types of opponents. Even a member of the Nazi Party could be 'outed' in a carefully orchestrated scandal. When Helmut Brückner, a Nazi Party regional leader in Silesia, complained about a number of mur-ders carried out by SS officer Udo von Woyrsch, Himmler had him arrested on a swiftly concocted trumped-up charge of 'gross indecency with an army officer' and he was sacked and then tried and sentenced to eighteen months imprisonment.[14] On 1 October 1936, a Reich Central Office for Combating Homosexuality and Abortion was established. Gestapo officers all over Germany received instructions to recruit informers to find homo-sexuals – especially those operating in opposition and dissident groups.

In the autumn of 1937, the Nazi authorities decided to mount a major nationwide crackdown to break up all banned youth organisations. The drive to root out youth subversion was led by the Gestapo. In Ulm, the local Hitler Youth leadership already knew about Hans Scholl's d.j.1.11-style group. In the middle of November 1937, the doorbell rang at the Scholl apartment. Outside stood two men wearing overcoats. When there was no answer, they knocked on the door and one shouted, 'Gestapo! Open the door'. Robert Scholl finally opened the door and invited them in. The officers had come not to arrest the parents, but the children. Hans was not at home so Sophie, Inge and Werner were taken away and transported to Gestapo headquarters in Stuttgart. Inge recalled that 'in Stuttgart each of us was put in a cell and no one knew what was going to happen.'[15] At first, the Gestapo thought Sophie, with her short bob haircut, was a young boy, but as soon as they discovered she was a girl she was released. Elisabeth was not arrested in the raid. Inge, a devoted member of the BDM, was soon released and fifteen-year-old Werner Scholl, who had been involved in Hans' d.j.1.11 group, was interrogated and then released. The Gestapo also arrested the rest of Hans' 'A Squad' during extensive raids in the Ulm area. Sophie seemed to take the whole thing in her stride. A few weeks later, after returning from a late night out, accompanied by Inge, the door to their apartment on Olgastrasse was locked. 'We quaked and trembled and boldly rang the bell', she explained to Fritz Hartnagel, 'My father peered out of the window, thinking it was the Gestapo. He was agreeably surprised to find it was only us two and we didn't get told off.'[16]

But the Gestapo interrogations of the young men arrested in Ulm for *bündische* activity was getting ever more serious. At the beginning of November 1937, the local gossip mill in Ulm was putting out a rumour that Ernst Reden had been expelled from his Hitler Youth group in Cologne for same-sex activity. Hans Scholl reported this rumour to the regional leader of the Hitler Youth in Ulm in an attempt to distance himself from Reden. During the Gestapo interrogations, a teenager claimed that Reden had made improper sexual advances towards him, but he brushed them off.[17] The Gestapo was most concerned about Reden's sexual behaviour. After all, he was a twenty-three-year-old man and the boys making the allegations against him were under sixteen. During the early stages of investigation Reden confessed to making improper sexual advances towards two teenagers in Ulm.[18]

But another young man, 'Teenager X', claimed that he had been involved in a brief 'gay' relationship with Hans Scholl while they were both in the Hitler Youth.[19] These allegations led to Hans Scholl's immediate arrest.

At the time he was undergoing military training at his army barracks at Bad Cannstatt. He was handcuffed, driven to Gestapo headquarters in Dusseldorf and placed in solitary confinement. In a letter to his mother, shortly after his arrest, Hans said a great deal of 'mudslinging' was now going on among the arrested members of his d.j.1.11 youth group, but he gave no details as to what he meant.[20] Sophie sent Hans a Christmas present while he was in prison, but the Gestapo would not let him even open it.

In a series of lengthy interrogations, Hans fully confessed to a 'close relationship' with 'Teenager X'.[21] 'I am so very sorry to have brought all this misfortune on the family', he told his parents a few days before Christmas 1937, 'I was often close to desperation during my first few days of custody. I promise you, though, I'll put everything right. When I'm free, I'll work and work – that and nothing but – so you can look on your son with pride once again.'[22] Robert Scholl made a strenuous effort to get his son released. He lobbied Captain Scrupin, an officer in Hans' cavalry unit who regarded the Gestapo investigation into a promising young recruit as unwarranted. On 20 December 1937, Captain Scrupin told Robert Scholl 'I called on Judge E. [Eckert, Director of the Regional Court] on Friday afternoon and also spoke with the judge advocate on Saturday. The main problem is that, as a youth leader, your son may be held to have abused his senior status [as Hitler Youth leader].' But for this, the whole business would probably have been dropped.[23] On Christmas Eve 1937, Captain Scrupin visited Hans in Stuttgart, and reported to Robert Scholl: 'I found your son quite calm and composed … He has undergone some further questioning about his membership in the *bündische Jugend*, but he feels confident that no charges can be brought on that score.'[24] It seems Scrupin's lobbying of the Special Court did have some influence as the case was subsequently transferred to the jurisdiction of the Superior State Court in Stuttgart. This was extremely important for Hans Scholl; Stuttgart was a city where the German army had great influence.

Hans told his sister Inge:

I often forget the whole thing and try to act carefree and exuberant, but then the dark shadow looms up again and makes everything seem dismal and empty. When that occurs all that keeps me going is the thought of a future that'll be better than the present. You've no idea how much I look forward to going to university.[25]

In this period, Hans' mood alternated between increasing anxiety about his plight and a youthful optimism that he might walk free. In March 1938, he told his parents:

I've a feeling that everything is going to turn out alright. I now look forward to the day when all this will be forgotten and I'll be a different person again … Last Monday, I sneaked into a nice café … Then I took a bus to Leonberg, where we spent an enjoyable evening. I was back in barracks just before midnight … On Friday, I told our lieutenant the whole story. He's entirely on my side … All the non-coms know about the foreign exchange business by now, of course, which is why I'm seeking a transfer to another squadron as soon as possible.[26]

At home, Sophie appeared outwardly to be coping with all the pressure. Sophie felt the charges were 'totally unjustified' and she could not understand why Hans was being put through such an endless ordeal by the Gestapo.[27] At times of stress, Sophie would often retreat to the comfort of her bed, go to sleep and have vivid dreams. 'They say dreams depend on the noises you hear in your sleep', she told Fritz Hartnagel, 'Maybe it's true. Anyway, I really enjoy dreaming. I live in peculiar world (while I'm dreaming) where I'm never entirely happy.'[28]

In the midst of this anxiety-ridden family crisis, German troops marched into Austria on 12 March 1938. The next day Hitler drove through the streets of Vienna in an open-topped limousine in front of hundreds of thousands of cheering Austrians waving swastika flags. The union of Germany and Austria – known as the *Anschluss* – was achieved without firing a shot. It was more of a Nazi victory parade than an invasion.[29] But the sound of a jack-booted German army on the march in Europe brought no joy to Hans Scholl: 'A lot of sabre rattling going on here', Hans told his parents:

In general, I refrain from commenting on political developments. My head feels heavy. I don't understand people anymore. Whenever I hear all that anonymous jubilation on the radio, I feel like going out into a big, deserted plain and being by myself.[30]

At the end of March 1938, Hans faced a further court appearance: 'I've just come from the district court', he told his parents in a letter on 28 March 1938:

All they did was take down my personal particulars. I asked the official what would happen next. He told me I'll be served with the indictment in the next few days and then the trial will open … That's what I find the worst part. If only it was over at last.[31]

As the day of the trial grew closer, Hans seemed resigned to his fate. He told his parents that he was 'not afraid of going on trial. Even if I can't justify myself in open court. I can justify myself to myself.'[32] The pressure on Hans must have been immense in this period. A conviction on a 175 charge would ruin him and he knew it. Yet he showed great fortitude in spite of the seriousness of the charges he faced and the negative stigma attached to them by the Nazi regime.

The Special Courts – set up in each judicial district in March 1933 to deal primarily with 'political opponents' – became infamous during wartime for brutal sentencing. They were staffed by professional judges selected by the legal authorities. Few judges were 'old comrades' – meaning those who had joined the Nazi Party during the early 1920s. These courts administered fast-track justice with no appeal system, except a plea for 'clemency' that was rejected in almost every single case. But the judges were expected to administer justice leniently to a 'national comrade' and deal more harshly with 'community aliens'. Middle-class 'ordinary' Germans were rarely seen in these courts. Most were acquitted or given very mild sentences – on average less than six months in prison. It was very rare indeed for a 'national comrade' to be sent to a concentration camp. The judges had incredible latitude in sentencing and they still retained enormous autonomy. They could convict an innocent person or they could acquit someone whose guilt was clear. The punishment did not fit the crime so much as each judge's subjective views and prejudices. Judges often completely ignored rules of evidence and any principles of fairness or equality.[33]

Even Adolf Hitler thought that a 'national comrade' who had 'tripped up' just the one time deserved a second chance. After all, Hitler had served a lengthy prison sentence himself in the 1920s. What the Nazis feared was that by putting a 'decent national comrade' in prison they might come into contact with those defined as 'community aliens' – especially hardened criminals – and become 'corrupted'. Hence, first offenders tended to be treated very leniently, provided their crimes were not seen as a threat to the national community.[34]

The Ulm *Bündische* Trial took place on 2 June 1938 in the Special Court in Stuttgart. The judge appointed to adjudicate in the case was Hermann Albert Cuhorst, who was the son of the chief prosecutor in Stuttgart in the Weimar era.[35] Cuhorst had trained as a lawyer and joined the Nazi Party on 1 December 1930. During the Nazi era he became a propaganda speaker for the party. In October 1937 he was appointed as the Chief Justice of the Special Court in Stuttgart.[36] At the end of the Second World War Cuhorst went into hiding, but he was captured by US forces in November 1946. He was eventually put on trial at Nuremberg at the 'Judges' Trial', conducted by the US allied authorities, which took place between 5 March and 4 December 1947. The sixteen defendants were prominent German judges and lawyers, most of whom had operated the Special Courts and People's Courts of Nazi Germany. Ten of the defendants were found guilty of 'crimes against humanity' and membership of the SS or Nazi Party leadership groups, but four were acquitted, including Cuhorst.[37] Oral evidence presented during the trial showed that Cuhorst was a fanatical local Nazi and a very ruthless judge, especially when dealing with cases involving Jews, opponents of the regime and foreign workers.[38] Unfortunately, the records of the Stuttgart trials were destroyed by fire towards the end of the war.[39] In passing judgement, the rather benevolent US judge said Cuhorst was criticised by committed Nazi officials because of the lenient and inconsistent sentences he often passed and because of the lost records there was insufficient evidence to convict him.[40]

But when the people of Stuttgart heard about Cuhorst's acquittal they found it quite incomprehensible. The US authorities had obviously blundered badly. So Cuhorst was put on trial again during the de-Nazification trials in 1948. At this trial, it was shown that he had passed 120 death sentences between 1937 and 1945. In one case, Cuhorst said to his fellow judges, 'Well, today, we have three cases, which must be at least two heads' (for the executioner). In another, he ordered the death of a man for stealing the Christmas bonus of a Stuttgart man in a local beer hall. Many witnesses said Cuhorst commonly described defendants as 'pigs', 'racial scum' and 'degenerate traitors'. He often dealt with cases that resulted in execution in less than thirty minutes. At this trial Cuhorst was found guilty and sentenced to four years. He appealed, but then his sentence was increased to six years. For the rest of his life, Cuhorst went on moaning that he had been tried twice for the same crime and he went to his grave refusing to face up to his dreadful role in the Nazi terror machine.[41]

The trial of Hans Scholl took place in a single day. 'Teenager X' helped Hans tremendously by saying that he had totally forgiven him for starting their 'brief' same-sex relationship, which he depicted as a few instances of very mild teenage fumbling. The Regional Director of the Hitler Youth helped too by telling the court that the Hitler Youth had actually given the go-ahead for Hans to set up his d.j.1.11 'A Squad' in the first place. In his testimony, Hans Scholl said his group had just wanted an outlet from the Hitler Youth, but none of the members were really opposed to the ideals of National Socialism.

Hans made a very 'favourable impression' on the judge. He was further helped by an excellent testimonial from Captain Scrupin, his commanding officer. In his judgement, the judge did briefly criticise Hans for continuing to lead a circle of friends whose activities were independently *bündische* in 'character' and 'contravened the law', but he put these indiscretions down to Scholl's 'youthful exuberance' and 'obstinate personality'. Cuhorst concluded that Hans was not really '*bündische* in spirit', but was really a 'national comrade' who would never take actions that would place the state in 'any danger'. He had made just made a few silly mistakes which he now deeply regretted. Cuhorst passed off Hans' relationship with 'Teenager X' as a youthful 'failing', instigated by a headstrong young man who was 'normally heterosexual in nature'; nor had Hans abused his role as a Hitler Youth leader, as the two teenagers were too close in age for this to apply.

There was even better news. Following the union with Austria, Hitler had announced there would be an amnesty to everyone charged with *Bündische* offences. So the judge announced to the court that Hans Scholl was acquitted on all charges and could leave the court a free man without a stain on his character. A few days after the trial, a mightily relieved Hans told his sister Inge, 'You know what I've been through in the last few days. That puts me under an obligation to thank you all, and you especially.'[42] All the other defendants in the case, except one, were also acquitted of all charges.

Ernst Reden was the only defendant found guilty. Cuhorst concluded that Reden's 'inexcusable' sexual actions against the two young boys were 'premeditated' and psychologically harrowing for one of the boys ('Boy B'). Reden was found guilty of one 175 charge, but acquitted on the charge against the other boy involved in the case. He was given a very mild three-month prison sentence.[43] Cuhorst concluded that Reden had exercised a 'great influence' over the *Bündische* group in Ulm, but in mitigation he said that Reden had been a good soldier during his military service and he was convinced he was a loyal comrade. Reden was asked to pay the full costs of the case, as he had been convicted.[44]

It seems Cuhorst defined Hans Scholl from beginning to end as a respectable and highly educated 'national comrade' who was not a danger to the Nazi state. Cuhorst concluded that Hans Scholl was a young man from a good family who had already suffered enough humiliation and punishment, freely admitted his mistakes and could be trusted to behave well in the future. It is clear Hans had suffered some ostracism from some of his army colleagues. In a letter, dated 27 June 1938, Hans wrote in a tone obviously tinged with a residual bitterness:

I keep a rosebud in my breast pocket. I need that little flower because it's the other side of the coin, far removed from soldiering, but at odds with a soldierly frame of mind. You should always carry a little secret around with you, especially when you're with comrades like mine.[45]

This lengthy drama affected the whole Scholl family. At school, Sophie suffered a great deal of verbal abuse from her classmates who constantly asked her 'what on earth have you people been up to?' It says something for her strength of spirit that Sophie weathered this storm with calm dignity. The BDM charged Sophie with 'disloyalty' just for being related to someone charged with *bündische* activities. Elisabeth, who had not even been arrested by the Gestapo, was also disciplined by the BDM.[46] According to Inge Scholl:

Our family at this time was a sheltering island. Since [Hans'] arrest the fights between him and my father stopped altogether ... We children often went for walks with our father. I could sense how hard he had been hit by our imprisonment. One night, as Sophie and he and I were walking, he gave vent to his feelings ... 'If those bastards harm my children in any way, I'll go to Berlin and shoot him', meaning Hitler.[47]

These events add a vitally important new personal ingredient to the complex motives that propelled Hans and Sophie Scholl towards outright opposition to Hitler. During her interrogation by the Gestapo in February 1943, Sophie Scholl said the arrests in the autumn of 1937 were the 'most important reason' for her subsequent opposition towards the Nazi regime.[48] Elisabeth Hartnagel says that the affair had a traumatic effect on the whole family and the Nazis were never forgiven for the trauma they had inflicted on the Scholls.[49] During his terrible ordeal, Hans had displayed honesty and courage. He had met adversity and disappointment head on and was not found wanting. The outcome of the case had left Hans and Sophie Scholl, who had supported him throughout his ordeal, with a clear choice. They could conform to the existing Nazi order and become respectable 'national comrades' or they could be true to their obvious free-spirited and individualistic approach to life. The movement towards outright opposition did not begin the next day or the next week, but all enthusiasm for the Nazi regime was now draining away. The seed that was to result in the active involvement of Hans and Sophie Scholl in the White Rose was planted during this crisis.

FIVE

IN THE SHADOW
OF WAR

In the summer of 1938, Sophie Scholl went on a pleasant and much-needed holiday with her school friends, Annelies Kammerer and Lisa Remppis, along with her younger brother Werner and the rest of the Kammerer family. It was enjoyable for Sophie to sit lazily in the open air, go swimming, go on boats drifting on slow-moving rivers and walk in the beautiful green countryside. Sophie's love of nature intensified during periods of personal pressure. Later in the holiday the party met up with Inge Scholl, who had been strawberry-picking on a nearby farm. Sophie blew hot and cold on Annelies. 'It's often quite an effort for me to put up with her at all' she told Inge:

> The atmosphere when we are together is often tense. I keep thinking I'm going to snap, but I hope Annelies does not catch on. Sometimes we can have such a good time together and that cancels out some of the arguments.[1]

This sort of letter is quite typical of Sophie's alternating feelings towards her few close friends.

During the holiday they were driven to various places by the long-suffering 'Herr Kammerer', including Giessen and Lesum, near Bremen.[2] Sophie always felt slightly uncomfortable with the people of northern Germany. She sensed a lack of warmth, which she often contrasted unfavourably with the more 'warm and friendly' regions of Swabia and Bavaria in the south. When Inge – who was still a devoted member of the BDM – finally showed up, Sophie had difficulty not bursting out laughing when her big sister, without a hint of cynicism, greeted her – as she did most 'loyal national comrades' –

with the well-known 'Heil Hitler' salute. A few days later, while on a stormy boat trip aboard a trawler in the North Sea, Sophie got irritated when 'four Hitler youth leaders and a young married couple' started a conversation, but in the end the teenage Hitler Youth leaders, according to Sophie, 'turned out to be very nice' and she had a pleasant chat with them.[3]

When Sophie returned home from her holiday to Ulm, at the end of August 1938, Adolf Hitler was threatening war unless the 3.5 million German-speakers who resided in a border region of Czechoslovakia (the Sudetenland) were granted self-determination. Czechoslovakia, a democratic state created by the 1919 Paris Peace Settlement, had diplomatic agreements with France and the Soviet Union. The crisis held out the prospect of war if a negotiated settlement could not be found.[4] Step forward Neville Chamberlain, the British prime minister, following a policy of 'appeasement', which aimed to satisfy German grievances over the 'hated' Treaty of Versailles and almost anything else Hitler wanted. Chamberlain flew to meet Hitler three times during September 1938, thereby single-handedly creating what is now called 'shuttle diplomacy'. All this had one aim: to bring about the peaceful transfer of the Sudetenland to Nazi Germany on Hitler's terms. On 22 September 1938, Hitler made new demands and the talks broke down. 'How horrible, fantastic, incredible it is', Chamberlain said in a speech on BBC radio on 27 September 1938, 'that we should be digging trenches and trying on gas masks here because of a quarrel in a far away country between people of whom we know nothing'.[5] For once, Hitler backed down, but still got everything he wanted under the terms of the Munich Agreement signed on 30 September 1938, described later by Sir Winston Churchill as 'the blackest page in British history'.

What Sophie Scholl thought about these events is not recorded in either her letters or her diaries. But we can glimpse what Hans Scholl felt about the Munich crisis in a letter to Inge Scholl:

> Now that all the excitement is over I've time to write to you … I've never been such a patriot, in the true sense, as I was in the early days of October. Only when you're compelled to wonder if the Fatherland still means as much as it may once have done – only when you've lost faith in banners and speeches because pervading ideas have become trite and worthless – does true idealism assert itself.[6]

But this sudden brief surge of patriotism was not strong enough for Hans to decide on a career in the armed forces. After his compulsory military service ended on 1 November 1938, Hans decided to study medicine. Any person called up for military service who decided to study medicine at university had their two-year compulsory service shortened by six months. All that was required to gain this useful concession was to attend a six-month medical pre-liminary course. Hans completed this at Tübingen University, 50 miles from Ulm. For his degree studies, Hans opted for the more prestigious Munich University.[7] Sophie was now determined to go to Munich University too.

But the Nazi regime did not approve of women going to university at all. The number of female students fell from 17,000 in 1932 to a mere 6,000 in 1939. From April 1938, all girls who managed to gain the coveted *Abitur* had to undertake a 'domestic year', in which they had to complete a course in a practical subject linked to their future roles as mothers. In addition, they also had to endure a six-month period of 'labour service'. For Sophie the prospect of unskilled labour service was very unappealing. But she was prepared to endure it to go to university.[8]

Hans found university life very enjoyable. 'It's all so different from a year ago', he told his parents, 'but I can't help brooding on the year that has gone by since then. Have I really improved? Have all my efforts borne fruit and resulted in progress?' Hans was seeking some sort of spiritual regeneration at this point in his life. He became much more brooding and philosophical and confessed honestly: 'there are times when you feel petty and ridiculous in your human frame'.[9] At these moments of bleak depression, Hans could turn morose, speaking of a 'burning emptiness'.[10] In November 1938 he wrote:

Yes, the autumn has arrived. That means ... wild windswept skies ... delicate veils of mist that enshroud everything in melancholy. It means dying itself. The dying [you] can't evade because you're young and believe in the return of spring. You have to pass through the process of dying, which doesn't after all mean death itself.[11]

Hans Scholl increasingly looked for answers to the human predicament in philosophy, literature and the words of the Bible. He found the works of St Augustine inspiring and uplifting, especially his view that barbarians could not prevail against the truth of God. Another major source of inspiration was the writings of St Thomas Aquinas. Hans was particularly inspired by Aquinas' view that the state existed to serve the individual, not the other way around. Hans would frequently share his views with Sophie when he came home and they developed a great love of discussing philosophical and spiritual writings and trying to find answers to the big questions: morality, conscience, belief, life and death.

Sophie Scholl, now seventeen, began the studies, in September 1938, that would eventually lead to the coveted *Abitur* – the passport to university. Before the new term was due to begin Sophie was enjoying what she called the 'love of my dear old bed'. Lying in soothed her and she was soon bemoaning the fact that 'this vacation has seemed incredibly short – shorter than the Easter vacation'.[12] Sophie also loved her bath tub and could stay in there soaking and reading for ages until her mother knocked on the door to get her to come out. At school, Sophie often seemed to become increasingly disinterested or distracted. 'Sometimes school is like a film – a film I watch but can hardly act in.'[13] At other times, she berated herself for 'working too little' or 'daydreaming' and not achieving 'what I should'.[14] Sophie was much too realistic to give in to enthusiasm and her moments of optimism were increasingly fleeting. Behind her frequent self-mockery and love of speculation lay a lively and curious mind. Dr Else Fries, one of her teachers, said that whenever she asked Sophie a question 'she was immediately alert and knew the answer'.[15] To stress her individuality she would often wear a flower behind her ear, while dressed in the same school uniform as all the other girls. It was a small and discrete act of non-conformity, but it pleased her nonetheless. At BDM meetings, which remained compulsory, Sophie was feeling more and more alienated. She found the meetings were repetitive and boring. There were also frequent disagreements between Sophie and her local BDM squad leader over how to make the activities of the group more intellectually stimulating for the members.[16] By now, Sophie was already strongly opposed to Hitler's aggressive foreign policy. She asked all of her male friends who were conscripted never to kill anyone.[17]

The Ulm Gymnasium Sophie attended employed some teachers who were known to be 'reserved' from National Socialism.[18] All the evidence suggests that most teachers at Sophie's school tried to keep Nazi indoctrination to a bare minimum. Some teachers did not even wear the obligatory Nazi Party badge on their lapel. One of Sophie's history teachers often used examples from history to provoke more open debate. In one discussion, concerning the death of Mary, Queen of Scots and the role of Queen Elizabeth I in her execution, most of the pro-Nazi students in Sophie's class argued that Elizabeth was justified in her actions as she had wanted brutally to crush all opposition. Sophie argued that the state had to operate within the terms of the law and protect the right of individuals to protest against what they felt was tyrannical rule. Of course, this topic had an obvious parallel with what was going on in

Nazi Germany, but only by using these past events obliquely could any meaningful moral questions ever be debated in an otherwise rigidly prescribed conformist curriculum in the German schools.[19]

Most of the Scholl family thought Sophie – who had excelled at art in her teenage years – would opt to study that subject at university. There is no doubt that Sophie was a very gifted artist. In life study classes she preferred to draw women as she thought their bodies were more beautiful. Her art teacher in life studies class called men the bread and women the cake – to which Sophie quipped 'I would so much rather have cake.' In the end, Sophie decided that 'art is not something you learn'. She picked biology and philosophy as her joint degree subject, if she passed her exams.[20] Sophie's favourite subject was biology. At school, she looked forward to the practical biology lessons, conducted by her favourite teacher, Dr Else Fries. 'Biology is tremendous fun these days', she told Fritz Hartnagel:

> I've already dissected an ox eye. And when I did the fish, I displayed all the
> inner parts ... so beautiful ... Fish have golden eyes and lovely circular lenses.
> Awfully nice creatures. I felt so sorry for them.[21]

Meanwhile, the Nazi terror against the Jews finally spilled onto the streets of Germany on the brutal and destructive night of 9–10 November 1938. The spurious pretext was the murder of a German diplomat in Paris a few days earlier by a Polish Jew named Herschel Grynszpan. The night was called *Kristallnacht* (Night of the Broken Glass), as the streets of most towns and cities in Germany were littered with broken glass from shop windows and business premises owned by Jews. On this night, thousands of Jewish shops were vandalised, hundreds of synagogues burnt down, in the region of ninety-one Jews murdered, thousands violently assaulted and 30,000 more put in 'protective custody' in concentration camps.[22]

In Ulm, synagogues were set on fire, shops vandalised and Jews attacked. A local Ulm newspaper ran the approving headline of the pogrom 'Just Vengeance of Outraged Citizens', but it also reported that many citizens were 'whimpering and complaining' about the brutality of the attacks on Jews.[23] Unfortunately, there is no written evidence about how the Scholl family felt about the violence. A number of Jewish families were living in the apartment block at 81 Olgastrasse (now renamed Adolf Hitler Ring) on *Kristallnacht*, but there is no record as to what happened to them. Fritz Hartnagel later recalled that the Scholls were sympathetic with the plight of Jews in Nazi Germany. 'I was particularly shaken by the persecution of the Jews', he later commented, 'that escalated, in the *Reichskristallnacht* of November 9, 1938, into an explosion of violence, with officially organised assaults on Jews'.[24] A lack of documentary evidence should not lead to the conclusion that the Scholl family were not equally shocked and outraged by *Kristallnacht*. Everything we know about Sophie Scholl indicates that she would have been extremely angry about the violence.[25] The secret Social Democrat reports (known as SOPADE) concluded that the popular reaction to *Kristallnacht* in most German towns and cities was one of private revulsion and horror.[26] In general, there was no meaningful opposition in Germany to what had occurred.

With the benefit of hindsight, we can now see that a great many Germans wittingly and unwittingly benefited from the Nazi regime's economic plunder of Jews. In 1933, there were approximately 100,000 Jewish-owned businesses in Germany, but by July 1938 only 30,000 remained. Few hands were completely clean. No doubt Robert Scholl's financial business was helped by Nazi economic policies – even though he disapproved of them personally. It would also be naïve to think that Robert Scholl's taxation work did not bring him into close professional contact with the leading Nazi officials. As one estate agent put it: 'To do business under the Nazis, you had to have a friend in every government office.'[27] In his professional life, Robert Scholl did his job, tried to earn a living for his family, but in private he detested the Nazis.

During 1939, the relationship between Sophie Scholl and Fritz Hartnagel was getting ever closer. On 1 February 1939, Fritz told Sophie: 'We are becoming closer and getting to understand each other more.'[28] In another letter, dated 15 March 1939, Fritz told Sophie he was pleased to be her 'little drummer boy'. He urged her to 'tell me everything and don't hide your feelings' and wanted her never to think 'I would ever laugh at your feelings'.[29] Fritz was accepted into the Scholl family circle. On 27 March 1939, for example, Fritz asked Sophie to thank her mother for sending him a delicious home-made cake.[30]

In the summer of 1939, with Europe on the verge of war because of a messy dispute between Germany and Poland, over the free port of Danzig, Werner Scholl became the first member of the Scholl family to undertake open acts of public opposition to the Nazi regime. He resigned from the Hitler Youth, in the full knowledge that this act of defiance meant he could not take the *Abitur* examination and would not be allowed to go to university. But Werner's most daring act of opposition was to climb to the very top of the statue of Justice, outside the courthouse in Ulm, late one night and to place a swastika blindfold over the eyes of the lady holding the scales of justice.[31]

By now, Hans Scholl had started his medical studies at Munich University and the Scholl family had moved into a spacious and lavishly furnished seven-room rented apartment on the fifth floor of 33 Münsterplatz, in the affluent cathedral square, overlooking the imposing Münster.[32] In the same period, Sophie was forced to abandon her plan to go on a summer holiday to Yugoslavia with Fritz Hartnagel because 'young people are not allowed to go abroad during this critical period'.[33] This did not mean Sophie was going to be denied her annual summer holiday. In August 1939, she went with Fritz on a two-week holiday to north Germany, beginning on the Baltic, then moving on to the North Sea coast, finally ending up at Worpswede, near Bremen. The weather was gloriously sunny during the summer of 1939. They went on walks together in the countryside, took pleasant boat trips, enjoyed lavish meals – paid for by the affluent army officer – and visited art galleries. The town was still a thriving area for actors, writers, artists and sculptors. Sophie told Inge about the brilliance of some of the art she had viewed in Worpswede, but she was even more impressed by the natural environment: 'The landscape made a deep impression on me, it was so dark and peaceful.'[34] She also found time to go swimming and commented:

> I fell in love with the North Sea all over again. The breakers were simply ter-
> rific. I'd feel I was in seventh heaven, bobbing around on the waves, if only
> the salt water didn't keep disillusioning me so cruelly.[35]

But once again it was the inhabitants of north Germany that left her feeling disappointed. 'I can't get close to north Germans', she said, 'which is why I'm looking forward to Ulm again.'

With the imminent threat of European war, Fritz Hartnagel was recalled to his army unit one week into the holiday. Hans Scholl was also ordered to return to report for military duty as a student-medic at Grabnik in Masuria.[36] Even all this gloomy news did not make Sophie cut her summer holiday short. She went back on her own to the youth hostel in Worpswede which she had stayed in with Fritz, because she had left some of her belongings. She told Fritz:

> While we were gone a man [had] slept in my bed and had looked through
> my books. He proposed to go to the police at once and report us (for having
> banned books). Frau Ötken (the hostel manager) managed to stop him
> because we were guests ... Now they're [the hostel owners] taking an interest
> in my books and becoming very suspicious.[37]

'I am so happy when we spend vacations together', Fritz told Sophie a few weeks later, 'It makes me feel able to face my work again.'[38]

Just days after Sophie returned home, the Nazi–Soviet Pact was signed between Germany and the Soviet Union. The agreement came after the British and French governments failed to agree a military alliance with Stalin's communist regime. Poland complicated matters by not wanting Soviet assistance anyway. Neville Chamberlain, the British Prime Minister, had already made a monumental blunder by offering to defend Poland after Hitler had occupied Czechoslovakia five months earlier. Of all the European leaders, Stalin was the only one Hitler admired: 'That fellow Stalin is a brute, but you must admit, he's an extraordinary fellow.'[39] As for Chamberlain, Hitler frequently mocked the fact that he always carried an umbrella around with him.

It was about to start raining bombs. At dawn, on 1 September 1939, the German armed forces crossed the Polish border. They were about to open a new terrifying chapter in the history of warfare: *Blitzkrieg* (Lightning War). This consisted of rapid assaults by tanks, motorised infantry and screeching Stuka dive-bombers. Poland was about to pay a terrible price in blood for defying Hitler. Two days later, Britain and France reluctantly declared war on Germany. Hitler wanted to dominate Europe by force and the British government finally decided to resist. In Berlin, William Shirer, the leading US correspondent, stood on Wilhelmplatz while loudspeakers announced the British declaration of war:

> When it was finished there was not a murmur ... I walked in the streets. On the faces of the people astonishment, depression ... no excitement, no hurrahs, no throwing of flowers. No war fever, no war hysteria.[40]

On 3 September 1939, after hearing the news of the outbreak of war, Fritz informed Sophie: 'We will now be separated for long periods, but feel free to write whatever comes into your head and as often as possible.'[41] 'I just can't believe that people's lives are now under constant threat', Sophie replied two days later, 'I'll never understand it, and I find it terrible. Don't go telling me it's for the sake of the Fatherland.'[42]

SIX

KINDERGARTEN TEACHER

The outbreak of war coincided with the start of Sophie's last year at the Ulm Gymnasium. She soon noticed that once the war had started 'nobody could talk openly about anything anymore', but she still hoped it would be brought to a swift conclusion, even though she doubted that 'Germany will blockade England into quitting'.[1] Hans Scholl was similarly depressed about the start of war in Europe. He could not predict how long 'this mass murder will go on for', but believed that all the hopes of Germany, for good or ill, 'are pinned on this awful war'.[2] Less than six weeks later, Poland was under a brutal Nazi occupation which would kill millions.

The total lack of military activity in the winter of 1939–40 prompted the British press to describe it as 'The Phoney War'.[3] Anglo-French military chiefs decided to sit on the defensive. The British government felt the Nazi-Soviet Pact would not last and that all that was needed was a naval blockade, BBC radio broadcasts to Germany and dropping anti-Hitler leaflets by aircraft. The Germans responded with the infamous 'Germany Calling' propaganda broadcasts, delivered by William Joyce, an Anglo-Irish fascist – soon called 'Lord Haw-Haw'.[4]

In October 1939, Sophie recounted to Fritz Hartnagel a recent strange dream she had: 'I dreamt I sat in a prison cell' with a 'heavy iron ring around my neck'.[5] The next month, Sophie was speaking positively about her relationship with Fritz: 'How exquisite when two people can have a relationship without having to promise. Let's meet at such and such a place, or always stay together.'[6] Her thoughts soon turned towards Christmas – her favourite time of the year. Sophie enjoyed every aspect of the festive season:

singing carols around the piano, candle-lighting, wrapping presents, making Christmas cards, Advent calendars, flower wreaths, family get-togethers and going to church in the snow, as Ulm nearly always had a white Christmas.[7] Sophie had created a special Advent wreath and a calendar for Fritz. In a letter on 20 December 1939, Fritz wrote that he hoped they could arrange another ski trip together during the winter and admitted: 'The first thing I look for is a letter from you.'[8] But the highlight of that Christmas for the Scholl family was the return of Hans Scholl from military duty. Sophie and Hans were developing a very close bond. With Sophie now eighteen, they could chat more openly. 'While Hans was here', Sophie wrote, 'I often went walking in the woods with him. We tested the ice on the [River] Iller back-water. We even made it to the other bank without falling through.'[9]

In January 1940, Sophie began revising for her school-leaving examination.[10] But the Nazi educational authorities, not wishing young people to go to university in wartime, would not tell students the dates of exams. 'They just don't want to make things easy for us', she commented bitterly.[11] By now she had grown tired of school. She could not wait to get her exams over and done with as soon as possible. In March 1940, Sophie, with a gift of focusing on a clear goal, passed the *Abitur* examination, thereby securing a much-cherished place at Munich University to read biology and philosophy.

It was time for some fun. In March 1940, Sophie went on a skiing trip to the Austrian Alps with Fritz Hartnagel, who had been granted army leave. Her mother was not happy about Sophie going on a trip with her boyfriend without a chaperone. Nevertheless, she was allowed to go. The snow-capped mountains gave Sophie the joyful sense of freedom she craved. The 'gentlemanly' German army officer wined and dined Sophie in expensive restaurants with what Sophie described as 'meals fit for a king'. The weather was fine and clear during the whole break. One day she went on an exhilarating ski run down a steep mountain in zigzag fashion wearing just her swimming costume.[12]

Shortly after her return to Ulm, Sophie was off on holiday again. This time it was an enjoyable two-day cycle trip with her close friend, Lisa Remppis. They cycled through the rugged Swabian hills, south of Ulm, and then visited three monasteries. On the second day they stopped for coffee, cake and ice cream at a café at Ehingen. Then they took off their shoes and stockings to wade in the Danube, before picking some flowers to put in their hair, and then cycled along the beautiful Swabian country roads all the way back home.[13] These outdoor holidays offered Sophie access to the normal and free life she so desperately craved. Even Hitler could not conquer the sun or destroy the mountains.

Days later came the harsh reality of what Hitler could do – with the help of the armed forces. On 9 April 1940, German panzers rolled into Denmark and Norway, gaining swift victories. 'There are times when I dread the war', Sophie wrote after hearing the war in the west was finally and spectacularly underway, 'and I feel like giving up completely. I hate thinking about it, but politics are almost all there is, and as long as they are so confused and nasty it would be cowardly to turn your back on them.'[14] Sophie took out her anger about this surge of German militarism on Fritz, advising him impatiently: 'whatever you do, don't turn into an arrogant, uncaring lieutenant … It's so easy to become callous and I think that would be a shame.'[15]

In spite of the escalation of the war, Sophie was still determined to begin her degree studies in the summer semester of 1940. But all potential undergraduates needed to complete a six-month stint in the National Labour Service – known as RAD. Sophie bitterly resented this Nazi intrusion into her life. She tried to avoid it by enrolling on a practical course in kindergarten teaching at the Lutheran Fröbel Teachers' Seminary for children in Ulm-Söfingen, beginning in May 1940, in the naïve hope this would satisfy the Nazi labour service requirement.[16]

On 9 May 1940 Sophie enjoyed her nineteenth birthday in the company of Fritz Hartnagel, after the army had granted him another brief period of leave. After a pleasant day together, sitting out in the sunshine near the Danube, Sophie walked with Fritz to Ulm's central train station before he departed for military service in the Netherlands. On the platform, holding a bunch of daffodils he had bought for her earlier in the day, she kissed and embraced him and waved to him as his train pulled away.

The very next day, German troops – including Fritz's own unit – invaded the Netherlands in another lightning assault. The same day, Winston Churchill, a strong critic of the Nazi regime, replaced the broken, tired and ill Neville Chamberlain. If ever there was a man born to be a war leader it was sixty-five-year-old Churchill, who became the human embodiment of uncompromising defiance against Adolf Hitler's regime. 'We shall fight on the beaches', he told the House of Commons, 'we shall fight on the landing grounds, we shall fight in the fields and in the streets, we shall fight in the hills, we shall never surrender.'[17]

On 16 May 1940, Sophie wrote to Fritz Hartnagel. 'We notice the war, even here (Ulm) because scarcely a minute passes without our ears hearing the sound of aircraft.' With Fritz's life now in danger, Sophie told him what she now needed from their relationship 'is love, not friendship and companionship' and she candidly confessed: 'My dearest wish is that you should survive this war and these times without becoming a product of them', ending with heart-felt words: 'Think of me sometimes, but don't dream of me. I'm often with you in spirit, wishing you well and loving you.'[18] The same day, Fritz wrote hurriedly from the midst of the battle raging in Holland. 'I've very little time to write', he wrote, adding, 'The [Dutch] population is very friendly and agreeable'.[19]

On 28 May 1940, King Leopold III of Belgium, without informing his British and French allies, surrendered to the German forces without a fight. 'It's not easy to banish all thoughts of the war', Sophie commented to Fritz the next day. The successive victories of Hitler's armies made Sophie feel at a low ebb, and she admitted:

> I don't know too much about politics and I've no ambition to do so. I do have some idea of right and wrong, because that has nothing to do with politics and nationality. And I could weep at how mean people are and how they betray their fellow creatures, perhaps for the sake of personal advantage. It is enough to make a person lose heart sometimes. I often wish I lived on a Robinson Crusoe island.

Sophie questioned whether being romantically involved with an officer in the Wehrmacht – the embodiment of Hitler's militarism – was advisable and these doubts, based not on who Fritz was, but on what he represented, crop up in her letters to him during this period. In a demanding tone, Sophie also wanted to know from Fritz whether her strong feelings towards him were reciprocated: 'You do sometimes think of me at night, don't you? … Don't just think of me as I am – think of me as I would like to be.' Then, in an even more distant tone, Sophie questioned their compatibility in an off-hand way. 'We don't know one another anything like well enough and I'm a lot to blame … If much of what I say seems silly, hurtful, and unnecessary, remember I judge things from my own viewpoint and I may be crediting you with many of my own characteristics.'[20]

The Wehrmacht now began the military assault on France via the heavily wooded and poorly defended Ardennes region. This military masterstroke allowed the German panzer units to drive swiftly through the French countryside, without ever facing a major counter-attack. The French and British defending forces were outfought and soon in complete disarray. The British Expeditionary Force abandoned a futile struggle, leaving all their equipment behind and fleeing to the coastal town of Dunkirk. Between 27 May and 4 June 1941, 338,226 troops – including 140,000 French troops – were evacuated back to Britain on a flotilla of small ships.[21] Churchill dressed up this terrible, humiliating retreat in another brilliant speech as the British Empire's 'Finest Hour'. On 10 June 1940, Italy decided to enter the war on the side of Nazi Germany – mainly because Mussolini thought Hitler was going to win it. On 14 June 1940, German troops triumphantly entered Paris without meeting any resistance at all. 'To tell the truth', Sophie wrote, 'I'm now pretty unmoved by each new turn of events', but 'I'm always worried about Hans in particular. He's so vulnerable'.[22]

Her much-loved older brother was serving as a medic in a field hospital, close to the French town of Reims.[23] From this point onwards, Hans combined periods in term time as a medical student at Munich University with stints during the vacations in the 'Student Medical Corps' of the German army. As a student-medic, Hans was required to treat and heal people – not to kill them. In the field hospitals he treated wounded soldiers, assisted in limb amputations and other major and minor medical procedures. The Student Medical Corps was composed of prospective doctors, drawn mainly from the middle classes. For many, the Medical Corps provided an ideal opportunity to meet fellow dissidents and opponents of the Nazi regime. Most of the student members of the White Rose resistance – apart from Sophie – were student-medics or female trainee doctors.

On 22 June 1940, France, now led by the Marshal Henri Pétain, signed an armistice with Germany, in the very same railway carriage at Compiégne where the Germans had signed the armistice in 1918. Adolf Hitler visited the city on a whistle-stop tour. 'It was the dream of my life to visit Paris', he told his favourite architect, Albert Speer, 'I cannot say how happy I am to have fulfilled that dream.'[24] Days later, German troops marched triumphantly through the streets of Paris in a victory parade. The war on the mainland of Western Europe had resulted in a swift and stunning victory for Nazi Germany. Fritz Hartnagel was part of the German victory party in Paris. Hans also served in a Paris hospital during the summer of 1940. Fritz went on a sight-seeing trip in Paris, taking in the Eiffel Tower and the Invalides, but when he got to the Louvre it was closed. 'I was not impressed with the rest of Paris', he wrote to Sophie, 'apart from the gothic splendour of Notre Dame Cathedral'.[25]

In the summer of 1940, Adolf Hitler stood at the pinnacle of power in Europe and popularity in Germany. On 6 July 1940, over a million people congregated outside the Reich Chancellery in Berlin, cheering boisterously as Hitler came out on to the balcony. This was nothing less than 'Hitler mania'. But Sophie Scholl was completely unmoved at this seminal moment of German national triumph. She was outraged by the feeble French capitulation. 'It looks as if the French were only interested in their home comforts', she told Fritz:

> I would have been more impressed if they had defended Paris to the last round, regardless of all the treasures housed there … But expediency is everything these days and true honour no longer exists … Saving your own skin is the main thing.

Once more, Sophie pressed home to Fritz her implacable opposition to the war and she raised the issue as to whether two people could live together in marriage if their views on war differed so greatly.[26] As much as Sophie wanted to appear detached and intellectual about love, her outlook was romantic in so many ways. For Sophie, love implied shared ideals and interest. Not for her a marriage of opposites or one based solely on outward physical attraction. Once the war started, she found it increasingly difficult to accept Fritz's role as an army officer, as she was so opposed to warfare. She wanted to convert Fritz to her way of thinking. She wanted to turn a Wehrmacht officer into a pacifist!

Not surprisingly, some of Sophie's letters often shocked Fritz. He must have feared the consequences of them being opened by his army superiors or even inadvertently by a loyal Nazi postal worker, who might have reported the often dissident comments to the Gestapo. In one letter, Sophie wrote:

> A soldier must swear an oath [to Hitler] as his job is to carry out the wishes of the government's orders. Tomorrow he might have to comply with an order completely different from the one issued yesterday. His [a soldier's] profession is obedience … You were not that in favour of war, to the best of my knowledge, but you spend your time training people for it … If a soldier's commandment is to be loyal, sincere, modest and honest he certainly cannot obey it, he has to carry it out whether he considers it right or wrong. If he does not carry it out he is dismissed, isn't he?[27]

Fritz Hartnagel later said of these frank exchanges:

> We often debated, and at first did not agree on anything … We argued vehemently … Only after much hesitation and reluctance did I find myself ready

to follow her ideas … Step by step I came to admit that her attitude was correct … What a tremendous plunge for me to take – to say in mid-war. 'I am against this war' or 'Germany has to lose this war.'[28]

In the midst of the series of incredible German victories in Western Europe in 1940, Sophie began her course as a kindergarten teacher at the Fröbel Institute. Susanne Hirzel, the daughter of an Ulm clergyman, was on the same course and recalls:

> Most of the time Sophie was quite reserved, quiet: a bit introspective. She spoke in a very low voice. Some people thought she was very shy. But, if you got to know her much better, you could tell she was very self-confident and rightly felt intellectually superior to some of the others, though she never let them feel it. She usually kept her distance. You always felt her main interest was in something else, not in kindergarten teaching.[29]

The course was a practical one: students looked after pre-school age children in the nursery and then went on residential placements in other childcare institutions. Sophie was able to live at home for most of the time. On her days off she often went on cycling trips, swam or engaged in other outdoor pursuits. After one enjoyable day out with her sister Inge in July 1940, Sophie told Hans: 'We enjoyed the cycling so much and there was a wind blowing. We felt like officials of God, sent on a mission to find out if the earth was good – and we discovered it was.'[30]

Sophie took her role as a trainee kindergarten teacher very seriously, even though she often admitted it was 'terribly tiring trying to think on the same wavelength as children, but remain detached from them at the same time.' Sophie found her response to the children more complicated than she had imagined at the beginning. 'I'd be lying', she frankly explained in a letter to Fritz, 'if I told you that the children give me unadulterated pleasure. Almost every face conveys so clearly what it promises to become in future: in other words, the kind of people (Nazis) that exist today.'[31] The actual experience of looking after children for lengthy periods made Sophie realise:

> how superficial my attitude to children really is. You need more than the kind of emotion children so readily arouse. I now realise what kind of unconditional love is required to look after these unpredictable, spiteful but often very warm little creatures.[32]

In July 1940, Sophie went on a ten-day holiday with Lisa Remppis to the same mountain region of Austria she had visited earlier in the year with Fritz and described it to him in a letter:

> Today I saw the ski runs we did together ... in their summer finery. I was pleasantly surprised because the mountains are very beautiful in summer too, but in a different way ... It's a long time since I got as much pleasure out of flowers as I did today. To tell the truth, it is a long time since I have felt as happy as I did this morning when Lisa and I were sitting on a hill in the Gamstal pass[33]

One of her friends later recalled: 'She enjoyed life to the fullest and simple nature – a bunch of flowers or blossoms on the tree, or flowers in the field completely changed her.'[34]

Sophie's only residential placement, outside the Fröbel Seminary, was at the Kohlermann Children's Sanitorium in the spa town of Bad Dürrheim, in the Black Forest. It took Sophie an hour to get there by train from Ulm. She worked there between 10 August and 11 September 1940. The home was a very exclusive, fee-paying, private children's sanatorium, reserved for the sons and daughters of the upper middle classes, aged between two and seventeen, who were suffering from childhood illnesses, particularly breathing disorders. But Sophie found even these sick children to be demanding, noisy, spoiled and arrogant. She did not like the disciplinarian rules imposed by the strict Kohlermann family either. She described the matron who ran the home as a very 'disagreeable Prussian'[35] who issued frequent 'angry reprimands, but hardly any compliments'.[36]

This was the very first time that Sophie had ever lived away from home. She felt a great sense of isolation and alienation while she was there. She found it very difficult to fit in with her work colleagues and thought the children were very noisy. Today, it would be said that she did not act like a team player. One day after arriving, Sophie was already complaining in a letter to Fritz that the children in the home spent most of their time 'kicking up a terrible racket'. She thought the experience would be a test of endurance and was looking forward 'to the end of my time here'.[37] Just days later, the poor discipline of the children was getting on her nerves even more: 'The little rascals are a handful', she confessed, 'All I do is tell them off the whole time'.[38] The fact that most of the children came from north Germany made it even harder for Sophie to warm to them. The work in the home consisted of washing and feeding the children, telling them stories, getting them to learn things, putting them to bed and getting them up, and taking them for walks. After ten days in the home, Sophie concluded that she was not relaxed or patient enough to cope with so many sick children. She seemed to get on much better with the older girls. Sometimes she would sit and chat with the girls she liked until very late in the night, which went against the strict rules imposed in the home. She found the younger boys in the home were always having fist fights with each other, while 'the little girls of six and seven spend the whole evening arguing'.[39]

Sophie quite deliberately set herself apart from the other young female workers at the home. These were mainly local young women, mostly working class and certainly not – like Sophie – heading to university. Sophie shared a small room during her placement with someone described as 'an overweight young women'. Sophie said her room-mate enjoyed reading frivolous paperback romances, snored incessantly, chattered non-stop and according to Sophie had 'the brain of a hen and eleven stone of fat to go with it. On top of that, she never gets washed but considers herself a beauty … I had a row with her straight away just so she would leave me in peace.'[40] Sharing a room with this young women made Sophie feel 'uncomfortable at night', as 'she bursts out laughing usually for no reason at all. She's the talk of the entire home.'[41] 'I hope that you are not feeling lonely there', Fritz, wrote sympathetically on 21 August 1940, and went on to comment that he hoped she had now been given a separate room and hoped she was coping better with 'the loud environment'. He also promised to comply with her request to write more often.[42]

As her placement at Bad Dürrheim drew to a close, Sophie's attitude towards the children softened. She even admitted – near the end – that she was 'deriving great pleasure from the little children more and more'. One young boy in the home had grown very attached to her and he was 'disconsolate' on the day she left.[43] In a letter on 12 September 1940, she reported to Fritz: 'I was released at lunch time yesterday', but admitted she had 'found it harder to say good-bye than I thought possible'. At the end of her placement, she was paid 50 marks in wages, which she joyfully described as 'the first money I've ever earned'.[44]

Sophie now returned to the Fröbel Seminary for the remainder of the course. 'The [Fröbel] seminary head, Miss Kretschmer' Susanne Hirzel later recalled:

> was not an out and out National Socialist. She knew how to seem more non-committal. So one day when we were all supposed to listen enthusiastically

... to a Hitler speech on the radio, we dared to just read our books just to see how she would react. Miss Kretschmer did notice our lack of interest, but just cheekily wagged a finger at us.[45]

Sophie was increasingly finding comfort in reading the Bible at this point in her life. Many of her letters contain quotations from it.[46] Sophie's mother was a committed Christian and she greatly influenced and encouraged her children to seek solace in biblical study. It is noticeable how many letters from the Scholl family to friends contain religious presents, most notably new copies of the Bible and books on theological matters, and often have lengthy reflections about questions of morality and religious belief.[47] In a very typical letter, Fritz acknowledges receipt of a copy of the New Testament from Sophie's mother while on military duty in France, and he tells Sophie: 'When I've got more time I'll write to your mother and offer detailed thanks.' In many other letters, Sophie emphasises that Christian values and the right to religious freedom are key elements in any moral regeneration of Germany. A key component of her revulsion towards Hitler was a firm belief that he wanted Nazism to be a secular ideology, which was antithetical to the humanistic teachings of the Bible.

On 23 September 1940, Fritz told Sophie that he would soon be allowed leave. He was eager to fix a date to visit her. But Sophie wanted to make sure Fritz's visit did not clash with Hans' period of leave as 'Then I could devote myself exclusively to each of you.' The letter shows how important the time she spent with Hans was becoming. In the same letter, Sophie offered her frank views – now at Fritz's request – on the question of patriotism in a time of war. Sophie thought the position of a soldier fighting for his nation in a war was no different to a son who stands by his parents and his family in an unconditional manner, but 'justice takes precedence over all other attachments', adding, 'I have always thought it wrong for a father to side with his children on principle even if they were in the wrong ... It's just as wrong for a German or a Frenchman, or whatever else a person may be, to defend his nation just because it's "his"' as she thought such 'emotions can often be misleading'. For Sophie, the Nazi version of nationalism was 'subjective and partisan'. It was attempting to usurp religion for its own cause. What Sophie wanted was a patriotism that was 'objective, impartial and even handed' and especially one that 'tolerated spiritual and religious feelings'.[48]

Fritz Hartnagel later admitted that he was often very 'shocked' by such candid letters – as he still supported the German cause – and he thought a decision to oppose Hitler 'could not be made overnight'.[49] This helps to explain why most of the surviving letters written by Fritz during this period are quite reserved, circumspect and non-committal. Fritz mostly described the places he visited in a very matter-of-fact manner by simply announcing some town or other had been 'decimated by the air force' and he offered no details of the brutality of the German army. 'As I went through the countryside', wrote Fritz in a typical letter from the Western Front, 'I was reminded of our holiday in Worpswede'.[50]

The differences in outlook towards the war between Sophie and Fritz clearly caused tensions in their relationship. In the autumn of 1940, Sophie was frequently complaining to Fritz that he was not replying to her letters often enough. On 4 November 1940, Sophie writes: 'You've been so silent. I've absolutely no idea how or where you are. Do write me however things are with you, good or bad. Is anything wrong?'[51] On 10 November 1940, Sophie turned up the heat further. 'I've been debating whether to dispense with your letters, because the motive that prompts me to write is a selfish one ... because my assumption (which may not coincide with yours) is that you're alone in an atmosphere that has nothing in common with the one I'd like to win you over to', ending with the blunt question: 'Do you still enjoy writing to me?'[52] In another letter, Sophie writes: 'If you're angry with me, be angry if you want, but vent your anger on the wind or on me, just don't bottle it all up inside you.'[53] In general, Sophie's complaints about the lax response of Fritz to her letters do not seem justified. Fritz wrote to Sophie – even though he was an army officer commanding troops in battle – about twice a week.

At the end of November 1940, Sophie sent Fritz an Advent parcel as a sort of romantic peace offering. It contained a flower wreath, candles and the story of Christmas.[54] But on 11 December 1940, Sophie was once more urging Fritz to write more often:

> your last letter was written sixteen days ago. Now I'm permanently on ten-terhooks waiting for another. It is not that I am urging you to write more often.[55] I don't mean to influence you anymore from that point of view, because I know you're aware of what you are doing, but I'd like to have a far bigger share of you. It's worrying hearing so little ...[56]

During the festive season of 1940, most Germans decorated their Christmas trees in an atmosphere of great optimism. It had been a year of unprecedented military success. Germany looked poised to win the Second World War. The only barriers to complete Nazi dominance over Europe were the

Soviet Union and Britain. The Nazi–Soviet Pact was still in place, if somewhat strained. But the British Empire still 'stood alone' and had survived a fight for air supremacy over the British Isles dubbed 'the Battle of Britain'. Hitler now abandoned his plan to invade Britain.[57]

After an enjoyable Christmas break, Sophie went on the annual family skiing holiday. The group this time consisted of Sophie, Inge, Werner, Lisa Remppis, Otl Aicher and a biology student named Willy. They stayed in a luxurious skiing lodge in the Lech valley. Sophie gave a summary of the holiday in a letter to Fritz: 'We lived on tea and bread, went to bed late and got up late as well', but on the train home, Sophie suddenly experienced a sense of unease in the company of the other young Germans aboard, who she felt were 'exploiting their youth for pleasure's sake. But my brother and sisters and friends, though often more gauche and unsophisticated were brimming with goodwill.'[58]

At the beginning of 1941, Sophie was now counting the days until the end of her course in kindergarten at the Fröbel Seminary. She was more eager than ever to begin her degree at Munich University. 'Wouldn't it be wonderful', she wrote in her diary, 'if Hans and I could study together for a time? We are bursting with plans – irrepressible.'[59] Sophie believed that studying with Hans would be beneficial to both of them as she felt 'I wouldn't slack in front of Hans ... The same goes for him and that's the best educational incentive of all.'[60]

In February 1941, Fritz Hartnagel returned to Ulm on leave from his army duties. They were able to spend some real quality face-to-face time together rather than their usual pen-friend relationship. Sophie's positive views towards Fritz were always increased by his presence. The visit left Sophie 'bubbling over with high spirits' and she was sorry when he left because she had 'grown accustomed to your warmth and affection', but then to put a dampener on these compliments when she told Fritz she would have liked 'a note from you, meant specially for me. Something I could carry round unseen by others.'[61] The visit put Sophie back on good terms with Fritz. 'I know I can depend on you', she confided in him:

> and that you love me. That's why we needn't tie each other down. I can tell you I'm growing fond of you all over again, in a different way. I'm fond of you – because of what makes you a human being. That can form a special bond.[62]

The alternating moods of Sophie within her relationship with Fritz, expressed in their correspondence, not only reveal her own alternating feelings about

the strength of the bond, but also show that Sophie often placed a psychological screen in her friendships to protect herself from disappointment. In
other letters, it is clear that Sophie and Fritz did have sex outside marriage,
which was not common in 'courting' couples at the time – especially those
from strongly religious backgrounds.

In March 1941, Sophie duly passed her exam and graduated as a qualified
kindergarten teacher.[63] She could now – she fervently hoped – begin her
studies at Munich University. But the Nazi authorities flatly refused to recognise her teacher training at the Fröbel Institute as an acceptable substitute
for labour service. To her dismay, she was told she must complete six months
'proper labour service' – all of it away from home. Shortly after hearing this
depressing news she told Fritz:

> I've already come to terms with my immediate future. I always try to acclima-
> tise myself as quickly as possible (mentally too, and to new ideas). It's an aid to
> maximum independence from all outward circumstances pleasant or unpleas-
> ant. I've become so expert at self-adjustment that I got over my call up to the
> RAD [Labour Service] in five minutes flat and when I left school Fräulein
> Kretschmer defined my most salient characteristic as imperturbability.[64]

SEVEN

IN THE LABOUR SERVICE OF THE FATHERLAND

In the spring of 1941, Adolf Hitler's regime was busily making detailed plans for a massive military attack on the Soviet Union. Hitler told his generals that the war in the east would be a racial war of destruction and annihilation. The Nazi regime was also trying to find a 'Final Solution' to the 'Jewish Question'. Jews were already confined to horrendous sealed-off ghettos in Poland, but in less than a year the Nazis were attempting to exterminate all of Europe's Jews. At the centre of SS activities in the preparations for 'Operation Barbarossa' (the German codename for the attack on the Soviet Union) was the *Einsatzgruppen* – the mobile killing units – who were to follow the German army as it swept through the Soviet Union, round up communists and Jews, march them to the edges of towns, order them to strip naked and mow them down with machine gun fire. The Second World War was about to enter its most horrific phase.[1]

On 6 April 1941, German forces invaded Greece and almost simultaneously attacked Yugoslavia. Within weeks, both nations were part of Hitler's 'New Order' in Europe. On the same day Germany attacked Greece, Sophie began her six-month compulsory labour service at the Krauchenwies labour camp, located on the upper Danube, about 45 miles southwest of Ulm. Sophie spent six lonely and depressing months there, billeted with eighty other young women aged between eighteen and twenty-five, in an old dilapidated manor house near to some parkland.[2] Sophie's sense of isolation increased dramatically in this period as most of her fellow uniformed 'RAD girls' were committed National Socialists, who talked non-stop of their love and devotion to the Führer.

The Labour Service involved doing a variety of jobs on local farms in a predominantly rural area. Sophie's many letters from this time record her misery in full detail. The camp leader, a fervent Nazi devotee, insisted on calling Sophie a 'Labour Maid'. Sophie knew she could not disagree, but often wished she could yell back at her: 'My name is Sophie Scholl – Remember that!' She wisely kept such feelings to herself.[3] She described the high-handed camp leader to her sister Inge: 'She is sarcastic to everyone all the time, never friendly, and does not seem to have any pleasant characteristics that would help to create a harmonious atmosphere ... I think she would make life easier if she was less angry.'[4] In April 1941, Fritz's Wehrmacht unit was fighting in Yugoslavia. Nevertheless, he still found time to write her a letter in which he said he fully realised 'she might be a bit lonely at this time' but that, due to the war, he might not be able to write very frequently.[5]

Sophie had to share a communal dormitory with ten other young women. For a high-minded member of the middle class, this was very much an unfamiliar environment. The sparse rooms were draughty, cold and damp and there was no hot water. The staple diet was dominated by potatoes. 'The most noticeable thing is the coldness', Sophie wrote in a letter to Inge, 'Lots of dear little mice are another noticeable feature. I'm getting to know them really well during my hours of insomnia.'[6] Sophie made very little effort to fit in. She quite deliberately kept her distance from her co-workers:

> I often have to close my ears to their chatter in the evening. Every time I join in, it seems like a concession and I regret it. I've managed to stay pretty much in the background, thanks to my shyness ... I'm forever catching myself showing off. It's awful, my craving for recognition.[7]

Less than a week after arriving she had this to say to her old friend, Lisa Remppis: 'I am always horrified to think that I'm going to be stuck here for six months'.[8]

Sophie made very few friends during her time at the camp, largely out of choice. For most of the time she behaved in a rather idiosyncratic manner. The other girls did not hate her, but they thought she was aloof, bookish and undemonstrative. Sophie, for her part, disliked the sexually crude banter of her female colleagues. She hated the frequent 'snide comments' they often made about her love of art, highbrow books, novels and poetry, but she thought they were 'quite ordinary decent girls' at heart.[9] Her one source of refuge from her frivolous, socially incompatatible companions was reading the book by Thomas Mann she had smuggled in (*Magic Mountain*) and a much-thumbed selected volume of writings by St Augustine. In *Confessions of St Augustine* she found a quotation that she felt was in keeping with her own views, 'Thou hast created for us Thyself, and our heart cannot be quieted till it find repose in Thee.'[10] The camp leader did not allow any of the other young women to have books at all, but in Sophie's words: 'she lets me have them (why I've no idea)'.[11]

In her first week Sophie had a major row with one of the other girls in her dormitory, who came from the working-class coal-mining area of the Saar. Sophie graphically, no doubt accurately, described her as 'crude, big and fat', with a face that 'would make her look thoroughly at home in a waterfront tavern', but who was 'universally popular because of her brazen impudence and the infectious laugh that she often lets out quite uninhibitedly at the top of her voice'. Sophie hardly eased the tension by deciding to draw a pencil line across her cheek as she walked past her just to rile her. Not surprisingly, the young woman did not see the funny side of this and let off an angry and spiteful torrent of ceaseless abuse, which Sophie admitted left her completely 'defenceless'.[12] For once, Sophie's calm, self-contained and unflappable personality had no answer to the rough-and-ready style of this type of vitriol. She retreated to her isolation, to her bed and her books.

In an attempt to maintain her inner strength, Sophie went for long walks in the nearby park. 'I spent an hour in the park this evening', she told Fritz Hartnagel, 'the clumps of trees looked so lovely in the evening light that I walked home backward just to prolong the sight of them'.[13] Sophie's increasing isolation from the other girls in the labour service was soon recognised by the initially frosty camp leader, who decided to offer her preferential treatment by allowing her to read books and sit and sketch in her office. She was even allowed out of the camp, unaccompanied, and strictly against the rules, to buy art materials at nearby Sigmaringen. This excursion cheered Sophie up greatly and she told her parents: 'It was my nicest day here to date', and although she had not made any special friends, she now felt 'on fairly good terms with everyone'.[14]

But this feeling of belonging did not last very long. Only two days later she told Lisa Remppis:

> Today is my third Sunday here and I'm feeling thoroughly miserable. However objectively I view this place, I'm bound to say it isn't pleasant … It almost horrifies me to find that not one of the eighty-odd girls here is remotely cultured … The sole, favourite and most frequent topic of conversation is men. I get sick of it sometimes.[15]

Sophie's feelings of homesickness and isolation soon led to the return of her familiar concerns about the strength of her relationship with Fritz Hartnagel. In her diary, on 1 May 1941, she noted: 'I've only had two letters from Fritz in the whole of the four weeks I've been here.'[16] But Fritz found some time to write Sophie a letter later in the month. He found the idea of Sophie wearing her RAD uniform (which had a swastika on it) very strange as it 'contradicts your true nature' and he thought she must be 'feeling like a prisoner in the company of prisoners'.[17] To ease her anxiety about not fitting in, he observed reassuringly that 'it is always hard for anyone to fit in with a group of rowdy people, as they tend to dominate and lower the tone'.[18]

At the beginning of June 1941, Sophie was assigned to work outside the camp during the day at local farms. This involved hard physical labour alongside local workers, but being out in the fresh open air in the bright sunshine lifted her spirits. In a letter to Lisa Remppis in June 1941 she commented:

> I've been doing outside work for a farmer since the beginning of the week. It's odd, but now the Labour Service has taken on a different complexion. Perhaps it's because of the glorious sunshine we've had since Pentecost which has made the whole countryside blossom out wonderfully. My route to work is simply lovely – eight kilometres up the hill and down the dale through open woodland. I've a genuine feeling of happiness and find myself once more wanting someone to share it with.[19]

In the early hours of 22 June 1941, 3 million German troops launched the largest military attack in human history. The German-Soviet War in Eastern Europe was the most decisive, horrific and brutal battle of the entire Second World War. Hitler staked everything on destroying the largest communist regime in the world. Inge Scholl was actually visiting Sophie with Otl Aicher on the day when news came through on the radio of the German attack on the Soviet Union. 'In spite of the shocking newscast', Inge later recalled, 'that Sunday turned into a beautiful day for us. The valley of the upper Danube is one of the loveliest in southern Germany. We walked in the woods near the Danube. At night Sophie had to return to the camp.'[20] The next day Sophie wrote to her brother Hans and inquired: 'What does the immediate future hold for you, I wonder? We live in interesting times. I, too, get to hear what's been happening now and then.'[21] In a letter to Lisa Remppis, Sophie summed up her feelings about the importance of what became known in Germany as 'the war in the east': 'I think the war is starting to have its full effect in every regard. Sometimes, and especially of late, I've felt that it's grossly unfair to have to live in an age so filled with momentous events.'[22]

There was more bad news. Sophie was informed that her Labour Service, due to end in October 1941, had been extended for a further six months. Her dream of going to university was once more put on hold. In a letter during this period, Fritz told Sophie in a concerned tone: 'I hope you stay healthy. I'm often concerned about your health and your stomach aches', adding plaintively, 'I can only help you with my heart.'[23] She was briefly in despair about the extension of her labour service, but in a letter to Hans on 2 August 1941 she had recovered her usual calm composure:

> I'm still reeling under the impact of the latest, appalling piece of news: We're to do another six months' compulsory war work in camps, under the auspices of RAD, which intends to organise our leisure time as well. I'm ready to contract any reasonably tolerant disease or do anything that would spare me this fate ... So much for my rosy prospects! Instead, it's another dose of this ridiculous boarding school.[24]

A circumspect and resigned Sophie was soon telling Lisa Remppis that she had been really looking forward to starting at Munich University and studying there with her brother Hans, 'but it's no use clinging to my own personal desires when every other circumstance conspires against them'.[25] A few days later she told Hans 'I'll be an old crone before I can start university. But I won't abandon the struggle in a hurry. I'd rather take poison.'[26]

At least Sophie's isolation at Krauchenwies castle was made more tolerable due to the arrival of an intelligent young woman with whom she was to develop a close friendship. Her name was Gisela Schertling and she intended to study art history at the University of Munich. Sophie was soon telling her younger brother, Werner:

> I can talk more freely with her than I'd had ever thought it possible to talk with anyone during these six months and I doubt if our friendship will be restricted to the RAD. It does me good, and I often feel glad to have such a person around ... She's younger than me in many ways. It's only here that I realise how much another friendly person can mean. Heavens if she could see this letter! Our relationship is actually very matter of fact and unemotional and that's the way it must stay. Otherwise it will lose its value.[27]

Above all, Sophie felt Gisela Schertling was on her wavelength – even though she was not opposed to Hitler's regime. Sophie invited Schertling to stay at the Scholl apartment on Cathedral Square in Ulm when they had a weekend break. On one of these visits Gisela met Hans Scholl. He was pleased to hear she would be enrolling at Munich University some time in 1942. The experience of enduring labour service was now serving to make Sophie more truly independent, determined and mature. 'I feel strong inside', she confided to Lisa Remppis, 'Not always, but willpower is what counts and I'm getting to know my own moods well enough to assess them accurately'.[28]

Also during this period, Otl Aicher, a close friend of the Scholl children – who had been denied the opportunity to take his *Abitur* because he had bravely resigned from the Hitler Youth – came up with the idea of producing a clandestine dissident journal called *Windlicht* ('Storm Lantern') in which individuals – mostly opposed to the Nazi regime – could write articles and reviews about art, literature, religion and culture. Aicher had already submitted an original article to *Hochland* ('Highland'), an underground journal edited by an elderly Catholic scholar named Professor Carl Muth, a non-violent but principled opponent of the Nazi regime, who had consistently attacked the Vatican for continuing what he thought was an incestuous relationship with fascism in Italy and especially National Socialism in Germany. *Hochland* was not approved of by the Vatican and banned by the Nazi regime. This was not surprising as the Catholic Church had been under attack by the Nazis for many years already. Most of its newspapers and all of its youth organisations had been closed down. Many Catholic clergy were imprisoned. All of this occurred in spite of the 1933 Concordat between Hitler and Pope Pius XI, which was supposed to have protected the independence of the Catholic religion in Nazi Germany.

Windlicht was very much in the spirit of Carl Muth's *Hochland*. Hans Scholl contributed an article which compared Hitler to Napoleon and ended by stating: 'Remember what happened to Napoleon and have hope!' In another essay, Hans attacked the general apathy of the Christian churches to Nazi attacks on religious practices and especially the failure of the churches to speak out more forcefully against the Nazi euthanasia programme, which had led to the systematic murder of thousands of the mentally and physically handicapped in German hospitals. Hans wrote:

> It's high time that Christians made up their minds to do something …
> What are we going to show in the way of resistance – as compared to the
> Communists, for instance – when all this terror is over? We will be standing

empty-handed. We will have no answer when we are asked: What did you do about it?[29]

In the summer of 1941, Hans Scholl knocked on the door of Carl Muth's large house in the leafy Munich suburbs. He was immediately invited in by the grey-haired seventy-four-year-old scholar. A near neighbour was Werner Bergengruen, a philosopher and writer who was described in a local Gestapo file as 'politically unreliable'. Another frequent visitor was Theodor Haecker, a sixty-three-year-old Catholic scholar who was forbidden by the Nazi authorities from publishing, but who continued to spread his 'subversive' humanist views among like-minded individuals. Haecker believed that National Socialism was 'sent as a plague on Europe' and was intent on establishing itself as an 'alternative religion to Christianity'. The idea of the need for a 'spiritual resistance' to National Socialism – which informed the views of Muth, Bergengruen and Haecker – was a very important philosophical influence on Sophie Scholl's own moral, intellectual and spiritual journey towards active opposition.[30]

Hans became a close friend of Muth, visited him regularly and was fascinated by his ideas. Hans agreed to come around to Muth's house to catalogue his vast library of books and articles. Most of his collection contained books banned by the Nazi regime, but Muth didn't care. He had endured ostracism from academia, the hierarchy of the Catholic Church and the Nazi authorities, but none of this had broken his spirit. He believed that freedom of thought, religion and free speech were principles that had to be defended, but in a non-violent manner. All of this aimed at a moral and spiritual regeneration of Germany – through Christian values – derived from deep reading, but also a restoration of religious toleration, which meant, in turn, a restoration of a democratic form of government and the non-violent strands of his thinking represented a desire for peaceful international co-operation – not war. These ideas were not a fully worked-out political programme, but they amounted to a basis to mount an opposition to the regime, in the hope of attracting like-minded people.

What form such an opposition could take was – at this time – still hazy. But during the summer of 1941, an anonymous leaflet was delivered in a brown envelope to the Scholl apartment on Cathedral Square. It was produced on a duplicating machine. It contained the full draft of a sermon given by the German Catholic bishop, Clemens Graf von Galen, which had denounced Hitler's state-organised euthanasia programme (codenamed T4) which the Nazi regime had secretly established in August 1939 – and which was systematically killing thousands of mentally ill and physically handicapped adults and children in a number of German mental hospitals.[31] The T4 programme used lethal injections, gas vans and shower rooms converted into gas chambers. The leaflet added personal comments supporting Galen's sermon. It asked every recipient to make six copies and mail them to their friends. Hans Scholl seemed deeply impressed by this anonymous, but clever act of opposition. 'Finally', Hans told Inge Scholl, 'a man has had the courage to speak out' and after reading it in detail he commented: 'We really ought to have a duplicating machine.'[32] The anonymous leaflet provided a useful blueprint for a non-violent opposition group to influence opinion and hope to avoid detection by the Gestapo.

In the sermon, Galen told his congregation that people were not like animals, to be slaughtered when they ceased to be of productive use:

> Once it [state-sponsored killing] is allowed … then fundamentally the way is open to the murder of all unproductive people, of the incurably ill, of people invalided out of work or out of the war, then the way is open to murder all of us, when we become old and weak … Who can trust his doctor anymore?[33]

The speech was not reported in the press, but it was mentioned on BBC Radio's German service. Hitler decided that to arrest such a high-profile Catholic bishop might create a martyr. Joseph Goebbels thought that a better method to gain public support was subtle propaganda. In August 1941, the Nazi Propaganda Ministry sponsored a feature film called '*I Accuse*' in which a young and beautiful German woman with multiple sclerosis says she would like to die to prevent further suffering. There are long discussions in the film, seen by 18 million Germans, about the rights and wrongs of such an assisted suicide, but in the end she is helped to die by her husband and a family friend.[34] Eventually, the Nazis decided to halt the programme of killing mentally and physically handicapped adults, but the killing of children continued in much stricter secrecy and was eventually moved out of hospitals and into the extermination camps.

It was also during the summer of 1941 that Hans and Sophie first heard details about the mass murder of Jews in the Soviet Union. Manfred Eickemeyer, a young Munich architect, met Hans Scholl that summer after being told about him by a friend of Carl Muth. Eickemeyer had worked on many construction projects in Krakow, in German-occupied Poland, and he rented a large basement studio in a very secluded street, not far from Munich University. While travelling around Poland, Eickemeyer had seen the terrible conditions in the

Jewish ghettos. But the news from the Soviet Union about German atrocities was even more gruesome. Eickemeyer told Hans that the *Einsatzgruppen* were fully engaged in mass killing of Jews on a monumental scale, a prelude to the six purpose-built death camps in Poland: Auschwitz-Birkenau, Belzec, Chelmno, Majdanek, Sobibor and Treblinka.[35] What Eickemeyer told Hans Scholl about the mass murder in the east did not shock him. He knew enough people who had served in Poland and the Soviet Union to know what was happening anyway.[36] The meeting with Eickemeyer was significant for another important reason. It was Eickemeyer's studio that Hans later used as the base camp for the production of leaflets of the White Rose.

In early September 1941, Fritz Hartnagel's unit was transferred from the German assault on the Soviet Union to the German spa town of Weimar. Fritz had been asked to put together a signals company to support the Afrika Korps in Libya. But Fritz's unit did not receive any marching orders and he remained in Weimar between September 1941 and April 1942. This allowed Sophie and Fritz to meet on many weekends in nearby Freiburg. 'Religion', according to Inge Scholl:

> became more important in this phase of her life. She sensed that God was very much relevant to her freedom that in fact he was challenging it ... God was your insight into yourself. He was the only mirror in which you could see yourself with any clarity.[37]

Robert Scholl wrote a long, pleading letter begging the Nazi authorities to allow Sophie to start at Munich University rather than endure another six months of enforced labour, but his pleas were flatly rejected. In October 1941, Sophie was assigned by the National Socialist Public Welfare Service (PSV) to work as a kindergarten teacher in a nursery school in Blumberg, a small farming town near to the Swiss border. The work was very exhausting. In one letter Sophie describes scrubbing 150 chairs and 20 tables in a single morning.[38] The only consolation was that she was allowed more free time at weekends.

On 10 October 1941, German newspapers were carrying banner headlines suggesting the German army had won the war in the Soviet Union. It now seemed Adolf Hitler was on the verge of total domination of Europe. Sophie's mood always darkened into depression when the Nazis seemed in sight of total victory. In her diary, in the autumn of 1941, she wrote: 'All that I'm left with is melancholy, incapacity and a slender hope.'[39] In November 1941, she confessed in her diary:

Yesterday I was delighted, but today I can't summon up the energy to be delighted anymore. I'm so tired, I'd like nothing better than to go to bed right now and sleep forever … I'd like so much to believe in miracles. I'd so much like to believe that I can acquire strength through prayer. I can't achieve anything by myself.[40]

This was a very low period in Sophie's life. She suffered feelings of deep melancholy and bouts of depression. 'I'm all mixed up I can tell', she told Lisa Remppis, 'That's because I'm tired. I feel so homesick.'[41] For solace – and in search of some spiritual and philosophical enlightenment – Sophie began writing to Carl Muth and often sent him little presents of food.[42] 'He must have a kindly heart', Sophie wrote in her diary, 'to find room in it for lesser people whose only connection with him is quite superficial. I couldn't appreciate it more. That in itself puts me under an obligation to better myself.'[43] Although Sophie was brought up a Lutheran, she was drawn towards certain aspects of the Catholic faith. In some of her letters she described Protestant churches as cold, but viewed Catholic ones as much warmer places. 'One must not lose heart', Sophie wrote in her diary on 10 November 1941:

once when I lost heart because I kept backsliding, I didn't dare pray anymore. I decided not to ask more of God until I could enter his presence again. That in itself is a fundamental yearning for God. But I can always ask him (through prayer), I know that now.[44]

'She sensed God was very much relevant to her freedom', Inge Scholl later recalled:

That freedom became more and more meaningful for her. In those years of total bondage, questioning about God opened her eyes to the surrounding world … God was your insight into yourself. He was the only mirror you could see and understand yourself with clarity.[45]

During the autumn of 1941 Fritz made frequent weekend visits to meet Sophie, mostly in Freiburg. Fritz took a morning train from Weimar to Freiburg every Saturday and returned on Sunday evening. Once the couple visited a local beer hall and the landlord and his wife commented to Sophie that Fritz would make an ideal marriage partner.[46] Her growing devotion to prayer became apparent during this meeting. She took Fritz by the hand at one point during the visit and said, 'We must pray, and pray for each other.'[47]

It is clear from his letters to Sophie that Fritz desperately wanted to become the soulmate Sophie desired. He did read many of the same religious and philosophical works as her and they discussed them at length in their correspondence, but he once admitted frankly: 'So much of your innermost thoughts are unknown to me.'[48] Apart from these visits from Fritz and her reliance on prayer, Sophie's only other refuge from her enforced labour was – as always – her love of nature. 'I delight every morning', she told Otl Aicher, 'in the pure air and the sky'.[49] In a letter to Hans on 20 November 1941, Sophie observed that 'it's been ages' since they corresponded with each other and she lamented: 'So now my university course will have to wait until spring (if they let me go then).'[50]

On 7 December 1941, the USA entered the war following Japan's surprise air attack on the US fleet at Pearl Harbor. On 11 December 1941, Germany declared war on the USA, thereby conveniently relieving President Roosevelt of the need to do so. In military terms, Germany now faced a very powerful coalition of the Soviet Union, Britain and the USA. But it must be understood that the dangers faced by any potential opponent of Hitler's regime inside Germany – even at the end of 1941 – were actually much greater than ever before. Hitler's grip on the German state and the public had grown stronger since the war began. The will of the German people to resist the Nazi leadership was less powerful than their determination to resist their foreign enemies. The Western Allies were soon demanding the 'unconditional surrender' of the German armed forces. If the Allies won, Germany would be occupied – possibly forever. This meant that internal opponents could expect very little popular support within Germany. The People's Court and the Special Courts were now conducting lightning-speed trials in which most opponents were brutally ridiculed and increasing numbers were executed. Hitler was determined to avoid the collapse of public morale which had occurred in the latter stages of the First World War. In a letter from the Justice Ministry, circulated to all the regional Special Courts on 28 October 1941, the following 'instructions' were issued:

The administration of justice must proceed with the most severe measures against all habitual and professional criminals, all anti social parasites and all those who commit crimes damaging the war economy, in short, all those who weaken, undermine or endanger the fighting efforts of our people.[51]

At the end of 1941, Sophie's sense of isolation in such an increasingly repressive society was extremely powerful. Sophie told Otl Aicher she felt bored and unhappy at the kindergarten in Blumberg, as her work was very constricting and offered no intellectual stimulation whatsoever. She even doubted whether she would ever be happy again. She was feeling 'miserably weak' and was doubting if she could give love to another person fully or even to love God.[52] 'My sole sustenance is Nature', she noted in her diary in December 1941, 'the sky the stars and the silent earth', adding, 'I realise that when I love people very much I can't do better than include them in my prayers. If I love people in all sincerity, I love them for God's sake. What better thing can I do than take that love to God? God grant that I come to love Fritz too in His name.'[53] Inge Scholl believed Sophie's love of nature was linked to her growing conviction 'that behind all living things there must be a creative force at work'.[54] Otl Aicher believed a strong sense of justice and morality were also key parts of Sophie's personality and her striving for spirituality was an addition to this world view.[55]

Sophie was only allowed to leave for a short Christmas break from the kindergarten in Blumberg on Christmas Eve 1941. For the very first time she had failed to make it home in time to complete the annual ritual of opening Christmas presents with her family.[56] She was not looking forward to her return to Blumberg, describing the newly appointed kindergarten leader as 'a 150 per cent Nazi'.[57] Sophie was able, however, to attend the annual family ski trip – this time to a log cabin high in the Coburg Mountains. The group consisted of Sophie, Hans, Inge, Traute Lafrenz, the new 'girlfriend' of Hans, a young man called Wulfried and a music student named Ulla, a friend of Traute and also a great admirer of Hans. Lafrenz had met Hans at the Odeon, a concert hall in Munich, after listening to Bach's Brandenburg Concertos. She came from the lively seaport of Hamburg. She was highly intelligent, witty and strikingly beautiful. She was studying medicine at Hamburg University, but took supplementary courses at Munich. At Hamburg she had been a member a student group that opposed National Socialism.

During the trip, the weather was extremely stormy and there were several terrible snow blizzards. But the party, egged on by the adventurous Hans, backed up by a now lively Sophie, went on several memorable but extraordinarily dangerous ski runs down the steep mountains. At night, the party discussed matters philosophical, political and spiritual over several glasses of wine, as the elements lashed the windows of their cabin. According to Traute Lafrenz the party discussed questions literary, philosophical and religious, and strong anti-Nazi views were expressed, especially by Hans and Sophie, but there were no detailed discussions about a programme of resistance.[58]

But the trip did much to lift Sophie's spirits. In a letter to Otl Aicher, Sophie claimed the party had debated their 'spiritual hunger' and emotions in great depth. These discussions had led her to a conviction that 'a hard mind without a soft heart is necessarily as barren as a soft heart without a hard mind'. Sophie emphasised how 'music softens the heart', relaxes tensions and leaves the listener having a 'liberated heart, a heart that has become receptive to harmony and things harmonious, a heart that has opened its doors to the workings of the mind'.[59] Hans described the trip to his sister Elisabeth as a 'monumental experience' because the group had been exposed to great danger due to all the storms and blizzards, but had managed to 'discuss our troubled times, the cross and salvation'.[60]

In the first week of January 1942, Sophie returned to Blumberg in a very positive mood. 'I've become a pretty experienced nursery school teacher during my three months here (nearly four now)', she told Lisa Remppis, 'I doubt if many people get as much of an opportunity to learn as I do here and I'm having a certain amount of success.' She had started to listen to music more often and commented: 'If anything can raise a stolid heart, it's music.'[61] 'I've decided to pray every day', she noted in her diary:

> so that God won't forsake me. Although I don't yet know God and feel sure that my conception of him is utterly false, he'll forgive me if I ask him. If I can love him with all my soul, I shall lose my distorted view of him … O Lord, I need so badly to pray, to ask.[62]

But Sophie's good mood did not last long. In February 1942, her father Robert Scholl was arrested by the Gestapo for offering criticism of the regime. In an unguarded moment in his office, he had said to his young secretary: 'This Hitler is God's scourge on mankind' and then told her 'If the war does not end soon, the Russians will be sitting in Berlin within two years.'[63] The secretary later admitted to being 'fond of Herr Scholl' and grateful to him for giving her a job, but she felt she could not allow such critical comments on the Führer to pass. She reported what he had said to the local Gestapo office. The Gestapo relied overwhelmingly on such accusations from the public to find and prosecute opponents and critics of the regime. Such comments were an offence under the Treacherous Attacks on the State Law (*Heimtücke*), established in 1934. Before the war, very few 'national comrades' were charged under this law, but during wartime prosecutions increased. Even long-tolerated minor dissidents like Robert Scholl ended up in a prison cell. After a couple of weeks he was released, but told he would face a trial in Stuttgart before a Special Court later in the year. Magdalene Scholl was distraught about the prospect of her husband going to prison. The upcoming trial was another source of pressure for the whole family.

On 1 April 1942, Sophie's long period of labour service duty was finally over. In her last letter from Blumberg, Sophie admitted that she had grown fond of the children in her charge and promised to take them on a 'grand outing' before she left, but she ended by admitting 'I'm going home in a week's time. I can't tell you how much I'm looking forward to it.'[64] At last, Sophie could now finally look forward to beginning her degree in biology and philosophy at Munich University. In the meantime, she could enjoy a long break at home. On 4 April 1942, Sophie attended the Easter service at Söflingen Catholic Church and admitted:

> Much as I need that kind of service – because it's a real service, not a lecture like you get in a Protestant church – I'm sure it takes practice or habit to participate fully … My trouble is, however, I'd like to kneel down, as it accords with my feelings, but I'm shy of people seeing, especially people I know. I'd like to bow down before an effigy of God, because you shouldn't just experience such feelings but express them as well, but again I'm too inhibited.

The next day Sophie told her friend, Lisa Remppis: 'I've been back home for a whole week. It's a tremendous change and a tiring one, finding your way back into a circle of friends after a solitary and self-reliant way of life.'[65]

At the end of April 1942, Sophie Scholl was packing a large suitcase in eager anticipation of her journey to Munich by train on the following day finally to fulfil her hard-fought and cherished ambition to go to Munich University. 'I can't believe that tomorrow I'm starting my studies', she said to her mother as she packed her belongings. 'I can still see her, my sister, standing there the next morning', Inge Scholl later recalled, 'ready to travel and full of expectation … She looked upon the world with her big, dark eyes questioning yet with a lively sympathy. Her face was still very childlike and delicate.'[66]

EIGHT

MUNICH UNIVERSITY

In the first week of May 1942, Sophie travelled by express train to Munich.[1] Her mother had baked a cake to take with her and packed two bottles of red wine. In a few days, Sophie would be twenty-one years old.[2] When her train arrived at Munich's central station, waiting patiently on the platform was Hans Scholl, accompanied by Traute Lafrenz.[3] They all greeted each other very warmly. It had taken a great deal of determination for Sophie to get to university at all.

Munich was the capital of the German state of Bavaria. It was called the 'birthplace of National Socialism'. Adolf Hitler had moved there in 1913, renting a spartan room in the arty Schwabing district. Hitler loved the elegant classical Italianate architecture of Munich. He made his reputation as a charismatic rabble-rouser in its local beer halls during the 1920s.[4] The Nazi party headquarters, *Braunes Haus* ('the Brown House'), Hitler's lavish apartment and his favourite restaurant – the Osteria – were all located there. His now legendary Bavarian mountain retreat, the Berghof, was within easy commuting distance.

Yet in spite of so many links to Nazism, Munich still retained much of its distinctive Bavarian charm and character even during the Nazi years. To begin with, the Nazi Party was far less popular in Catholic Bavaria than in the small rural northern Protestant towns. Munich is a predominantly Catholic city. The dominant figure on the city coat of arms is a monk. The colours of the city flag – black and gold – are the same as the flag of the (Catholic) Holy Roman Empire. During the Protestant Reformation, Munich was a centre of opposition to Martin Luther. In spite of the fact

Hitler was baptised a Catholic, the regime he led viewed Catholics as 'non-believers' in National Socialism and therefore suspect. So Munich was not as unusual a location for an educated opposition to the Nazi regime to develop as it may first appear.

The University of Munich was founded in 1472 by Duke Ludwig of Bavaria-Landshut and is one of the leading universities in Germany. It began in Ingolstadt, but in 1800 was relocated to Landshut. In 1802 it was renamed *Ludwig-Maximilans-Universität*, in honour of King Maximilian I and King Ludwig the Wealthy. In 1826 it relocated to Munich, where it has remained ever since. It played a pioneering role in the education of women; in 1900, two Scottish-born scientists – Marie Ogilvie-Gordan and Agnes Kelly – were the first women to receive doctorates from the university. In 1903, Munich was the second university in Germany, after Baden, to offer full admission to female undergraduates. In 1918, Munich awarded a professorship to Adele Hartman, the first chair ever given by a German university to a woman.

Unfortunately, the university's role in the treatment of Jews was less exalted. In 1920, the Jewish Albert Einstein, the world-renowned physicist, was prohibited from lecturing there. In 1925, Richard Willstätter, the Jewish Nobel Prize-winning chemist, resigned in protest at what he called the 'compulsive, intolerant and unconstitutional anti-Semitism' that pervaded the university administration.[5] The students' union was dominated by pro-Nazis even before Hitler came to power. On 10 May 1933, it organised a major book-burning ceremony on Königplatz, not far from the main university buildings, located on Ludwigsstrasse, a grand Italianate-inspired boulevard.

The rector of Munich University in 1942 was Professor Walter Wüst, an expert on a new Nazi-approved subject called 'Aryan Culture'. He was a loyal Nazi who held the rank of SS colonel. But Wüst did not impose Nazi ideological rule over the campus, except for ensuring the exclusion of Jews and communists. The Nazi-dominated students' union tried to instil loyalty within the student body, but it was still possible for independently minded students to go their own way and form small sub-groups based on shared interests.[6]

The Nazi leadership advised all universities in Germany to put Nazi ideology at the heart of their teaching and research. In reality, fewer than 5 per cent of lectures at German universities were overtly Nazi in title or content. Most academics retained a remarkable degree of independence when carrying out their research and publications.[7] A major study of doctoral dissertations in the Nazi era recently showed that fewer than 15 per cent could be described as Nazi in methodology and approach. German professors and lecturers were never sent on Nazi indoctrination courses, unlike schoolteachers.[8] Academics in some subjects were – of course – despised by the regime, but most were left alone. The star name in Munich's chemistry department was Heinrich Wieland, who never hid his indifference to Nazi ideals. Another well-known professor at the university, Arthur Kutscher, actually read passages by the banned playwright Bertolt Brecht during lectures. Some lecturers openly called the Nazis 'great simplifiers' of complex ideas and pointed out the anti-intellectual nature of Nazi ideology. By and large, there were many more committed Nazis among the young students – most of whom had just left the Hitler Youth – than among the highly intellectual academics.[9]

In her first month at university, Sophie lived as a lodger with Professor Carl Muth, the elderly Catholic scholar who had become a close friend of the Scholl family.[10] Sophie was grateful for Muth's hospitality. In a letter to her parents, dated 6 June 1942, she asked them to send some food for the old professor, as 'our wartime nutrition is not exactly helpful to general health'.[11]

There is mention in some books on the White Rose of a birthday party for Sophie, which took place at Hans' rented apartment at 1 Mandelstrasse in Schwabing, which was supposedly attended by the leading figures of the group later known as 'the White Rose'.[12] Traute Lafrenz-Page, who lived with Hans Scholl in this period, did not recall it.[13] But there may have been a social gathering on the first night Sophie arrived, attended by Hans, Traute and two of Hans' closest university friends, Alexander Schmorell and Christoph Probst.[14] In the next few weeks, Sophie also met Wilhelm ('Willi') Graf, a self-effacing young medical student, and attended lectures by Professor Kurt Huber, the star philosophy lecturer on campus. Sophie was able immediately to feel part of an established group, all of whom were trusted and close friends of her beloved brother. 'There was a certain seriousness about all of them', recalls Traute Lafrenz-Page:

> but otherwise we were kind of happy, talking to each other, taking walks. I guess we were not that different from young people today, only our fun was a little different. It was a time without TV, without much emphasis on outward appearance … We read together and that was fun.[15]

Some of the people Sophie came into contact with during her first few weeks at university must be introduced at this point. Alexander Schmorell was born at Orenburg, in the Russian Urals, on 16 September 1917. He was baptised in the Russian Orthodox Church. He was tall, popular, extremely stylish and charming. His mother was Russian, but died of typhus when he was just two years old. Alex was only four when his father, Hugo, a doctor, also born in Russia, moved the family to Germany and remarried a German woman, also born in Russia. Alex grew up speaking German and Russian with equal fluency. His favourite writers, composers and artists were all Russians. His childhood nickname was 'Shurik' and it stuck with him for the rest of his life. His family was affluent, cultured and lived in a large villa in the smart Munich suburb of Harlaching. In spite of this comfortable background, Alex was attracted to the edgy artist, the disaffected outsider, the bohemian radical and the downtrodden.

'Alex was the most complex of all', a friend recalls, 'because he was torn between his Russian ancestry and his German ancestry'.[16] Alex was always opposed to the Nazi regime and never joined the Hitler Youth. When he was called up for military service in the German army, he refused to take the oath of loyalty to Adolf Hitler, but his commanding officer did not report this act of defiance. The German invasion of the Soviet Union in 1941 intensified Alex's long-standing hatred of National Socialism. In the autumn of 1940, George Wittenstein – a fellow medic in the student medical company – introduced Hans Scholl to Alexander Schmorell. They struck up a firm friendship, reading and discussing philosophical, theological and literary works together. These conversations soon developed into a determination to 'do something' to oppose the Nazi regime. In Elisabeth Hartnagel's opinion, Alex was the 'closest friend Hans ever had during his entire life'.[17] Alex invited Hans to the regular discreet 'reading evenings' he organised at his home. At first, these discussions were just confined to literature, philosophy, religion and music, but most of the guests held dissident views on the Nazis.

It was Alex who introduced Hans Scholl to Christoph ('Christl') Probst. He was born on 6 November 1919, in Murnau. Christoph was dependable, restrained and self-deprecating, with a ready smile for everyone he met. His sensitivity and intelligence made him the most well-loved and highly respected member of the whole group. His father, Hermann, came from a wealthy merchant family. Due to a substantial inheritance, he lived his life as 'a private scholar', independently researching eastern religions. Christoph grew up surrounded by books, and met a host of eminent expert scholars and talented artists throughout his childhood. His parents divorced during his early infancy, but his father soon remarried. Christoph developed a very close bond with his sister Angelika, who recalls 'We had many Jewish friends and our stepmother was Jewish.'[18]

In 1935, Christoph first met Alexander Schmorell at the Neues Realgymnasium in Munich. They soon became inseparable friends. In school reports, Christoph is described as 'mature, lively minded and thoughtful'. He was never enthusiastic about Nazism, due to his love of freedom of thought and religion. But the stability Christoph had enjoyed as a child was shattered in 1936 when his father suddenly committed suicide, following a bout of severe depression. Without an 'Aryan husband', his Jewish stepmother was now in real danger from Nazi anti-Semitic policies, but she managed to remain in her home, escaping persecution and deportation to a death camp.

In 1939, Christoph began a degree in medicine at Munich, but also took courses in Strasburg and Innsbruck. He combined his studies with service in the Luftwaffe. At the age of twenty-one, he married Hertha Dohrn, the daughter of Harald Dohrn, another 'private scholar' who was a long-standing opponent of the Nazi regime. By 1942, this devoted young couple had two children and another on the way. Christoph became very agitated when he heard news about the Nazi euthanasia programme against the mentally ill and the disabled. The escalation of Nazi terror towards the Jews was another basis of his anger towards the regime, and he was increasingly attracted towards Catholicism. Sophie Scholl had a touching fondness for Christoph and his family, and she felt he was 'a good influence on Hans'.[19]

Christoph introduced Wilhelm ('Willi') Graf to the small circle of like-minded friends, after meeting him at a Bach concert in Munich in June 1942. Willi was born on 2 January 1918 in Kuchenheim, but his family soon moved to the Rhineland town of Saarbrücken. Willi was extremely devoted to the Catholic religion and had always opposed the Nazi regime. In 1934, he joined the 'Grey Order' (*Grauer Orden*), a religiously based youth group, part of the *Bündische* youth movement. During the Gestapo crackdown on non-conformist youth groups in 1937–38, Willi was arrested and served three weeks in prison accused of 'subversive activities', but due to the amnesty announced by Hitler after the *Anschluss* in March 1938, the case was dropped.

Graf started his medical studies at Bonn University in the academic year 1937–38, but also served as a medical orderly in field hospitals during the German military attacks on Poland, Yugoslavia and the Soviet Union. 'The war here in the east', Willi wrote in a letter home, 'leads to things so terrible I have not thought possible and I wish I had not seen what I have seen'.[20]

In April 1942, he was able to continue his medical studies at Munich University. His strong dislike of National Socialism was also motivated by a growing feeling that the Nazi regime was undermining Christianity in general, but the Catholic Church in particular. His religious devotion gave him a tremendous inner strength that ultimately proved remarkable.

One of the most popular lecturers at Munich University was Dr Kurt Huber, who ran a philosophy course which Sophie attended twice a week in her first term. Huber's lectures were 'must-see' events for undergraduates, often attracting over 250 students. They were all cleverly punctuated by satirical remarks, designed to show his indifference to Nazi ideals. Traute Lafrenz-Page described Huber as 'a truly genial person, with a wonderful clarity of thought and precise language. He was kind and compassionate and would not fit easily into any organisation, certainly not a fascist one.'[21]

He was born on 24 October 1893 in Chur, Switzerland, of German parents, and he was forty-eight years old when Sophie arrived at the university. He had a pronounced limp in his left foot and numbness in his right hand due to the complications of rickets and diphtheria. He also had a noticeable stammer. At the age of four, his family moved to Stuttgart, where Huber attended the Eberhard-Ludwig Gymnasium. He showed exceptional musical talent as a child, which was encouraged by his parents. After his father's death, his mother moved her four children to Munich. He was excused military service in the First World War due to his disabled status, and opted for an academic career. He was awarded a doctorate from Munich University in the early 1920s. In 1926, he became an associate professor at the university. Three years later he married Clara Schlickenrieder and quickly established an international reputation as an expert on Bavarian, German and European folk songs. 'Without a doubt', wrote Dr Kurt Port, his academic publisher, 'Huber was of similar importance to German folk music [scholarship] as the Grimm brothers were to the German fairy tale.'[22]

Huber became a star turn at numerous international conferences. In 1936, he represented Germany at a prestigious folk music conference in Barcelona. In 1937, he was 'head-hunted' to the renowned National Institute for German Music Research at Berlin University. At this stage of his career, Huber's star was very much in the ascendancy, but he refused to produce new Nazi marching songs or become a musical propagandist for the regime. In 1939, Huber's request for permanent tenure in Berlin was rejected. He was forced to return to the much less exalted position of associate professor, back at Munich University. His career had come full circle. Of course, he remained a big name in his own specialist academic area, and students flooded to his lectures each week, but the 'lone-wolf' reputation stuck with him and his once promising academic career stalled. Huber's popularity with the students clearly became an important source of solace in the twilight of an unfulfilled career.

Kurt Huber was someone who was greatly admired by all the circle of friends who later became known as 'the White Rose'. They all wanted to get to know their friendly lecturer much better. They sensed he was a like-minded opponent of the Nazi regime. Traute Lafrenz-Page wrote 'if you listened to Huber's lectures you could detect his [anti-Nazi] political position'.[23] Other students also remember Huber fondly. 'His open and warm hearted personality', recalls Mirok Li, 'always filled me with joy' and Angelika Probst remembers: 'Sophie attended his lectures, but students from other faculties crowded into the hall: it was often difficult to get a seat.'[24]

This small group of friends who Sophie had joined all came from very affluent middle-class backgrounds. They met in student flats, paid for by their parents. They attended musical concerts, plays, movies, bars and restaurants. If they had not wanted to oppose Nazism, they could easily have slipped into a 'Brideshead Revisited' student lifestyle of self-gratification. But they were all deeply committed Christians who were also intellectual, humanist and democratic in outlook. They could talk for hours in a serious manner on complex literary, theological and philosophical issues – and found such conversations rewarding. Even before Sophie arrived these discussions were already evolving into a concrete plan to engage in active opposition to the Nazi regime. In effect, these students were crossing a very dangerous line. Crossing that line would turn them from being regarded as 'national comrades' to 'enemies of the people'. 'It was not a political organisation you could join' says George Wittenstein of the White Rose, 'It was a group of personal friends with shared interests.'[25]

NINE

WHITE ROSE

By the time Sophie arrived at university, Hans and Alex had already decided to mount an active resistance campaign against the Nazi regime. The plan had developed over many discussions in the previous months. There is no conclusive evidence to show who was the chief author of the plan. According to Traute Lafrenz-Page, 'Hans was the prime mover, then Alex', but she feels the decision 'had grown out of our discussions'.[1] Lilo Ramdohr, a close friend of Alex, remembers witnessing a conversation just before Christmas 1941 between Hans, Alex and Christoph Probst, during which the idea of forming a passive resistance group against Hitler was openly discussed.[2] Sophie Scholl later claimed it was Hans and she who had jointly hatched the plan.[3] The exact origins of the leafleting campaign of the White Rose, which began in the summer of 1942, remain tantalisingly indefinable. In the words of Franz Müller, 'Sophie Scholl, she was the heart – and Hans and Alex were the thinking behind the White Rose.'[4]

There were many eclectic philosophical, theological and literary influences on the group, but it is very difficult to highlight any one primary influence. But one thing is for certain: devotion to God was a unifying and dominant factor. These young people searched for a spiritual definition of humanity. The writings of the theological scholar St Augustine made a deep impression upon Sophie and Hans and made them realise that serious philosophical thinking had to take place before real faith could begin. The constant encroachment by the Nazi regime against organised religion was undoubtedly a key motivation in the decision to mount active opposition. They all emphasised Christianity as the basis for moral regeneration in a post-Hitler Germany.

But devotion to religion does not fully explain the protest. Hans Scholl was influenced by meetings with the sociologist Alfred von Martin, who promoted the idea of a federal and pluralistic Europe. Hans and Sophie also met Josef Furtmeier, whom they dubbed 'The Philosopher', who had suggested a need for active resistance to the Nazi regime by rousing the German population through propaganda. 'In the evening', wrote Sophie Scholl on 30 May 1942, 'Hans and I went to a friend whom we call "The Philosopher". There we had a continuous and exhausting conversation. In fact, I need to spend some time alone, since I feel the urge to realise through action, what has been inside me only as thoughts and recognised as the right thing.'[5] They all believed basic freedoms had to be restored through a restoration of democratic government – which was a political objective.

They felt that common humanity counted more than the nation state. They thought some kind of international community of states would reduce the risk of war ever happening again. They wanted individuals to have free choice and not become the tools of the will of a secular dictator, using mass propaganda to dupe the people and trample on basic civil rights. They were a group of individuals living under a dictatorship. In the view of Traute Lafrenz-Page, this small circle of friends all viewed the Nazi regime as composed of 'criminal war makers'. It was, she recalls, primarily a 'Christian' and 'moral' protest rather than one with a clear political agenda.[6]

It is very important to stress that these anti-Nazi views were not shaped by the downturn of Germany's fortunes in the war. The leading student figures in the White Rose in Munich had all opposed Nazism long before the war began. They were not swept away by the incredible military successes of Hitler's regime. Sophie became most agitated and depressed after the defeat of France in 1940 and in the months following the attack on the Soviet Union – when the rest of Germany was rejoicing. News of the increasing criminal irresponsibility of the Nazi regime, especially the euthanasia programme and the appalling genocide against the Jews and other minorities in Eastern Europe, was also extremely important in driving the group forward towards outright opposition.

In the end, they decided to express their views in leaflets and distribute them using the German postal system. It was a non-violent form of passive resistance. They were protesting against tyranny and for a free society. 'I think it is characteristic of the Munich students', Inge Scholl later recalled, 'choosing leafleting with its paper thin chance of mobilising passive resistance … They could have chosen to throw bombs, but that would have been at the cost of human lives.'[7] It might seem a very mild form of resistance to send anonymous anti-Nazi leaflets through the post. But any form of opposition carried the risk of death. 'I always understood', Alexander Schmorell later explained, 'that I could lose my life in the event of an investigation. I ignored this all because my deep urge to combat National Socialism was stronger.'[8] George Wittenstein said 'You had to keep everything secret. You could not even trust your friends.'[9]

The choice of the name 'White Rose' for the early leaflets is still unclear. It may have been adopted to stress that the members of the group were peaceful and not inspired by any recognisable political colour, as red was the dominant colour in the flags of communism and National Socialism. It has also been suggested that the name 'White Rose' comes from a novel of the same name, written in 1929, by a mysterious novelist who used the *nom de plume* B. Traven. It depicted a poor Mexican farmer fighting against the brutal and dictatorial policies of a large oil company. No one was ever able to establish the real identity of Traven.[10] Hans Scholl offered the following explanation:

> The name White Rose was chosen arbitrarily. I proceeded from the assumption that powerful propaganda has to contain certain phrases which do not necessarily mean anything, but sound good, and give the impression of a political programme. I may have chosen the name intuitively since at that time I was under the influence of the Spanish poetic ballad 'Rosa Blanca' by Brentano.[11]

Alexander Schmorell provided a portable US-made Remington typewriter, borrowed from a neighbour (Karl Pötzl), to type the first leaflet, but Hans wrote it on his own, possibly in March 1942, copied it on a duplicating machine he purchased for 32 marks, with paper and stencils he bought from a local office supply shop. Hans posted just 100 copies of the first leaflet to addresses he had copied straight out of a Munich telephone directory.[12] This small mail-out just went to middle-class professionals and a few beer-hall owners in the hope they would pass them on to their customers.

The first leaflet appeared in the last days of June 1942 and began with the words: 'Nothing is so unworthy of a civilised nation than to allow itself to be governed without opposition by an irresponsible clique that has yielded to base instinct.' It urged German people to engage in 'passive resistance' towards the Nazi regime 'before it is too late' and ended with a quotation from the poet Goethe's *The Awakening of Epimenides*, Act II, Scene 4:

Now I find my good men
Are gathered in the night
To wait in silence, not to sleep
And the glorious word of liberty
They whisper and murmur
Till in unaccustomed strangeness
On the steps of our temple
Once again in delight they cry
Freedom! Freedom!

Finally, the recipients of the leaflet were encouraged 'to make as many copies of this as you can and distribute them'.[13] A Gestapo report on the leaflet, written by language expert Professor Richard Harder, suggested that the author, although deeply influenced by Christian ideals, was not 'an embittered loner' but most probably part of a group. He concluded that the leaflet did not have a 'positive agenda', nor explain how 'passive resistance' was going to be organised or co-ordinated.[14] It was – according to the expert – the work of a young romantic idealist rather than the leader of a dangerous resistance movement. Most loyal 'national comrades' dutifully handed the leaflets they received by post straight to the Gestapo.

Traute Lafrenz was not told about the decision to send the first leaflet, but when she saw a copy: 'I could tell at once that it must have been written by "us", though I wasn't sure if Hans himself had done it.'[15] It is not clear when Sophie first became involved. In the transcript of her Gestapo interrogations she offered two conflicting versions. In one exchange, Sophie claimed that she was given the fourth leaflet by Traute Lafrenz in the middle of July 1942. She apparently read it with Hans leaning over her shoulder, but doubted whether Hans was the author. A few days later she asked Hans who 'he thought the author was' and he replied: 'it's not a good idea to ask who wrote the leaflet as that person's life might become endangered'.[16] But in another admission Sophie said 'I could not tell you when my brother or I first came upon the idea of producing the leaflets', but she claimed that they had been discussing for at least a year how to, 'effectively communicate' their opposition to the war to the German public.[17] One of the first things Traute Lafrenz-Page noticed about 'quiet and reserved' Sophie was how strongly she opposed Nazism.[18] Fritz Hartnagel later claimed that in May 1942 Sophie asked him to try and buy a duplication machine – an indication that she knew very early on.[19] Elisabeth Hartnagel is convinced Sophie was involved in the leafleting operation from beginning to end.[20]

Clara Huber, Kurt Huber's wife, later recalled she had no idea Sophie Scholl was involved in opposition activities against the Nazi regime and she saw 'nothing of a rebel' in the polite, reserved and intelligent young student who sometimes visited her home.[21]

The second leaflet was co-written by Hans Scholl and Alexander Schmorell. It opened with the assertion, 'It is impossible to engage in intellectual discourse with National Socialist philosophy, for if there is such an entity, there is nothing rational about it' and it revealed that 'three hundred thousand Jews had been murdered' in Poland 'in the most bestial way' and called these killings 'the most frightful crime against human dignity, in the whole of history'. It then asked directly: 'Why do German people behave so apathetically in the face of these abominable crimes so unworthy of the human race?' and claimed it was 'the sole duty of every German to defy these beasts'. It ended with a quotation from Lao Tzu, the founder of Taoism, a philosopher who argued against violence and war.[22]

The second leaflet was first received by unwitting members of the public in the first week of July 1942. It was far more strident and polemical than the first one. It attacked the German people for offering blind allegiance to an obviously criminal regime and revealed that Nazis were carrying out genocide on a mass scale in Eastern Europe. But once again, the 'unknown' authors of the leaflet offered no concrete proposals for action. A Gestapo report in Upper Bavaria concluded that the authors of the leaflets 'could not be determined' and nor could their location.[23]

The third leaflet also appeared in the first week of July 1942. It once more attacked the 'dictatorship of evil' that was Hitler's Third Reich and contrasted this with 'God's will', which it claimed was for 'earthly happiness, in self-reliance and self-chosen activity, within the community of life and the work of the nation'. This contrast between the 'good' of Christianity and the 'evil' of Nazism was a central belief of all the leading figures in the White Rose group.

The third leaflet once more emphasised 'passive resistance' as the best means to 'topple National Socialism', but it did not rule out 'any action' and advanced the following advice to those who supported their ideas, urging:

Sabotage in armament plants and war industries. Sabotage in all gatherings, rallies, public ceremonies and organisations in the National Socialist Party. Obstruction in the smooth running of the war machine ... sabotage in all areas of science and scholarship which further the continuation of the war - in universities, technical schools, laboratories, research institutes or

technical bureaus. Sabotage in all artistic institutions which could potentially enhance the 'prestige' of the fascists among the people. Sabotage in
all branches of the arts ... Sabotage in all publications, all newspapers that
are in the pay of the 'Government' and defend its ideology and help in disseminating the brown [Nazi] lie ... Try to convince all your acquaintances,
including those of the lower social classes, the senselessness of continuing,
of the hopelessness of the war, of our spiritual enslavement at the hands of
the National Socialists, of its destruction of all moral and religious values
and urge them to passive resistance.

It ends with a quotation from Aristotle that 'the tyrant is inclined to engage
in constant warfare in order to occupy and distract his subjects'.[24] Once
more, it urged recipients to 'please make copies and pass them on'.

The third leaflet was by far the most provocative to date. The frequent
references to 'sabotage' of the war effort were obviously the work of Alex.
It not only offered a negative attack on the Nazi regime, but recommended
ways to 'topple' Hitler. There was even a request for recipients to influence 'the lower social orders', which emphasises once more that the group
viewed its target audience as the educated members of the middle class.
In Nazi legal terms, the leaflet was much more dangerous as it was urging
'high treason' at a time of war.

The fourth leaflet, primarily written by Hans Scholl, soon appeared at a
time when the German army was once more scoring a number of military
victories in the Soviet Union and North Africa. It focused primarily on
attacking Adolf Hitler's leadership, claiming at one point that:

Every word that comes from Hitler's mouth is a lie. When he says peace, he
means war, and when he blasphemously uses the name of the Almighty, he
means the power of evil, the fallen angel, Satan.

It urged every German to 'attack evil where it is strongest and it is strongest
in the power of Hitler'. There was the return of a theological dimension,
with a biblical quotation from Ecclesiastes:

So I returned and considered all the oppressions that are done under the sun
and beheld the tears of the oppressed and they have no comforter: and on the
side of the oppressors there was power, but they had no comforter. Therefore
I praised the dead that are already dead than the living that are yet alive.

The leaflet ended with a promise: 'We will not be silent. We are your bad conscience. The White Rose will not leave you in peace.'[25]

In the fourth leaflet, the fight against the Nazis is once more viewed as a struggle between God and the Devil. The leaflet is directly aimed at influencing 'Christians' to rise up against the godless Nazis. To counteract claims that the White Rose leaflets were the work of allied saboteurs, the leaflet stated: 'we wish to expressly point out that the White Rose is not in the pay of a foreign power'. There was also a recognition that the Nazi regime would ultimately be broken, not by leaflets or sabotage, but by 'military means', and before then it was vital for Germans to recognise 'the guilt with which the German people have burdened themselves through their support of Hitler's regime'. For young Germans in the midst of war, this was a far-sighted recognition of what later became known as collective guilt.

By now, the Gestapo thought they were dealing with a large organisation, possibly with links to the Allies. Sophie explained that in the period when the first four leaflets appeared in the summer term of 1942 'we wanted to give an impression this propaganda was the work of a large organisation' and she confessed 'we even made jokes about this falsehood'.[26] But the leaflets had not made much impact on public opinion. Even Hans Scholl was pondering at this juncture whether to abandon the leafleting campaign altogether.[27]

There was clearly a growing feeling within the group that the experienced academic writer Kurt Huber might be able to supply added gravitas and ideas. They decided to try and entice him to join them. Huber was invited by Alex and Hans to one of the regular 'reading evenings' at Alex's house. Huber accepted the invitation on the basis it was a pleasant social gathering.[28] He was met at the tram stop by Hans and Traute Lafrenz, who asked him if he had received a leaflet from the White Rose. He told her he had, but made no comment on the contents and swiftly changed the subject. Most of the leading figures in the White Rose – Hans, Alex, Christoph, Sophie and Traute – were present at this gathering. The talk eventually turned to politics, but Huber, who was normally negative about the Nazis in his lectures, was much more guarded in such an open social setting. He said 'active resistance' to the regime was 'impossible'. The only mildly radical suggestion he made was to say Bavaria should have greater autonomy from central government, a programme that had been advocated by the right-wing Bavarian People's Party (BVP) in the 1920s. Shortly after this muddled intervention, Huber made a polite early exit.[29] Sophie, Hans and the other members of the White Rose were disappointed.

In early July 1942, the student medics were told they would be sent to the Soviet Union at the end of the semester. On 22 July 1943, the night before their departure, a farewell party took place at Eickemayer's studio at which most of the leading figures in the White Rose were present, as was Kurt Huber. The Gestapo officers were later convinced that this event was some sort of resistance symposium or a future planning meeting of the group, not just the 'farewell party' they all claimed it was. Katharina Schüddekopf later said the partygoers talked about the wave of 'White Rose leaflets' that had recently appeared, but many people thought they were the work of 'Communists'.[30]

Manfred Eickemeyer mentioned the mass shootings of Jews by the *Einsatzgruppen* in Poland. Alex said German soldiers should engage in passive resistance too. Huber disagreed, saying every soldier should continue to follow orders. Huber also spoke up when the issue of 'resistance' towards the Nazi regime cropped up again. He said 'active resistance' was impossible for academics and students. The only way to get rid of Hitler was 'to assassinate him', but this idea was not endorsed by Hans, Alex or Sophie, who retained a non-violent stance. Hans Hirzel, a young Ulm high school student, was also invited to the party. He later recalled that nearly everyone present refused to offer any open criticism of the Nazi regime.[31] Once again, the students never got the chance to broach the subject of Kurt Huber joining the group and he left the party early.

The next morning Sophie Scholl went along with Hans Scholl, Alexander Schmorell, Willi Graf and their student medic friends George Wittenstein and Hubert Furtwängler to Munich's Ostbahnhof railway station. These young men were bound for the Soviet Union, via Poland, for a stint of medical duty that was to last three months. They all saw the consequences of the German assault on the Soviet Union that summer. For Alex, it was a journey of the heart and soul. He felt his 'homeland' had been violated by the Nazis. For Hans, it was a first opportunity to discuss with Russian people how the Germans had destroyed their lives. Willi Graf was outraged by the terrible treatment inflicted on the people of Eastern Europe by the Nazi regime. The trip to Russia undoubtedly acted as a further spur to carry on their resistance to Hitler and helped to push it into realms that had not been contemplated in the initial first phase of the leafleting campaign.

At the end of July 1942, Sophie returned home. It proved a very stressful summer for her. The trial of Robert Scholl for denouncing Hitler, which had been delayed, was finally set for 3 August 1942, in the Special Court in Stuttgart. In a letter to her friend, Lisa Remppis, Sophie was pessimistic about the outcome: 'there's little hope that he'll be allowed home', and she was already missing her new university friends. 'I never could have believed I would become attached to them all.'[32]

The presiding judge at Robert Scholl's trial was Hermann Cuhorst, who had granted leniency to Hans Scholl and the members of his d.j.1.11 group in June 1938. The case had been brought after a secretary working in Robert Scholl's office reported him to the Gestapo for saying Hitler was the 'scourge of humanity' and leading Germany to military disaster. In this case, it seems the secretary – as far as we know – did not have a vengeful motive. In some cases during the war judges punished such outbursts harshly – and in rare cases they inflicted the death penalty.[33] There were two different ways a judge could deal with a case like this. It could be seen as a mild outburst and classed under the *Heimtücke* law, which dealt with crimes regarding 'political slander and libel', or the far more serious *Wehrkraftzersetzung* law, which punished public attempts to 'undermine the will of Germany'. It was really up to the Gestapo to decide which route to take and then for the judge to decide the punishment. A study of 249 cases in the Cologne Special Court has revealed that over 80 per cent of such cases were dismissed before ever proceeding to trial, and those who did go to court received mild sentences.[34]

The case against Robert Scholl was dealt with under the mild *Heimtücke* law. The reason it went ahead at all was due to the increasing directives of the Justice Ministry in the summer of 1942, which urged judges to punish even minor cases of dissent. Cuhorst sentenced the well-known non-conformist Robert Scholl to the relatively lenient term of four months in prison. He concluded that Robert Scholl did not have a 'treasonous' attitude and was generally a law-abiding member of the 'national community'. He also gave him three weeks to sort out his business affairs before his sentence began.[35] But Cuhorst's judgement also deprived Robert Scholl of his right to practise law. The future of the Scholl family finances now looked bleak. Robert Scholl managed to persuade a business friend in Stuttgart – Eugen Grimminger – to take over his affairs and offer clerical work to Inge Scholl, who had worked in her father's office as an administrator for several years.

The imprisonment of her father was viewed by Sophie as yet another example of the injustice of the Nazi regime. On many of the summer evenings in 1942, Sophie stood outside the prison wall and played on her flute a tune her father loved called '*Die Gedanken sind frei*' (Your thoughts are free).[36] A distraught Magdelene Scholl asked Hans and Werner, who were both serving in the Soviet Union, to write clemency letters. They both initially refused, but eventually intervened, and so did Fritz Hartnagel. The reluctance of Hans to bring himself to the attention of the Nazi authorities during a time when he was engaged in dangerous opposition activity of his own is fairly understandable.

In August 1942, Ernst Reden, who had remained friendly with Inge Scholl, was killed in action in the Soviet Union. On hearing of Reden's death, Sophie reportedly said, 'It's got to stop.'[37] Her worries were further increased because Fritz Hartnagel's unit was dispatched to Stalingrad, a major port and industrial city, located on the west bank of the River Volga. The German Sixth army, commanded by General Friedrich Paulus, was moving relentlessly towards the northern suburbs of the city. The intense struggle at Stalingrad would drag on for months and the outcome of the battle would be deeply significant.

Sophie had not seen Fritz since 20 May 1942. Her letters to him were much more guarded than before and much less revealing. This is hardly surprising as she was now living a secret double life. But there was another deep concern troubling her at this time. She had developed an infatuation for Alexander Schmorell. In October 1942 she admitted that 'I was still thinking my feelings for "Shurik" were stronger than for anyone else', but she felt this was a 'false delusion' and thought she had only become attracted to him because he was popular within the group.[38] During this period she also had a dream about Alex and Hans. In it she was being carried along with her feet off the ground with Alex on one arm and Hans on the other. Was this a sign she trusted both unconditionally and felt they were guiding her safely home? Or did she feel Alex and Hans were taking her on a journey over which she had no control?[39]

That summer Sophie felt under unremitting pressure. She was ordered to complete a further two-month labour service stint at a local arms factory. Most of her co-workers were female Russian slave labourers. 'How will I know I'll still be alive tomorrow?' she wrote in her diary, 'We could be killed by a bomb and my guilt would be no less than if I died in company with the earth and the stars.'[40]

In the same month, in a letter to Fritz Hartnagel, she described her work in the factory as:

> a soulless, loveless occupation, standing by a machine all day long going through the motions … You go home every night tired and bored. The sight of so many people working on machinery is depressing and very like slavery.[41]

1. Sophie Scholl at home in Münsterplatz, 1942 (© Manuel Aicher)

2. Sophie as a teenager, 1938 (© Manuel Aicher)

3. Hans Scholl, 1941 (© Manuel Aicher)

4. Sophie as a teenager, 1938 (© Manuel Aicher)

5. Sophie Scholl, near the Iller River, summer 1938
(© Manuel Aicher)

6. Sophie Scholl threw the leaflets into the Lichthof from the marble balustrade just below the clock
(© Weisse Rose Stiftung)

On 2 September 1942, Sophie told Lisa Remppis of her continuing unhappiness over the tedious nature of factory work. She hated the deafening noise from the machinery, but she was very touched by the Russian women slave labourers whom she described as 'more childlike in general than the German workers' and 'devoid of mistrust'. Even when vicious Nazi guards roared orders at them, Sophie noticed they did not understand and just burst out laughing.[42] Sophie's time in the factory was the first time she had endured the reality of working-class life, and she summed up their plight in the following way: 'The more they lack material things, the more they indulge themselves when they can, but the less is their satisfaction with this world and they hunger for life after death.'[43] During lunch breaks at the factory, Sophie often called in on Hans Hirzel and she gave him money to buy a duplicating machine.[44]

On 7 September 1942, Sophie informed her father that she knew 'his spirit' would not be broken by his period in prison, but she could not forgive the Nazis 'who made it happen'.[45] A few days later, Carl Muth's house was damaged during one of the first RAF bombing raids on Munich. The 'terror from the skies' – as Nazi propaganda called it – was bringing the war to German cities. Only on very rare occasions was Sophie able to enjoy nature, but one day she was able to get away on her own and observed that 'the sight of the evening sky above the mountains and the soothing sound of bells inspire another vision of humanity for me. I look forward to breathing fresh air again.'[46]

In early October 1942, her father was released from prison after serving just two months. The letters from Hans, Werner and Fritz had impressed the prison authorities. Meanwhile, Sophie's depressing factory work stint finally ended. She was finally able to rejoice in 'the last rays of the sun and the incredible beauty that was not created by man' and wonder why 'everything should be so beautiful in spite of the terrible things that are happening'.[47]

On 6 November 1942, Hans' student medical company returned to Munich, invigorated by their experiences in the Soviet Union and determined to expand their resistance activities. 'I think their love of Russia grew', says Traute Lafrenz-Page, 'They may have witnessed some atrocities by the SS troops. They saw the Warsaw ghetto.'[48] According to George Wittenstein, who went on the trip, what they saw in Russia – especially the abuses of the Russian people and Jews – left them with feelings of 'shock, horror and rage'.[49] The experience acted as a spur to further resistance.

The winter semester at Munich University would soon be starting. On 7 November 1942, Sophie told Fritz Hartnagel she was looking forward to seeing Hans and her friends from university again, but added in a worried tone: 'I can't be overwhelmingly happy. I'm never free for a moment day and night from the uncertainty in which we live these days, which excludes any carefree plans for tomorrow and casts a shadow over all the days to come.'[50]

TEN

SAILING INTO DANGER

In November 1942, the winter semester finally began at Munich University. Hans and Sophie had now moved into two separate rooms at 13 Franz Joseph Strasse in the fashionable Schwabing area, within easy walking distance of the main university building. They had the run of the place as their landlady had moved to her country house in fear of Allied air raids.[1] Sophie was excited about the prospect of meeting Gisela Schertling, who was due to start her art degree.[2] Hans' brief relationship with Traute Lafrenz had fizzled out. They both accepted their feelings had changed towards each other, but remained on friendly terms, and Traute remained active within the White Rose group. It was not long before the handsome Hans, with his melancholy dark eyes, caught the eye of Gisela Schertling and they soon became romantically involved. Hans had many female admirers, but most were brief and insignificant. A goodly number were close friends of Sophie. A new close friend of his sister usually turned into a new romantic partner for Hans. Schertling, a loyal supporter of National Socialism, had no idea whatsoever that Hans and Sophie were already involved in dangerous resistance activity.[3] In a frank admission to Rose Nägele, a previous 'girlfriend', Hans claimed that his inability to stay focused on any one person or interest for any length of time was 'the same impulse that makes waiting at railway junctions very appealing to me' and he compared this to a 'man who never takes off his coat when coming to visit, and is always the first to say "time to go"'.[4]

The time Hans, Alex and Willi had spent in the Soviet Union during the summer of 1942 had included lengthy discussions about how the campaign of the White Rose should proceed during the next academic year.

They all concluded that the first leaflets had only been distributed to a very small number of people. They had not had a major impact. They decided to build up a network of connections with other resistance groups and to raise money so as to expand their propaganda activity. But this outward-looking strategy ran greater risks of detection.

Hans Scholl heard from foreign radio broadcasts in August 1942 of the arrest of Arvid Harnack, a high-ranking civil servant in the Economic Ministry, and Harro Schulze-Boysen, an attaché in the Air Ministry, who were part of a resistance group based in Berlin called 'The Red Orchestra' (*Die Rote Kapelle*). The members of this group were not Soviet spies – as later depicted in Nazi propaganda – nor were they members of the German Communist Party (KPD), but they were sympathetic to socialist ideas and they did pass on military secrets to the Soviet government. The group produced a number of anti-Nazi leaflets. After a series of arrests, interrogations and trials by the Gestapo, a total of fifty members of the group were executed, including Harnack and his wife, Mildred, an American-born literary historian, and Schulze-Boysen and his spouse, Libertas, who worked in the film department of the Nazi Ministry of Propaganda.[5]

One of Alex's friends, Lilo Ramdohr, was friendly with Arvid Harnack's younger brother, Falk, and she arranged for Hans and Alex to meet him in November 1942, at a hotel at Chemnitz, near the old Czech border.[6] Falk Harnack was in his late twenties, talented, highly intelligent, clear-sighted: every inch the arty young intellectual. He had been the director of the National Theatre based in Weimar before the war, but was now serving as an officer in the army. In the safety of a hotel room, Hans and Alex showed him the first four leaflets. After reading them, Harnack said they were much too philosophical and literary to have any impact on public opinion. He emphasised that effective opposition had to appeal to the masses – but he was heartened to hear about the activities of the White Rose. He advised them to integrate their activities within the broader coalition of resistance groups opposed to Hitler's regime rather than working independently. This resistance was led by General Ludwig Beck, who had been chief of the Wehrmacht General Staff between 1935 and 1938, and Carl Friedrich Goerdeler, a former mayor of Leipzig.[7] The Beck-Goerdeler group had built up an impressive network of supporters inside the army and was developing diplomatic contacts abroad. Harnack told Hans and Alex something even more startling: the 'military group' – as he called them – were planning to assassinate Hitler and overthrow the Nazi regime. Among this group was Colonel Claus Graf von Stauffenberg, a Catholic

Bavarian, who made an attempt on Hitler's life on 20 July 1944 by planting a bomb under a table during a military meeting at his military headquarters at Rastenburg, East Prussia, during Operation Valkyrie.

The White Rose group next tried to raise extra money to fund a more extensive leafleting campaign. Hans and Alex went to Stuttgart to meet Eugen Grimminger, an accountant, a good friend of Robert Scholl and a trusted opponent of the Nazis. Inge Scholl was working in his office at this time – but it seems she knew nothing about the purpose of the meeting. Hans and Alex asked Grimminger for financial support and he sent them a cheque for 500 marks. To further expand the outreach of the group, Traute Lafrenz encouraged a group of her friends at Hamburg University to establish a complementary group there. The plans of the Hamburg group included discussions about blowing up a railway bridge that carried German troops and the local Gestapo headquarters. Willi Graf attempted to expand White Rose activities in the Rhineland area. In his home town of Saarbrücken, his friends warned him of the danger of engaging in resistance against the Nazi regime and he found little or no support there. In Bonn he got a more sympathetic hearing, but few tangible offers of support. At the University of Freiburg he found there already existed an established resistance group led by the twins Heinz and Willi Bollinger. Heinz was an assistant professor at the university and Willi was a medical officer in an army hospital in Saarbrücken. On a further trip, Willi Graf gave a duplicating machine and some White Rose leaflets to Willi Bollinger. In the last months of 1942, the White Rose was changing from an anonymous and secretive small Munich-based group run by high-minded young undergraduates, into a more dedicated and organised anti-Nazi resistance organisation, which was planning to expand greatly its field of operations. Sophie was fully aware of all these activities and she endorsed them fully. In practical terms, Sophie was placed in charge of the finances of the group. She kept detailed accounts of income and expenditure and allocated money to buy materials for the leaflet operation.

In December 1942, Hans Scholl met Kurt Huber on several occasions. At one meeting, accompanied by Willi Graf, Hans confessed to being the author of the leaflets and he asked the lecturer to provide advice and assistance.[8] Huber was surprised by this revelation from one of his own students. He even doubted whether leaflets alone would make any real dent in the Nazi state, as the communists had already used this method of propaganda with very little success. In spite of these reservations, Huber decided he would become involved.[9]

During this period, Hans also developed a close friendship with Josef Söhngen, the owner of a student bookshop located on Maximilianplatz, near the university campus. Söhngen, a deeply religious, middle-aged 'confirmed bachelor', lived in a flat above the shop. In spite of the age gap, Hans often called on him and they would share a glass of wine or a coffee, chatting into the small hours. Söhngen knew Giovanni Stepanov, an art historian with close links to the Italian anti-fascist resistance. Feelers were put out to arrange a meeting between him and Hans next time he was lecturing in Munich – but this came to nothing. Söhngen later recalled that Hans was very eager to expand the resistance activities of the White Rose, but he felt his powerful desire to see National Socialism destroyed drove him onward towards more 'reckless and dangerous actions'.[10]

Towards the end of 1942, the military situation facing Germany at Stalingrad suddenly turned very serious. At the end of the summer the Luftwaffe had bombed Stalingrad to the ground and the Wehrmacht seemed poised for victory. But on 19 November, the Red Army mounted a stunning counter-offensive, commanded by the brilliant Soviet general Georgi Zhukov, which linked up two vast armies, thereby trapping the German Sixth army outside Stalingrad and cutting it off from supply lines. The German army was now in a hopeless situation. This news had good and bad aspects. Sophie had long wanted Hitler's seemingly unstoppable war machine to be halted, but Fritz Hartnagel's unit was among those trapped at Stalingrad. Fritz told Sophie that clinging on to a strong belief in God and writing her letters were the only two things relieving his increasingly 'tragic mood'. He observed that most of his fellow officers saw the battle at Stalingrad as a life and death struggle, which Germany had to win.[11]

Sophie returned home to Ulm for a short Christmas break. On 30 December 1942, she wrote to Fritz describing a 'quiet evening at home' during which she had listened to classical music on the radio which 'soothes your senses and tidies up the turmoil of your heart'. She had not seen Fritz since the spring. 'I don't look the same these days', she wrote, 'my hair will soon be down to my shoulders unless Lisl [her sister Elisabeth] takes pity on it again.'[12] On New Year's Day 1943, Sophie updated Fritz on recent events. She told him she was sharing 'the little upstairs room with Hans' during this vacation as the family had taken in lodgers. Sophie and Hans were having deep conversations over the Christmas break consisting of 'retrospective comments on the day or questions raised by what we've discussed or read'.[13]

On 3 January 1943, Sophie told Fritz that she felt sorry for the plight of soldiers at Stalingrad who were 'undeservedly having to suffer so much more than I'.[14] Two days later, Hans Scholl returned to Munich and confessed: 'The Munich air has stimulated me like mad again.'[15] A few days later Hans told Otl Aicher about 'the circle of people I've brought together here ... All the energy one expends comes flowing back', and he candidly confessed that the group were united in their opposition to 'Prussians'.[16] But Sophie's mood contrasted sharply with her brother's ebullience. On 13 January 1943, Sophie wrote in her diary, 'As soon as I'm alone, melancholy suppresses any desire to do anything' and 'when I pick up a book, I do it without any interest' and she admitted 'extreme pain' would be preferable to 'this vacuous inactivity'.[17]

The year of 1943 was the 470th anniversary of the founding of Munich University. To mark the occasion, every academic and student was 'ordered' to attend a keynote speech to be delivered by Paul Giesler, the *Gauleiter* (local governor) of the district of Munich and Upper Bavaria, at the German Museum of Technology. Giesler was determined to use his speech as a sort of sermon of loyalty to the Nazi regime. He was already well known for his belligerent speaking style. As he rose to speak, before a hall packed with academic staff and university officials dressed in their full academic robes, and young students, including Traute Lafrenz and Kate Schüddekopf, there was a large contingent of Nazi storm troopers scattered liberally around the auditorium. Sophie, Hans and Alexander Schmorell were not present, as they had agreed to boycott all Nazi-sponsored events.

Giesler was supposed to be giving a speech celebrating the anniversary of one of Germany's greatest seats of learning. Instead he used the opportunity as an excuse to launch a bitter attack on students, whom he claimed were little more than lazy draft-dodgers, pampered by the taxpayers. He then singled out female students in the audience, saying in a pretty lecherous tone that instead of reading books they should be using their 'healthy bodies' to offer 'an annual contribution to the Fatherland of a child', and in an even more offensive tone, he added: 'If you girls lack sufficient charm to find a man, I will be glad to assign one of my assistants ... to undertake the task and I can promise you a thoroughly enjoyable experience.'

In the balcony, many of the students began loudly hissing, whistling and booing Giesler's speech. Most of the female students got up to leave the hall. At the exits, fights broke out between students and Nazi storm troopers. The students were soon out on the streets, staging the first major street demonstration in the history of the Third Reich. A state of emergency was declared over Munich. The protest had been a spontaneous response to Giesler's inflammatory speech, but news of it spread.

Even before the speech, discussions were already well advanced for the production of a fifth leaflet. The aim was to reach a much wider audience. On 13 January 1943, Willi Graf recorded in his diary: 'We are indeed starting our work, the stone is beginning to roll.'[18] The decision to produce a fifth leaflet occurred at a time when Sophie was feeling pretty low. 'I am just not myself at the moment', Sophie explained to Otl Aicher, 'My thoughts move back and forward and I can't control them.'[19]

The fifth leaflet was completed in separate drafts by Hans and Alex, but this time the experienced academic Kurt Huber was invited to offer his judgement. Also present at the meeting were Hans, Sophie, Alex and Willi. Sophie deliberately kept in the background, leaving Huber to conclude she was not fully involved. After reading the two drafts Huber felt Alex's version was much too sympathetic to the Soviet Union; he preferred to use the version written by Hans, which was a more tightly focused criticism of Hitler's regime.[20] It was finally agreed to use Hans' version.

The fifth leaflet was not printed under the name 'White Rose', but placed under the more ambitiously titled 'Resistance Movement in Germany'. It was called 'A Call to all Germans' and predicted that:

> Hitler is leading the German people into an abyss. Hitler cannot win the war: he can only prolong it. The guilt of Hitler and his minions goes beyond all measure. Retribution comes closer and closer.

The leaflet then asked the German people to 'Dissociate yourself from National Socialist gangsterism.' The long-term blame for the war was attributed not just to Hitler but: 'A one-sided Prussian militarism' that 'must never again be allowed to assume power'. The leaflet mapped out a political manifesto for a post-Hitler Germany, which it claimed had to be a Federal state, in which workers were liberated from their condition of downtrodden slavery under National Socialism. The basis for the moral regeneration of Europe, the leaflet argued, must be 'Freedom of speech, freedom of religion' and 'the protection of individual citizens from the arbitrary will of criminal regimes of violence'.[21]

The Gestapo estimated that between 8,000 and 10,000 duplicated copies of the fifth leaflet were distributed. The majority were left in entrances to apartment blocks and beer halls around Munich. But many were posted in Cologne, Frankfurt, Augsburg, Salzburg, Stuttgart, Vienna and Innsbruck. Sophie took part in the posting operation. On 25 January 1943, she posted

250 letters addressed to local people in Augsburg. Two days later, she stuck between 600 and 700 leaflets in several different post boxes in Stuttgart.[22] In another night-time visit, Sophie distributed leaflets in Ulm, aided by local supporters Franz Müller, Hanz Hirzel and Heinrich Guter.

The fifth leaflet soon came to the attention of the Gestapo, located at the Wittelsbach Palace, the former residence of the Bavarian royal family. The matter was deemed serious enough for the departmental head of the Gestapo in Munich (Schäfer) to establish a special task force, headed by Robert Mohr, to track down the group behind the leaflets. Mohr was born on 5 April 1897 in Bisterschied (Pfalz). His father was a master stonemason; during the First World War he was awarded the Iron Cross, 2nd class. In 1919 he joined the police force. Four years later, he married Martha Klein and a year later his son, Willi, was born. He joined the Nazi Party in 1933 after Hitler came to power. His membership number was 3,271,936 – so he was not an 'old comrade'.[23] Between 1930 and 1938, Mohr worked as a police director in Frankenthal. He personally applied to join the Gestapo in Munich in 1938. So Mohr's move from 'ordinary' criminal policing into ideologically driven 'political' policing was a personal one. As a Gestapo officer, he was noted for his professional, unflappable manner. In later de-Nazification cases, nearly all former Gestapo officers claimed they were highly professional 'ordinary' men – not very different from their colleagues in the criminal police divisions. In reality, many figures just below the level of commanding Gestapo officers played a crucial role in major investigations and commanding officers were very often guided by their judgements. Many were ambitious and committed Nazis – others were 'ordinary' policemen who joined the Gestapo to further their career aspirations. It was only a lack of a university degree that had prevented an officer like Mohr from being promoted to the more elite SS-SD apparatus run by Heinrich Himmler. It would be foolish, therefore, to suggest that how Mohr behaved in the White Rose case was how he behaved when handling other cases, especially those involving Nazi terror targets such as communists, foreign workers and Jews.[24]

Mohr was given the task of bringing about the 'speedy arrest' of the leaders of the White Rose. The fifth leaflet had been widely distributed in a number of cities. Mohr discovered the paper used to print the leaflets, the envelopes and the stamps were all purchased in Munich. Local post office clerks were warned to look out for people buying large number of postage stamps. A linguistic expert – asked to give a psychological profile of the author of the leaflets – later concluded that the author probably had an academic or theological background. As so many had appeared in Munich in public places, Mohr felt the author was based in Munich, but there was no definite lead and the group was never put under Gestapo surveillance.[25]

Meanwhile, Hans and Alex, without consulting the other members of the group, decided to paint anti-Nazi graffiti around the streets of Munich. This was a very high-risk strategy, as it placed Munich firmly at the centre of White Rose activity. Suddenly, graffiti – with slogans such as 'Down with Hitler', 'Freedom' and 'Hitler the mass murderer' – were painted in bold letters on public buildings throughout the city centre. Hans, Alex and Willi all took part in the graffiti operation. Some of the slogans were three feet high. This adventurous style of protest carried enormous risk.

Sophie only found out about the graffiti operation afterwards. On 4 February 1943, when she walked to the university campus to attend a lecture by Kurt Huber she noticed the word 'Freedom' was painted in large letters at the entrance to the main university building. When Sophie went back to her apartment she told Hans, who accepted it as an 'interesting' piece of news, but gave no indication that he was the painter. A day or so later, Sophie, feeling certain Hans was involved, said bluntly to him: 'You did that didn't you?' and he nodded. Sophie's reaction was not to tell Hans to stop or warn of the dangers, but to ask if she could go on future graffiti operations.[26]

Hans Scholl later claimed the idea of the graffiti campaign was his, but it was Alex who created the stencils with the slogans hollowed out of them. On the evening of 3 February 1943, Hans and Alex went out together after midnight, painting graffiti throughout Munich city centre and on the university campus, using black tar paint that proved difficult to clean off.[27] There were subsequent graffiti operations on the nights of 8 and 9 February and 15 and 16 February, involving Hans, Alex – and on the last night – Willi Graf. When Christoph Probst was told about the graffiti escapades he said they were very foolish as they carried great risk and he refused to get involved, but he did agree – at the suggestion of Hans – to produce a draft for the seventh leaflet.[28]

Meanwhile, the Red Army inflicted the most decisive and significant defeat Germany had suffered since the war began. The Russians had killed or captured 235,000 Germans and allied troops during the battle of Stalingrad and 200,000 soldiers had been killed. A total of 91,000 unshaven, starving troops were marched out of the rubble of the city, under the supervision of the Red Army, which had encircled, then destroyed Hitler's best troops. On 3 February 1943, German radio announced that the Sixth army had surrendered. The aura of German military invincibility ended on this day. Germany never won another significant battle during the Second World War.

Kurt Huber's anger towards the Nazi regime intensified after he heard the news about the defeat at Stalingrad. He was so angry he decided to write the sixth leaflet of the White Rose. Huber's leaflet was entitled 'Fellow Students'. It began by placing the blame for the debacle at Stalingrad on Adolf Hitler, gloomily predicting that 'the day of reckoning has come – the reckoning of German Youth with the most abominable tyrant our people have ever seen' and he denounced the Nazi regime for swindling youth of personal freedom and destroying 'all the moral fibre of the German people' and plunging Germany into a bloody war.

The leaflet went on to denounce Paul Giesler for making 'lewd jokes' which 'insult the honour of the women students'. This was a clear refer-ence to Giesler's speech in January. It ended by claiming that the name of Germany would be 'dishonoured for all time' if 'youth does not finally rise, take revenge and atone, smash its tormentors, and set up a New Europe of the spirit'. It was the most stridently rebellious of all the White Rose leaflets – but the author was a 49-year-old philosophy professor.

Huber had now moved from peripheral adviser to active participant in the resistance against Hitler. In spite of his academic standing, he was eminently expendable within the group. He was not really taken into the complete confidence of its key members, and did not even know who else was involved.[29] At the same time Huber was increasing his active role, Hans and Alex were taking more dangerous risks. The strain was starting to show. Hans was becoming increasingly paranoid and his fears of arrest were growing.

Sophie was also feeling the strain. Fritz Hartnagel had escaped from Stalingrad in one of the last flights out, and was recovering from frostbite at a military hospital. On 6 February 1943, Sophie, who had had been suffering severe headaches for days, decided to go home to Ulm because her mother was even more poorly. The following day, in a long letter to Fritz Hartnagel, Sophie promised to try and visit him 'provided I'm still free'. These words were used in reference to the amount of housework she was doing at home, but the phrase was probably unwitting evidence of the internal strain she was under at this time.[30]

On 8 February 1943, with Sophie away, Falk Harnack arrived in Munich, ostensibly to stay with Lilo Ramdohr, with whom he was now romantically involved. During the afternoon, he went to visit Hans Scholl, with Lilo and Alex in tow. He had a look at the fifth leaflet, 'A Call to all Germans', and said he thought it was much more like a genuine political leaflet than the previous efforts. But he once more questioned whether a leaflet operation aimed at a randomly selected cross section of middle-class professionals represented any real threat to the Nazi regime. It seems doubts about whether to continue with the leaflet operation were also expressed at this gathering by Alex and Willi. Harnack said that if the group wanted to become seriously involved in 'real' resistance, designed to threaten the regime, they should meet him on 25 February 1943 at 6 p.m. outside the Kaiser Wilhelm Church in Berlin. Hans invited Harnack to come along the next morning to meet with their 'mentor', Professor Kurt Huber.

The next day a meeting took place at the Scholl apartment in Franz Joseph Strasse to discuss the draft of Kurt Huber's leaflet. In an unusual role reversal, Huber's undergraduates were now judging *his* writing. Present at this important meeting were Hans, Alex, Willi, Kurt, and for the first part of the discussion, Falk Harnack. Sophie was still in Ulm and so did not attend. This was the first time Harnack and Huber had ever met. From the start, it was obvious they were not going to get on. Harnack told the meeting he thought a full-scale rebellion against Hitler was now possible, but for this enterprise to succeed, all opponents of the Nazis needed to put aside political differences and unite. He went on to say that if Hitler was overthrown then a new domestic constitution should be introduced, but only three political parties should be allowed – Marxist, Christian and Liberal. He urged state control of finance and industry, suggesting the Soviet system was more of a role model for a post-war Germany than western capitalism. Harnack made no reference to the strong Christian values which animated the White Rose group.

Kurt Huber was very angry about Harnack's diagnosis and even more perturbed about his solutions. He offered a lengthy attack on Harnack's arguments one by one. The end of private ownership, said Huber, would destroy the middle classes and create a system no different from the Bolshevik one. This bitter exchange between Harnack and Huber reveals how little the group had thought about the political implications of their opposition.

But Huber's vitriolic attack on Harnack shocked Alex, Hans and Willi. They all assumed – somewhat naïvely – that Huber's sideswipes against Nazism in his lectures were evidence of a firmly liberal and democratic outlook. Alexander Schmorell was the most angered by Huber's outburst, which he felt completely soured the atmosphere. He also felt Huber had wrongly interpreted his own sympathy towards some aspects of the Soviet Union as denoting a Bolshevik political outlook.[31] Hans Scholl took a Christian democratic line in these discussions, stating that he was opposed to state control of the whole economy. It was only on the question of freedom of religion and the press that there was some semblance of agreement.

Falk Harnack, with the mood of the meeting still very tense, made an excuse and left. The discussion now turned to the draft of Huber's leaflet. The group thought the leaflet was a very well-focused attack on how the Nazi regime was stifling free speech at Munich University. Hans, Alex and Willi objected to just one line, in which Huber had stressed that in spite of the military disaster at Stalingrad, students should still offer loyal support to what Huber called 'our glorious Wehrmacht'. This was an endorsement of the German army, which Hans, Alex and Willi felt was the instrument of Hitler's will. They all pressed for that line to be deleted. Huber said the leaflet must be published in full or not at all. Hans, Alex and Willi were equally united in their refusal to include the offending line.[32] Huber suddenly declared his involvement in the White Rose was over; he left the apartment, in an extremely angry mood, determined to take no further part in the activities of the group.[33]

Sophie had missed these dramatic events. She admired Huber's lectures more than any other member of the group. She liked him as a person and had been to his house for social events. It is probably no coincidence that Huber's rather dogmatic politics were displayed without his most fervent acolyte present. The theatrical performances of Huber in the lecture hall and his witty anarchic asides were clearly not a full reflection of his anti-Hitler – but essentially conservative – nationalist views. Huber's rather fragile ego seemed to splinter when confronted not just with the very mature and sharp-minded Harnack, but also in front of the equally clear-sighted arguments of Alex, Hans and Willi – his own undergraduate students. Huber was certainly against Hitler, but whether he was against a conservative–authoritarian state remains a matter of dispute.

It was probably a blessing that Sophie was not present to see her star lecturer behave in such a high-handed manner. Sophie's spirits improved greatly during her break from the increasing tension. She was even starting to think about the future optimistically, or at least appeared to. 'I've been too tired until now' she told Fritz Hartnagel in a letter on 10 February 1943 'to make plans, since the war would bring them all to nothing, but they are now springing up like a forest of flowers … they don't seem at all outrageous'.[34] In another upbeat letter to Fritz she wrote: 'I keep having vivid dreams about the future and they are predominantly optimistic.'[35] In her diary, which recorded her innermost feelings, her mood was much darker. 'As soon as I am alone sadness overwhelms me … I would a thousand times endure the worst pain, even physical pain, than feel so empty.'[36] The next day Sophie left the train station at Ulm, bound for Munich in the late afternoon. It was already dark, which seemed to fit her mood. Without Sophie's calming influence, the tension within the White Rose group had intensified.

In spite of Huber's exit, Hans, Alex and Willi had agreed to print his leaflet, minus the compliment to the Wehrmacht. They ran off between 1,500 and 3,000 copies.[37] Huber later claimed that he had told Hans and Alex to destroy his leaflet and he twice phoned Hans, but received no reply. Whether this is true cannot be fully verified.[38]

Meanwhile, the Gestapo, alarmed at the graffiti operations, had ordered the university authorities to watch out for suspicious behaviour on the campus. Increasingly, the White Rose circle was narrowing down to Hans, supported by Sophie. Alex and Willi had doubts, but their actions during the graffiti operations and in the distribution of the sixth leaflet suggest they were not as doubtful as they claimed in their later Gestapo interrogations. Christoph Probst continued to support the group, but protecting his family was now becoming paramount. The burden of trusting nobody, leading a double life, student by day, dissident at night, the constant fear of being discovered, all these factors were weighing heavily within the group. All members of the opposition to Hitler encountered a lonely and hopeless predicament: to continue or to abandon the struggle.

For Sophie there was no question of giving up the fight. Wilhelm Geyer, the artist, breakfasted with Hans and Sophie Scholl frequently in this period. He sensed in Sophie 'an absolute fearlessness' about her determination to resist Hitler's regime.[39] But the friends of Hans Scholl noticed that he was feeling the strain. He feared – wrongly as it turned out – that the Gestapo had him personally under surveillance. Josef Söhngen later recalled that Hans had a contact in the Munich Gestapo who told him his arrest was imminent. But there is no firm evidence for this post-war claim.

In spite of all the danger, opposition activities continued. Christoph Probst wrote the seventh leaflet. During this time, Probst was stationed with his Luftwaffe unit in Innsbruck and he could only visit Munich infrequently. In the hand-written leaflet, which was never typed up or distributed, Probst called Adolf Hitler a 'military charlatan'. He urged the opening of negotiations to end the war and claimed that once Nazism was eliminated a new world order would emerge, under the guidance of US President Franklin D. Roosevelt. The leaflet ended with a plea for peace, order and sanity to return to Germany.[40]

When Sophie arrived back in Munich, the printing of the sixth leaflet was in progress. Hans, Alex and Sophie worked flat out on Monday

15 February 1943, printing, addressing and putting leaflets in envelopes. The same day, Hans purchased 1,200 8-pfennig stamps from a local post office. His purchase was reported to the Gestapo by the post office clerk. During the evening, Hans, Alex and Willi took part in another graffiti operation, while Sophie mailed out leaflets. Later, Willi Graf claimed that it was on this day that he discovered that Hans and Sophie were planning to distribute leaflets outside the lecture halls of the main university building on Thursday 18 February 1943. Willi thought this was too risky.[41]

On 16 February 1943, Sophie wrote a letter to Fritz Hartnagel:

> Just a short greeting before I run off to my classes. I wrote you that I stayed
> at home for ten days. [It was eight] ... my father is so delighted when I came
> home and surprised when I leave, and my mother is worried about a thou-
> sand different things. The 150 kilometres between Ulm and Munich changes
> me so rapidly ... from a harmless, exuberant child, I turn into a grown-up
> with only myself to rely on.[42]

The same day, Hans admitted to Rose Nägele that his life:

> has become an ever-present danger, but one of my own choosing. I must
> head for my chosen destination freely and without any ties ... I've gone astray
> many times I know ... As Claudel so splendidly puts it: Life is a great adven-
> ture towards the light.[43]

During the afternoon, Sophie went to see Wilhelm Geyer at Eickemeyer's studio and posed while he drew a quick sketch of her. She told Geyer that she thought the Gestapo might soon arrest them. If this happened, she wanted her arrest to be in a public place. 'So many people are dying for this regime', she told Geyer, 'it is high time that someone died opposing it'.[44] In the late evening of 16 February 1943, Hans paid a visit to Josef Söhngen. He was invited upstairs to the bookseller's flat. They shared a bottle of wine together and talked. Hans showed him a copy of the sixth leaflet, then alleg-edly explained how he planned to place the leaflet outside the lecture halls later in the week. Söhngen told him such an escapade was 'far too risky', but Hans reassured him that he was fully aware of the danger and the pos-sible consequences. When Hans finally got up to leave, they shook hands. Söhngen felt it seemed like Hans was really saying a final goodbye.[45]

The following day, 17 February, Hans Hirzel was summoned to a Gestapo interrogation in Ulm and questioned about his possible involvement in subversive activities. After a brief interview, he was released. He thought his arrest was linked to White Rose activities. So he hurried along to the Scholl family apartment on Münsterplatz and told Inge Scholl – who answered the door – that she needed to get in touch with Hans quickly and tell him a book called *Machtstaat und Utopie* ('The Absolute State and Utopia') was out of print. The message was a prearranged code that Hirzel had been given by Hans to tell him the Gestapo had discovered the White Rose in Ulm. Inge Scholl passed this message to her boyfriend, Otl Aicher, who was in Munich.[46] But the Gestapo in Ulm had not linked Hans Hirzel or Hans or Sophie with White Rose leaflets. They had questioned Hans Hirzel because of a tip-off which alleged he had been bragging to friends about involvement in resistance activities. As Hans Hirzel was the son of a well-respected Lutheran church minister, the Gestapo officer felt it was a tall story.[47]

During the late afternoon of 17 February 1943, Gisela Schertling arrived at the Scholl apartment. She went for a walk with Hans and Sophie in the beautiful English Garden in Munich until it grew dark. Every Thursday at 10 a.m. – without exception – Sophie and Gisela went to Kurt Huber's popular lecture course on the philosopher Gottfried Leibniz. But while walking in the park, Sophie told Gisela she would not be going to the class the next day, but asked her to meet up with her at noon in her apartment. After the walk, Hans, Sophie and Gisela went for a meal at a local restaurant. Gisela later said Hans and Sophie seemed relaxed and happy. They made no mention of a plan to scatter leaflets at the university.[48]

Sophie and Hans returned to their apartment on Franz Josef Strasse. Before she went to bed, Sophie put a record of Franz Schubert's *Trout Quintet* on the record player.[49] Schubert was only 22 years old when he composed this uplifting piece of music, which is loved by pianists, requiring both hands to play the melodic line and the octave part. Sophie – an accomplished pianist – had played the piece many times. When the record ended, Sophie sat at her desk and wrote a letter to her old friend Lisa Remppis:

I've just been playing the *Trout Quintet* on the phonograph [record player]. Listening to the andantino makes me want to be a trout myself. You can't help rejoicing and laughing, however moved or sad you feel, when you see the springtime clouds in the sky, the budding branches, moved by the wind, in the bright early sunlight. I'm really looking forward to the spring again. In that piece of Schubert's you can positively feel and smell the breeze and hear the birds and the whole of creation shouting for joy.[50]

ELEVEN

THE TIPPING POINT

On the morning of Thursday 18 February 1943, Sophie Scholl was in no great hurry to get out of bed. Outside her apartment on Franz Joseph Strasse it was one of the mildest winter days Munich had seen for years. The sky was blue, dazzlingly clear and the sun was shining bright. Sophie had already decided not to attend either a physics lecture at 8 a.m. or Kurt Huber's class timetabled for 10 a.m. Sophie and Hans breakfasted together. At around 9.30 a.m. the postman arrived, but left no mail.[1] By now Sophie was getting ready to depart for the university. Hans had started placing two neat stacks of leaflets into a large suitcase. Sophie took a small briefcase with her. In total they carried between 1,500 and 1,800 leaflets to the university. In spite of the good weather, it was still chilly outside. Sophie wore a thick woollen blouse, a calf-length woollen skirt, topped off with a warm overcoat. The plan of how and where they would distribute the leaflets at the university had already been extensively discussed and agreed over the previous few days. Hans and Sophie were very confident they could drop the leaflets and get away without detection. This helps to explain why Hans had a copy of a handwritten leaflet, written by Christoph Probst, in the inside pocket of his jacket and why Sophie put the key to Eickemeyer's studio in the pocket of her overcoat.

It was 10.30 a.m. when they finally left the apartment and began their familiar walk towards the main university building. They walked side by side, chatting amiably as usual. Sophie believed passionately that the sixth leaflet, addressed to 'Fellow Students', had to reach its target audience.

According to Lilo Ramdohr, Sophie and Hans met with Alex Schmorell at the Victory Gate on their walk to the university.[2] But Traute Lafrenz-Page is doubtful they saw him on the way.[3]

Sophie and Hans continued walking on towards the campus. The imposing university building was designed by Friedrich von Gärtner, the architect of King Ludwig I of Bavaria, in 1840. They reached the entrance at approximately 10.50 a.m. They bumped into Willi Graf and Traute Lafrenz as they entered the building, but they were hurrying along to attend a neurology lecture in another building and had no time to stop and talk.[4] Traute told Willi on the tram she had an 'uneasy feeling' about why Hans was carrying such a large suitcase into the building.[5]

Sophie and Hans skipped up a single flight of stairs into the entrance hall known as the 'Lichthof', which derives its name from the great glass-domed ceiling that casts light through the vast open space.[6] Dominating the entire floor at ground level is a giant stone staircase, which has two marble statues of men in academic robes at each side. There are no names on the statues. One is a statue of King Ludwig I and the other is Prince Regent Luitpold, both long forgotten figures of the Bavarian royal family. The hallway was quiet and empty. The lecture halls were packed with students. Sophie and Hans, working separately, were soon scurrying around placing small bundles of leaflets at each side of the statues. They next went up to the second and third floors and placed more leaflets at the top of the staircases and outside the lecture theatres. By this time they had reached the third floor. Hans put a large stack of leaflets on a marble balustrade, underneath a large clock. On impulse, Sophie pushed the leaflets off the marble shelf. They fluttered down like confetti at the exact moment the students started to pour out of the lecture theatres and seminar rooms. Jakob Schmid, a 46-year-old university porter and general handyman, saw the leaflets cascading down. He knew they had been thrown from upstairs and he started yelling 'stop!' as he ran up the stairs. His booming voice echoed around the vast space. Sophie heard the shouts, but she had enough time to dash into an empty room and hide the key to Eickemeyer's studio.

It took a breathless Schmid a minute to reach Hans and Sophie, neither of whom made any attempt to escape. It really made no sense to run away with so many potential witnesses in the building and outside it. 'I went straight up to them', Schmid told the Gestapo later the same day, 'I told them they had to come with me' as 'they were under arrest'. Hans reportedly questioned Schmid's right to arrest them. Sophie, who by now was carrying the suitcase, admitted she had thrown the papers into the Lichthof.[7] Schmid, a loyal Nazi Party member, took Hans and Sophie back down the stairs to the office of the building superintendent, Herr Scheidhammer, who then accompanied them to the office of Walter Wüst, the university rector. The incident was immediately reported to the Gestapo headquarters at the Wittelsbach Palace in a telephone call shortly after 11 a.m.[8] By this time all the exits to the university were locked until further notice.

There were numerous witnesses to the leaflet-scattering by Sophie. A good majority of them thought then and later her action was reckless. Sophie admitted later that it was a silly impulsive mistake. Schmid's eye-witness testimony – given to the Gestapo a few hours later – makes it clear that their plan was simply to deny everything in the hope they could talk their way out of trouble. As they were upstairs when Schmid arrived, with one of them holding a large suitcase, they had very few choices available. They would have been very lucky to escape detection after Sophie threw the leaflets off the balustrade.

Robert Mohr – the Gestapo officer given the task of finding the leaders of the White Rose group – was very eager to go to the university. In less than thirty minutes Mohr entered Wüst's office. He asked to see the student identification cards and identification papers of Hans and Sophie Scholl. He soon discovered they were brother and sister. Mohr's first impression was that Schmid had made a mistake. These two nice, quiet, middle-class 'national comrades' were surely not the leaders of movement calling itself the 'National Resistance Movement of Germany'. Mohr fired some questions at them. 'Why were you carrying a suitcase?' he asked Sophie. 'I was going home to Ulm for a few days and was going to bring some clean laundry back with me.' This seemed a plausible answer. They answered the rest of Mohr's questions in an equally matter-of-fact manner.

Meanwhile, two other Gestapo officers meticulously collected up all the leaflets the Scholls had either scattered or placed around the Lichthof. When the piles were placed side by side in the suitcase they fitted perfectly. Mohr now decided they had to be arrested and taken away for further questioning. Hans suddenly realised he had Christoph Probst's hand-written leaflet in his pocket. He started to panic. He took it out of his pocket and tried to rip it up into little bits under the chair he was sitting on while the backs of the Gestapo officers were turned. But he was spotted doing this by a Gestapo officer who quickly retrieved a major portion of the leaflet and also the ripped up section.[9] It would only be a matter of time before the fate of Christoph Probst, married, with three children, would become intertwined with that of the Scholl siblings. Mohr asked Hans why he had suddenly attempted to rip up the leaflet. Hans said it had been given to him by another student he did not know and he felt it might make him look guilty if he had not disposed of it before he was arrested. Suspects about to be unexpectedly arrested often behave in irrational ways. So Mohr did not interpret this panic-driven act as a definite sign of Hans' guilt.

Christa Meyer-Heidkamp, a student who attended Kurt Huber's philosophy course with Sophie Scholl, claimed she was standing in the Lichthof for nearly two hours before 'Hans Scholl and his sister were led away in handcuffs'.[10] As Hans and Sophie were being led out of the university building to the waiting green Gestapo van, Hans suddenly shouted 'Tell him [meaning Alex Schmorell] I won't be coming home this evening.'[11] The officers thought Hans was shouting to a male student standing in the crowd – Count Karl von Metternich – so they wrongly arrested him, then released him at 6 p.m. The warning for Alex was for Gisela Schertling who had been standing in the crowd. Sophie and Hans were bundled into the back of the van, which transported them to Gestapo headquarters.[12] As Sophie arrived at the opulent Wittelsbach Palace, which had been one of the residences of the Bavarian monarchy until the end of the First World War, but was now the HQ of Munich's Gestapo, the sun was shining brightly in a deep blue sky. Throughout the whole period since her arrest Sophie Scholl had remained extraordinarily calm and relaxed.[13]

TWELVE

QUESTIONS AND CONSEQUENCES

There was never a good day to be arrested as an 'enemy of the people', but this was one of the worst. It had been chosen by the Nazi regime to raise German morale after the military disaster at Stalingrad. A major speech by Propaganda Minister Joseph Goebbels at the Sports Palace in Berlin before a hand-picked crowd of 15,000 Nazi fanatics was being broadcast live on German national radio when Sophie Scholl arrived at the reception area at Wittelsbach Palace. At the end of the speech Goebbels put a series of rhetorical questions to the crowd: 'Do you want "total war"?' he asked; the audience roared back, 'Yes'. He then asked if any opponent of the regime should be executed, to which there was an even louder scream: 'Yes'.[1]

Else Gebel was the first person to see Sophie Scholl as she arrived in the reception area of Gestapo HQ. Gebel was born on 5 July 1905 in Augsburg, a city lying on the railway line between Munich and Ulm. She came from a well-to-do family. Before her arrest she had been the personal secretary to the owner of a large warehouse in Munich. Gebel was serving a 16-month sentence for acting as a courier for a communist resistance group. Many penal institutions in Nazi Germany thought some political prisoners could be 're-educated' as 'national comrades'. Most prison guards thought political prisoners were a cut above 'ordinary' criminals. A political prisoner capable of re-education was usually given undemanding clerical or library work.[2] This was what happened to Else Gebel, who continued her clerical work by day and occupied a cell at night. Gebel was what the Nazis called a 'privileged prisoner'. She had better conditions, better food and greater freedom of movement.

Gebel was ordered to share a cell with Sophie Scholl. A few years later she offered a detailed account of those four days, but her eyewitness testimony must be treated with caution.[3] To begin with, at the end of the war, Gebel tried to persuade the US occupying forces she was actually a member of the White Rose. She also claimed Hans and Sophie were beaten up during their interrogations and went on to say Sophie arrived in court on crutches. These claims were soon discredited, but were repeated in many otherwise respectable histories of the Third Reich.[4]

There is an even more troubling aspect of Gebel's account to consider. Many post-war trials – in similar cases – reveal that one of the most cunning and frequently used investigative tactics of the Gestapo was to give an important suspect a good cell, ample food and drink – then allocate them 'a special friend' to share their cell. The aim of this 'double agent' was to convince a prisoner that they were with a person they could trust. It does seem a fairly big coincidence that Sophie Scholl was given a cellmate who also happened to be a member of the resistance against Hitler. Sophie was a very intelligent person and was fully aware of this possibility, but she did inadvertently let slip a good deal of information to Gebel which in all probability was fed straight back into the investigation.[5] What makes this even more likely is that Gebel often reported details to Sophie about the other White Rose interrogations over the next four days that only an 'insider' in the investigation team could possibly have known about. So Gebel's account should be placed in the 'doubtful' category when judging its authenticity – but by carefully reading between the lines it still provides some very interesting insights.

There are some facts that can be verified more accurately. At the reception desk Sophie gave her personal details, handed over her belongings and was given a full body search by Gebel. She was then taken to be fingerprinted and to have her prison photograph taken by an old-fashioned box camera. She was photographed three times: front and right and left profile. In one image Sophie looks straight into the camera in a serious manner. After these formalities she was escorted to her cell which – according to Gebel – was reserved for 'the most privileged prisoners'.

Sophie and Hans were initially held under what the Nazi authorities called 'protective custody'. This open-ended term allowed the Gestapo to question a person suspected of crimes against the state and to detain them indefinitely or to bring a formal charge against them – known in the Nazi era as 'the indictment'. In the period before the indictment was drafted the Gestapo carried out its investigation, interrogated the accused, took statements from witnesses and diligently collected physical evidence. During the period of 'the investigation' the prisoner was denied access to a lawyer, could receive no visitors and was not informed of the likely charges or even the possible sentence. The whole process was designed to keep the suspect – and their relatives – in the dark, keep the pressure up and ideally end up with a confession and a list of new suspects the Gestapo could then track down.

Gebel's first impression of Sophie was that she was 'quiet, relaxed, and almost amused by all the excitement'. When Else was alone with Sophie she whispered: 'If you have a leaflet on you destroy it now.' In another bid to gain her confidence she said, 'I am a prisoner too.' Gebel's first thought was 'this sweet girl with the innocent child's face has never been involved in such reckless acts'. Sophie was reportedly allocated 'the best cell in the prison'. Gebel advised Sophie not to admit anything. 'Yes, that's what I've done up until now', replied Sophie, 'but there are many things that they may be able to find'.[6]

Robert Mohr took on the role of exclusively interrogating Sophie Scholl. Anton Mahler was given the task of interrogating Hans Scholl, with the support of other officers working in shifts.[7] From the earliest days of Nazi rule in 1933, Gestapo interrogations of political opponents of the regime often resulted in prisoners being beaten and tortured in order to extract a confession. It became such common practice that even Nazi judges were asking why prisoners always looked like they had been beaten up prior to trials. In June 1937, the Gestapo agreed to a Justice Ministry edict that if any physical punishment was administered it had to be no more than twenty strokes of the cane, administered in the presence of a doctor.[8]

On 12 June 1942, Heinrich Müller, the head of the Gestapo, introduced a new set of 'enhanced interrogations' to deal specifically with resistance activities.[9] These more brutal techniques included restricting the diet to bread and water, a hard bed, a dark cell, exhausting exercise routines, the deprivation of sleep and blows with a stick as a last resort. But Müller reminded Gestapo officers that such techniques could not be used 'towards persons who have temporarily been detained by justice for the purpose of further investigation'. In other words, only after the preliminary investigation had been completed and the indictment had been presented to a prisoner.

The evidence from Gestapo files, especially from cases involving German citizens, shows that officers favoured subtle interrogation techniques over brutal punishment. They believed such tactics produced better results. Some of the most successful Gestapo tactics – used extensively in the White Rose interrogations – included playing one person off against another, withholding vital evidence and using sleep deprivation by conducting interrogations all though the night.[10] In Gestapo interrogations the pressure was mostly mental and psychological. Gestapo files show interrogators usually worked in brief shifts.

But this did not happen to Sophie Scholl, who was interrogated exclusively by Mohr. This amounted to special treatment when compared with other cases. Hans Scholl's interrogation was of the textbook variety. One favoured Gestapo tactic was to produce evidence from other interrogations and ask an accused to explain the contradictory statements. Sometimes key evidence was withheld – then suddenly produced – often catching a suspect unawares. This was a good tactic to employ late in the night. Another method was to keep asking the same question over and over again. Many suspects have claimed this became a sort of mental torture. Interrogators were also encouraged to threaten, to coerce and to deliberately lose their temper – but only to increase the stress and the tension. This was cold, calculated anger. Many interrogators enjoyed playing out these pre-arranged and staged psychological games with suspects. The effect of all these devices was to make even the strongest and bravest resistance leaders feel uncertain and induce insecurity in the most confident individuals.[11]

Robert Mohr was a skilled Gestapo officer. His son, Willi, recalls that his father was a rigid disciplinarian at home, but he confirms that whenever his father spoke to him in confidence about the case of Sophie Scholl he said he was impressed by her and treated her well.[12] Sophie feared that she would face brutal treatment as she had heard rumours that the Gestapo often used extreme violence in order to extract a confession.[13] Mohr recalled that Sophie feared this would happen to her or more likely to her brother. Mohr says he laughed at this suggestion. In order to reassure her further that Hans was not being maltreated in the next room, he says he often opened the door so Sophie could see Hans was all right.[14]

Robert Mohr was clearly more than the 'ordinary officer' he tried to passs himself off as during the de-Nazification process after the war. Even so, in the specific case of his treatment of Sophie Scholl in her final days, there is no concrete evidence to doubt seriously that he was impressed by her or to question his own version of events. Mohr increasingly treated Sophie – as he got to know her better – like a concerned father dealing with an errant daughter who had fallen in with the wrong crowd, but would soon return to normal good behaviour after a stern ticking off. But Mohr's motives in writing his post-war memorandum to Robert Scholl in 1951 are a different matter alto-gether. This was a self-serving and personally motivated attempt to clean up his past by citing his good behaviour in this one very exceptional case.

The first interrogation of Sophie Scholl went on during the afternoon of 18 February 1943. When Mohr asked about her father's political views, Sophie said he had a 'democratic' outlook and was opposed to National Socialism, but never attempted to force his views on his children. She then told Mohr she had been a member of the League of German Girls until 1941, holding leadership posts between 1935 and 1938. She resigned as a leader – she claimed – in 1938 because of a quarrel with a regional leader over the internal organisation of the group. Her departure was personal and had nothing to do with National Socialist ideology.

Sophie said her estrangement from National Socialism began with the arrest of the Scholl siblings by the Gestapo in the autumn of 1937.[15] This was 'the most important reason' for her change of attitude towards the Nazi regime as she felt the arrests were 'completely unjustified'. As for her view now, she said she wanted 'nothing to do with National Socialism' because it limited intellectual freedom and 'contradicts everything inside of me'.

Mohr's polite and sympathetic questioning soon moved on to the events in the Lichthof. Sophie said she had arranged to meet Gisela Schertling at noon, but had decided to go home instead for a weekend break and then to bring some fresh laundry back with her. This was why had been carrying an empty suitcase. It seemed a plausible excuse, especially when delivered in a matter-of-fact manner. The reason she went to the university was to meet Schertling, who was attending Kurt Huber's lecture, which finished at 11 a.m. Hans went with her because she did not have enough money for the train fare and he was going to withdraw some from a nearby bank, once she told her friend about her changed plans. Sophie said that when she reached the third floor she noticed a pile of leaflets were lying on the balustrade and so she just gave them 'a little shove'. 'I now realise', she continued, 'it was a silly mistake that I now regret' but 'cannot change'. Mohr then asked her if she had recently purchased stamps from a local post office. She said she had purchased 'twenty odd stamps' about two weeks ago from a post office on Leopoldstrasse. She ended by saying that she had absolutely nothing to do with the production or distribution of the leaflets that were seized.[16]

Sophie's plausible explanations, delivered in a calm manner, completely wrong-footed the experienced Gestapo officer. He later claimed 'there was no reason to doubt the absolutely convincing statements made by Sophie Scholl'.[17] Even more helpful was a Nazi student leader who suddenly turned up at Gestapo headquarters, asked to see Mohr, and then told him Sophie was 'innocent and should be released'. The intervention by a loyal student 'national comrade' reinforced Mohr's view that a genuine mistake had occurred. He still thought the janitor had jumped to a wrong conclusion and he was now thinking she would soon be released.

Sophie was escorted back to her cell by Else Gebel and given a hot bowl of soup, a piece of bread and some coffee. At about 8 p.m. Else Gebel left Sophie alone in the cell and completed her remaining administrative tasks. When Gebel returned at around 10 p.m. she noticed Sophie had been taken away for a second interrogation. Before the second interrogation began, the results of the two extensive searches of the Scholl lodgings in Franz Joseph Strasse yielded a great deal of incriminating evidence, most notably a large quantity of unused 8-pfennig stamps, envelopes, letters and a notebook in Sophie's handwriting, which looked like an account ledger. It contained many names and listed amounts of money alongside them. When this flurry of evidence was communicated to Mohr he was deeply shocked.[18]

Meanwhile, new details emerged during the interrogation of Gisela Schertling which cast further doubt on the innocence of Sophie and Hans Scholl. Gisela said she had first noticed Sophie's 'negative' attitude towards National Socialism when they had been in labour service together. She felt Hans and Sophie believed Nazism was opposed to religious freedom and the freedom of the individual in almost every aspect of life. Gisela said she had disagreed with the Scholls whenever political matters were discussed. She then started to incriminate other members of the White Rose one by one. Alex Schmorell was 'with Hans all the time' and his other 'friends' included Kurt Huber, Josef Söhngen and Professor Carl Muth. The only reason she had not reported the opposition of Hans Scholl towards the Nazi regime was because 'I was completely under his influence.' Schertling further incriminated Sophie by revealing she had seen her buying large quantities of envelopes. Schertling said she had no doubt that Hans and Sophie had taken the leaflets in the suitcase to the university, distributed them and then thrown them down into the Lichthof.[19]

By this time, Sophie Scholl was undergoing her second interrogation. This marathon session went on until 8 a.m. the following morning. Mohr was now convinced she was guilty so he kept presenting Sophie with new incriminating evidence culled from her apartment, including the stamps, the account notebook and the allegations of other interrogations. One issue Mohr concentrated on for a great part of the time was Sophie's explanation of events in the Lichthof. Sophie kept cool and parried the questions. She kept on refusing to admit she was lying and stuck to her own version of events.[20]

Meanwhile, in the adjacent room, Hans Scholl's interrogation was not moving so smoothly. At 4 a.m., after hours of relentless questioning by alternating Gestapo officers, 100 8-pfennig stamps in mint condition were suddenly placed on the table in front of him. Hans was asked to explain what they were doing in his apartment. They also asked him to explain why all envelopes containing White Rose leaflets handed into the Gestapo by 'loyal' citizens all had 8-pfenning stamps stuck on them.[21] It seems all the pressure and anxiety which had been building up in Hans all day – and possibly for weeks – just proved too much. He suddenly – according to the interrogation protocol – decided to take full responsibility in the hope this would save Sophie and his other friends from a similar ordeal.[22] Hans was eventually taken back to his cell, which he shared that weekend with a young Bavarian labourer called Helmut Fietz, who had been arrested for making a joke comparing Adolf Hitler to a pig. Fietz noticed the Gestapo had left the light on in the cell all night and denied Hans a razor.

Robert Mohr was informed of the confession of Hans Scholl. Sophie now realised her position was hopeless and agreed 'to tell the truth'. Mohr claimed that Sophie was fully prepared to sacrifice her own life to save her brother. Hans showed a similar desire to do the same to protect his sister. Mohr said the strong love of Hans and Sophie he witnessed over those four days made 'a strong impression' on him and all the other staff in the Wittelsbach Palace.[23] In the dead of night Sophie told Mohr a partial version, in which she still tried to protect her friends. 'We were convinced Germany had lost the war', she explained. The military defeat at Stalingrad was the major spur to a more frantic period of resistance activity. She said the White Rose came into being after she arrived at Munich University. It was a joint venture with her brother, in which they were both fully involved at every stage. The idea of the leaflet campaign had been a topic of discussion between the siblings, claimed Sophie, for a very long time. It was only in June 1942 that Sophie and Hans made Alex aware of their already germinating plan.

The first leafleting campaign, she admitted, was a small-scale operation. It was only in December 1942 that Sophie and Hans decided to distribute future leaflets in much larger quantities. Sophie claimed she was the co-writer of the fifth leaflet, 'Call to all Germans', and also claimed authorship of the idea which appeared at the end of every leaflet, namely, to copy the leaflet and pass it on. It was just her and Hans who bought the duplicating machine, envelopes, stencils and stamps from local shops. After this, Sophie went on to admit she delivered leaflets in Augsburg, Ulm and Stuttgart. At this point, she admitted Alex had distributed leaflets in Munich. Sophie said Willi Graf 'in no way participated in the production or distribution of the leaflets'. She painted Willi as someone who knew about the leaflets, shared some of their views, but took no active part in the leafleting operation. Sophie made no mention at all of Christoph Probst or Kurt Huber.

She then provided further details on the leafleting operation. The duplicating machine was hidden in Eickemeyer's studio, she told Mohr, but the architect knew nothing about it, nor did her landlady, Mrs Schmidt. Wilhelm Geyer, who was renting Eickemeyer's studio, was – according to Sophie – similarly in the dark. In the case of her landlady Sophie was telling the truth, but Geyer and Eickemeyer had full knowledge of what was going on.

Sophie now told Mohr the truth about what really happened in the Lichthof. In 'my high spirits or stupidity I made the mistake of throwing between 80 and 100 leaflets from the third floor down into the Lichthof.' Sophie said the aim of the White Rose all along had been to rouse the German population to put an end to the Nazi regime. If they had not been caught, the campaign would have continued. They decided not to extend the group as they felt it was much too dangerous to do so. She had acted for purely idealistic reasons. They financed the whole operation themselves out of their own expenditure and through loans from friends who did not know for what purpose their money was being used.[24] The extent of Sophie's confession was limited to an admission that she and Hans were the co-creators and leaders of the White Rose and their only collaborator was Alexander Schmorell, whose real role was reduced to that of a help-mate in distributing the leaflets.

Sophie described her all-night encounter with Mohr to Else Gebel as 'exhausting but interesting' and said she had even been given a cup of real coffee. A well-spoken, calm, relaxed and highly intelligent university student was certainly a rarity in the German prison system and this helps to explain why Mohr played the 'good cop'. Gebel felt the long hours of interrogation had 'done nothing to your calm, relaxed manner' and her strong belief in God proved enormously important to her ability to weather the lengthy questioning. She also tried to reassure Sophie that her confession did not mean certain death. Gebel thought it would certainly take some time before the case came before the court. Of course, this was not what was being said behind the scenes. It may seem that Gebel was protecting Sophie from impending doom, but in reality the tactic of keeping a prisoner in the dark about their fate was quite a normal practice in Gestapo investigations.

By now, the Gestapo had printed a wanted poster of Alexander Schmorell offering a 1,000-mark reward for information leading to his arrest. Alex was holed up in Lilo Ramdohr's apartment. She managed to get him a Yugoslav passport. Alex had wanted to escape to Switzerland, but as he was now top of the Gestapo wanted list his chance of making it though the heavily guarded Swiss border was pretty remote. Late on the evening of 18 February, Willi Graf and his sister Anneliese were taken into custody. The softly spoken Willi proved a formidable character throughout his many interrogations. He denied everything, parried every question and left it up to the Gestapo to find definite proof of his involvement in the leafleting operation. Willi Graf is the unsung hero of the White Rose group and his bravery during his time in custody was truly remarkable and heart-rending.[25]

Events now moved at a rapid pace. Paul Giesler, the local Nazi gauleiter, informed Mohr that he wanted the case 'settled quickly'.[26] On the morning of Friday 19 February he telexed Martin Bormann, Hitler's private secretary, one of the leading figures in the power structure of the Third Reich.[27] Giesler outlined the 'highly treasonous activity' of the White Rose leafleting operation. He requested 'a quick trial' in the People's Court, even though the accused male students were members of the armed forces and subject to punishment by a special army tribunal.[28] At 4.20 p.m. on 19 February 1943 a telegraphed message, marked very urgent, was sent by Bormann's office to Giesler informing him that 'on my orders' Field Marshall Wilhelm Keitel, the leading figure in Hitler's General Staff, had discharged the accused soldiers from the army and he agreed to their swift trial in the People's Court.[29] The trial date was set for Monday 22 February. The presiding judges would be sent specially from Berlin to conduct the proceedings. The 'execution' was to take place immediately following the trial.[30] The main reasons why the Nazi authorities wanted to make a quick example of the White Rose case was because they did not know how large the organisation really was. A quick and brutal resolution would send a demoralising massage to those still at large and act as a deterrent to anyone thinking of following their example, which was especially important in the weeks after Stalingrad.

Sophie and her brother would stand trial in just three days' time. The fate of Hans Scholl had already been sealed. He was going to be executed. Sophie Scholl also faced trial, as she had confessed her guilt, and her position looked equally dire unless she changed her story. It was now established that Christoph Probst had written the seventh leaflet, so he faced trial as well. The Gestapo did not have any tangible evidence to try Willi Graf, but he was not being released. His ultimate fate was merely postponed. Willi Graf claimed in his interrogation that all he talked about with Sophie, Hans and Alex was religion, philosophy and literature. 'What about Hans Scholl?' he was asked. 'A loyal German soldier' was the swift reply.[31] Graf was presented with the evidence from Hans' confession and shown a copy of a leaflet. Willi just claimed to be 'shocked' that Hans Scholl could be involved in such activities.[32]

Mohr was not satisfied with Sophie's explanation. It seemed a highly contrived story, carefully designed to inflate her own role and lessen the responsibility of her friends. Sophie had to endure a further lengthy interrogation. Mohr asked Sophie to explain the role of Willi Graf. She admitted that he had 'shared our views', but insisted he was not actively involved in the leaflet operation. He did not even know about the leafleting or graffiti operations, Sophie claimed. The main subjects Sophie and Hans discussed with Willi Graf were Christianity and philosophy and only rarely political matters.

Sophie then offered a clever explanation as to why so many leaflets had turned up in so many cities, if only three people were involved. She said they had travelled around to so many places to give the impression of a much larger organisation. 'The National Movement' mentioned in the leaflets was simply a clever deception. The whole operation had been run by Sophie and Hans with a little help from Alex, and no one else was involved. Mohr then asked Sophie about Anneliese Graf. 'She was apolitical', replied Sophie, and 'had nothing to do with our propaganda activity'. Mohr then told Sophie that the Gestapo had searched Eickemeyer's studio and found the template with the words 'Down with Hitler' and a pair of gloves, paint and paintbrushes. He asked her who bought these items. 'I've never seen the template', Sophie replied.

Sophie said the recent focus of the campaign had centred on the students at the university. She claimed the idea of daubing anti-Hitler graffiti was hers and she even tried to diminish Hans' central role in the graffiti operation by saying her brother thought they should concentrate on the leaflet campaign alone. Mohr moved on to the matter of a notebook that had been found in Sophie's room, with a list of names and addresses. Sophie said it was a 'sort of account book' for the leaflet operation, listing income and expenditure.

The interrogation soon moved on to the typewriters used in the leafleting operation. The Gestapo had determined that more than the two typewriters they had found had been used and Sophie was asked to explain this.

She said only two were used: the one found in her room and a US-made Remington typewriter, provided by Alex, which had been borrowed from a friend or acquaintance of his. Sophie was asked when she had learned of the first White Rose leaflet. She said Traute Lafrenz showed her the fourth leaflet in the middle of July 1942, which she had received in the post. She was baffled about why the leaflet was headed 'The White Rose'. Hans explained the exiled French aristocracy – after the French Revolution – had a white rose on their flags. Sophie added that a few days later she questioned Hans about the leaflet and he told her not to ask such questions as 'the writer could be endangered'. Of course this explanation – which was possibly closer to the truth – contradicted her admission in the second interrogation the night before that she had been a co-author and collaborator in the leaflet operation from beginning to end. It seems Mohr's questioning at this point forced Sophie to outline the actual sequence of events. In other words, it does seem that Sophie was introduced to the campaign after it began.

By this stage, she probably realised that to concoct a story of the origins of her involvement would most probably contradict the story Hans was offering in the adjacent room. Sophie was now asked about how the group was financed. Mohr said the evidence pointed to donations from many 'third parties'. Sophie said this was not true. She said she had borrowed money from Alex and 'Captain Fritz Hartnagel', who had been stationed at Stalingrad, suffered severe frostbite and was luckily air-lifted to a hospital, and who she had 'planned to marry'. Fritz had given her 300 marks but he did not know she had used it to finance the leaflet operation.

Mohr now pressed Sophie on the role of Christoph Probst in the leaflet campaign. Sophie said Christoph believed that Germany could not win the war, but he had held back these views and took no part in the writing, production or distribution of the leaflets. Sophie described Christoph as a good family man, of above average intelligence. Sophie ended by saying: 'I have now confessed everything that is known to me' and 'I have not knowingly withheld information.' It was another brilliant performance. Sophie had emphatically claimed the White Rose was led by the Scholl siblings, with some help from Alex, and had diminished the role of Christoph and protected practically everyone else from any serious charges. Mohr finally asked her if she thought her actions were 'a crime against the common good' in a time of war. 'From my point of view no', Sophie replied, 'I believe I have done my best for the nation. I do not regret my conduct. I wish to fully accept the consequences of my actions.'[33]

Else Gebel claims that during this third and final interrogation – though it does not appear in the written summary – Mohr gave Sophie a stern lecture about the meaning of National Socialism and loyalty to the Führer, ending by saying Sophie had compromised Germany's armed forces by her deeds. 'You are wrong', Sophie reportedly told Mohr, 'I would do exactly the same thing again. It is you who has a mistaken worldview.' In his account, Mohr claims he brought Sophie in for one final 'off the record' interrogation. At this last meeting – not recorded – he claims that he 'tried to use my powers of persuasion to get Miss Scholl to say she did not agree with her brother's ideology' and to admit she had only been her brother's assistant. Mohr says Sophie rejected this deal, which would probably have saved her life, because she could not have 'betrayed her own brother'. Sophie chose to die for her principles and to stand with her brother.[34]

Otl Aicher, who was released from custody, returned by express train to Ulm on 19 February 1943 and told Robert, Magdelene and Inge Scholl about the arrests.[35] Traute Lafrenz also went to Ulm on the same day and she gave details of the events in the Lichthof.[36] According to Traute Lafrenz-Page the family were told by the Gestapo they could not visit their children after their arrests and they were kept completely in the dark about what was happening for the whole weekend.[37]

By Saturday evening – 20 February – Sophie Scholl was finally back in her cell. She was given a hot meal, presented with cigarettes, biscuits and sausages, and bread and butter.[38] In Gestapo custody, this was startlingly caring treatment. It was a sure sign that Sophie was now a firm candidate for execution. What Sophie did not know was that Christoph Probst had been arrested and was undergoing interrogation in the same building. Christoph soon admitted to the authorship of the draft leaflet found on Hans Scholl, but he offered mitigating circumstances: he suffered from depression; he had a sick wife and three children; he had only written the leaflet because Hans had asked him to; and he had not wanted it typed and distributed. Christoph said Alex was his best friend and Sophie was 'just a girl', under the influence of her brother.[39] But the Gestapo concluded that his draft leaflet amounted to written evidence of 'high treason'. The three accused in the first White Rose trial quickly narrowed down to Hans and Sophie Scholl, plus Christoph Probst.

By Sunday afternoon, 21 February, the indictment was being typed up for presentation. The chief prosecutor of the People's Court in Berlin had set the trial for the following day at 10 a.m. Sophie was escorted from her cell to be given the news that the investigation was complete. She was now formally arrested and charged with high treason, by creating an organisation to carry out treason, aiding and abetting the enemy in time of war and encouraging the demoralisation of the armed forces. Sophie was told the trial would take place the following day.[40] She was escorted back to her cell. Once inside she suddenly realised the gravity of the situation she now faced. Sophie broke down, but just as quickly pulled herself together. 'It is such a splendid sunny day', she told Gebel, 'and I have to go. But how many have to die on the battlefield in these days … what does my death matter if by our acts thousands of people are warned and alerted'. Else Gebel tried to suggest she might escape with a long prison sentence, but Sophie insisted: 'If my brother is sentenced to death, then I must not and ought not receive a lighter sentence.'[41]

The court-appointed lawyer assigned to Hans and Sophie was August Klein. He visited Sophie very briefly – not long after she had been given the indictment. Such lawyers could hardly be called a defence counsel, as they mounted little defence at all. Sophie emphasised that she would not plead mitigation. She wanted to have the same punishment as her brother. She said if Hans was to be executed he should face a firing squad, as he was still a soldier. In spite of this, Klein called for a 'mild sentence' for the serious charges Sophie faced.[42]

Meanwhile, the Ludwig Maximillian University held a hastily arranged disciplinary hearing, chaired by the university rector Walter Wüst, which punished Sophie Scholl for what it called her 'seditious activities', by prohibiting her from studying at any university ever again.[43] Robert Mohr visited Sophie in her cell and advised her to write final letters to 'her loved ones'.[44] She wrote to her parents, to her sister Inge and to Fritz Hartnagel. Sophie thanked her parents for all their love and kindness, and expressed deep regret for all the sorrow she had caused. She stressed her deep religious faith, said she would not have acted any differently and hoped that in future people would see that what they had done in fighting Hitler's brutal regime was right. The contents of the letters were reported to the Reich Security Office in Berlin, but they were never sent as the Nazi authorities were worried they might be used as propaganda for the resistance.[45] The letters did not survive the war. After Mohr left, Sophie read the indictment in detail and on the back she wrote a single word: 'Freedom'.

At 10 p.m. Sophie knelt down to pray before getting into bed. She then chatted with Else Gebel because it was hard to get to sleep as the lights remained on all night. Sophie told Gebel she was worried about how her mother would cope with the loss of a son and daughter, but she finally comforted herself with one consoling thought: 'Father has a better understanding of what we did.' Shortly afterwards, Sophie drifted off to sleep.[46]

THIRTEEN

THE PEOPLE'S COURT

Sophie woke just before 7 a.m. on Monday 22 February 1943. She described what she had dreamed to Else Gebel.

'It was a sunny day', Sophie told her cellmate, 'I was carrying a child in a long white dress to be christened. The path to the church led up a steep slope, but I held the child in my arms firmly and without faltering. Then suddenly my footing gave way ... I had enough time to put the child down before plunging into the abyss.'

'What does the dream mean?' enquired Gebel.

'The child is our idea. In spite of all obstacles it will prevail.'[1]

In his cell, Hans bade farewell to his eccentric companion of the past four days, Helmut Feitz. Before the prison guards arrived, Hans managed to write a single sentence from a poem by Goethe in pencil on the wall of the cell: 'Hold out in defiance of all despotism.'[2]

Sophie was allowed to change into her civilian clothes for the menacing ordeal that lay ahead. 'I promise you', Gebel told Sophie as the guards came for her, 'that later, in quieter times I will tell your parents about our days together'. Sophie briefly shook hands with Gebel, as the prison guards approached her cell. Gebel's parting words were 'God be with you.'[3]

At about 9 a.m. two plainclothes detectives from the regular criminal police escorted a handcuffed Sophie to a waiting police car. The Gestapo had passed the case into the supposedly 'normal' German legal system. Hans Scholl and Christoph Probst were both taken to the court in separate police vehicles. Their destination was Munich's imposing and improperly named Palace of Justice.

Meanwhile, the express train carrying the presiding judge from Berlin was delayed. The Scholl parents remained in Ulm over the weekend, in a state of utter helplessness and despair. The Gestapo refused to provide any official information to them. Years later, Inge Scholl described their predicament:

> In times like this, a time of great trouble, one's impulse is to rush in and try to batter the walls. Since the weekend intervened, when no visits were allowed, they waited until Monday to travel by train.[4]

Their train must also have been delayed or perhaps they were still in a state of denial because Robert and Magdelene Scholl did not arrive in Munich until noon, a full two hours after the designated start of the trial. Once again, why they left from Ulm so late on that day is very difficult to explain, other than by reference to a severe state of stress due to the exceptional circumstances. One possible reason may have been a fear of arrest under the Nazis' notorious kinship laws, which allowed the security forces to detain the whole family of someone accused of treasonable offences.

The limousine carrying the presiding judge finally arrived at the Palace of Justice not long before 10 a.m. – given the length of the trial transcript. The judge made his way to the robing room behind room 216, where the trial of Sophie Scholl, Hans Scholl and Christoph Probst had already heard some preliminary remarks from court officials.

The sign outside the door of the court had the familiar 'Public Not Allowed' written on it. Sophie, Hans and Christoph were seated in the defendants' area behind a wooden railing, flanked by uniformed armed guards, with fixed bayonets. They were all seated directly to the right of the judges' bench, facing large picture windows. There was no jury in the imposing court, decorated with numerous paintings in gold-braided frames.

The People's Court was presided over by a president, supported by two professional judges, and assisted by two legal representatives of the SS and SA.[5] It was a strict rule that no family members or friends were allowed in the courtroom. There were no witnesses for the defence. The whole procedure was based on the written and physical evidence collected during the Gestapo investigation over the previous days. The judge in such trials was present to decide what sentences were applicable, and to give reasons for them. The transcripts of these trials always read 'Verdict – with reasons.' There were tables and chairs for the court recorder, the chief prosecuting counsel and the so-called defence lawyers. The public seating at the back was filled with a specially invited audience of loyal Nazi Party officials, storm troopers and even some members of the armed forces. All of this added to the intimidating atmosphere.

Suddenly, into the packed courtroom strode a man, draped in blood-red robes trimmed in gold, wearing a red cap atop his bald head. The author of this carefully stage-managed entrance was Roland Freisler, the most terrifying judge in Nazi Germany. Everyone – except the defendants – rose to their feet, raised one arm and shouted at the top of their voices: 'Heil Hitler'. He was followed into the courtroom by two assistant judges and the two Nazi legal officials.

Freisler was born in Celle on 30 October 1893. He served in the German army in the First World War, but was captured by the Russians in 1915. While in captivity he learned Russian. After the Russian Revolution in 1917 he was attracted by socialist ideas, though he was never a convinced Marxist. In 1920 he returned to Germany to study law at the University of Jena. In 1925 he joined the Nazi Party as member number 9,679. In 1928 he married Marion Russegger and they had two sons, Harald and Roland. He defended many Nazi party members in criminal cases before 1933, the year in which he was appointed head of the Prussian Ministry of Justice. He was even a participant at the infamous Wannsee Conference in Berlin on 20 January 1942, which mapped out detailed plans for the 'Final Solution'. In August 1942, Hitler appointed him president of the People's Court, which had been set up in July 1934 to deal with serious political crimes, most notably high treason and acts of opposition which were thought to undermine the war effort.

Freisler not only acted as judge and jury in the cases he tried, but he also took his own hand-written notes – in very sloppy handwriting – and then used them to summarise his verdicts, rattled off in double-quick time. Freisler would often pronounce a death sentence, pause for effect, then shout 'off with his head'.[6] He mercilessly bullied defendants, showering them with rapid-fire insults issued at breakneck speed, so it was impossible to get a word in edgeways. His whole conduct was totally outrageous, highly theatrical, but coldly calculated. A man without any human feelings or empathy, Freisler would frame every question to have only two answers 'Yes' or 'No'. In films he is often depicted as a one-dimensional fairytale bully, but he was well-read, fluent in several languages and had tremendous mental agility. This skill showed in his stunningly effective brutal verbal attacks on defendants. He could take his voice from a very low monotone then crank up the volume to an ear-splitting high-decibel roar that echoed up and down the long hallways outside the courtroom.[7] His ill-tempered meanness was all part of a carefully crafted style.

At the outbreak of the war, Freisler had promised to deal with what he called 'any social parasite' – usually meaning an opponent of the regime – in the harshest possible way. As far as he was concerned, anyone who engaged in resistance ceased to be a 'national comrade'. Between 1934 and 1939, the People's Court had imposed the death penalty only 108 times. In 1942, Freisler's very first year as president of the People's Court, 1,192 people received the death sentence.[8]

With Freisler presiding, the trial of Sophie Scholl, her brother Hans and Christoph Probst would be brutal and brief. The verdict had been decided in advance. As in all trials in German courts, the chief prosecuting lawyer led the proceedings for the Reich. Weyersberg decided that, as the defendants had all confessed their guilt, the only witness he would call would be the university janitor and Nazi 'hero of the hour': Jakob Schmid, dressed in his best suit for his fifteen minutes of fame. In the end, Schmid, who had been paid a 3,000-mark reward for arresting Hans and Sophie in the Lichthof, was never asked to give his version of events.

The defendants were asked to stand up and gave brief personal details. The charges against them were then read out aloud to the court. Robert Mohr later recalled that Freisler conducted the trial with 'enormous severity'.[9] A young lawyer, Leo Samberger, also witnessed the proceedings. Years later, he remembered Hans Scholl standing upright, looking gaunt and pale and at one point suddenly turning white 'as if he were fainting'.[10] Sophie maintained a 'steadfast manner' as she explained to Freisler why she had participated in the leaflet operation. She defended her actions and offered no repentance whatsoever.[11] As each defendant gave their brief version of events they were constantly interrupted by Freisler, 'raging, screaming, roaring till his voice broke', Samberger recalls, 'jumping up again and again in red-hot explosions'.

What the defendants actually said is not recorded in the transcript – but given Freisler's rage, it is obvious they were defending their actions with great courage and refusing to bow to his bullying. It is also stated in the trial transcript that four White Rose leaflets were read out in full, but given how short the proceedings were this seems unlikely, and most probably only short extracts were read out. To emphasise Christoph Probst's guilt, his hand-written leaflet was most certainly read out. The chief inspector of the Munich Gestapo, Herr Möll, gave what must have been a short summary of the results of the investigation.

At the conclusion of the brief proceedings the chief prosecutor called for the death penalty for Hans Scholl, Sophie Scholl and Christoph Probst on charges of high treason, aiding and abetting the enemy and undermining the armed forces. Probst was additionally charged with listening to foreign radio broadcasts. The defence lawyer called for a 'just' sentence for Hans and a 'mild' sentence for Sophie. Christoph Probst's lawyer asked for a 'mild punishment', stressing the consequences of his execution for his young wife and children. Samberger observed that when Sophie, Hans and Christoph spoke during the proceedings, their answers were 'calm, composed, clear and unflinching'. Hans and Sophie's supposed defence lawyer told Freisler he could not understand why people would do things 'they ought to be ashamed of'.[12]

As was customary the defendants were allowed the 'last words'. Sophie stood up, but apparently made no comment. In some accounts, it is stated that Sophie reportedly said: 'What we wrote and said is also believed by many others. They just don't dare to express themselves as we did' and at another point she is supposed to have said to Freisler 'You know the war is lost. Why don't you have the courage to face it?'[13] In Mohr's memorandum and Samberger's account, there is no mention of Sophie saying these words. Hans reportedly asked the judge for a lenient sentence for Christoph Probst, but was told by Freisler to 'shut up' if he had nothing to say in his own defence. Probst asked for clemency on the grounds that he was suffering from depression at the time he wrote the leaflets and because his wife was suffering from a post-natal illness and his three children would be left orphaned by his execution.[14]

Freisler announced that the formal morning proceedings were over. There would be a brief adjournment for a working lunch, while the judges considered their verdicts. The defendants were allowed to stay in the courtroom during the intermission. Samberger observed that Hans, Sophie and Christoph had shown they 'were visibly and truly devoted to their principles'. He also noticed in the lunch break that Schmid, who he described as the 'loathsome janitor', dressed in his Sunday best, was being feted as a hero by the uniformed Nazi figures seated in the public seats.[15]

Given that the trial came so shortly after the humiliating German defeat at Stalingrad the verdict was never really in doubt. Freisler soon returned to the front bench of the court and delivered the verdict 'with reasons' in his usual staccato fashion, barely pausing for breath.

Each defendant was asked to stand while the verdict was read out to the court. For Hans Scholl, Sophie Scholl and Christoph Probst the verdict was guilty and the forfeit of their 'honour as German citizens for ever'. The sentence for all three was death. The verdict was designed to punish them for defying the Nazi regime and to send a warning to anyone else considering the dangerous path of open resistance.

Sophie remained calm and composed as Freisler explained the reasons for her verdict. She then stood as he gave his reasons for the sentence of death. He claimed Sophie's actions in participating fully in the leafleting and propaganda campaign had 'declared war' on the Führer, the party and the people, and had severely undermined the war effort. Sophie sat down.

Freisler asked Hans Scholl to stand. He depicted Hans as the leader of the group and Sophie as his committed and fully dedicated first lieutenant. Hans, as a soldier, said Freisler, had declared a special oath of loyalty to the Führer and had committed treason in the deluded belief his actions were the only way Germany could survive the war. In reality, Hans had committed treason, Freisler claimed, by stabbing his fellow soldiers in the back, and he had also severely undermined the morale of the German army and the people. 'I still remember', Robert Mohr recalled, 'that Hans Scholl's final words were "Today you will hang us, but soon you will be standing where I now stand" or something like that.'[16] Hans finally sat down.

Christoph Probst was asked to get to his feet. Freisler showed absolutely no sympathy for his tragic plight. Freisler said that if Probst was as 'apolitical' as he claimed then 'he is not a man at all'. The Nazi state had subsidised his education, Freisler continued, and his family had received generous state benefits and family allowance payments. All of this acted as little restraint on his decision to write a leaflet which had blamed the Führer for the defeat at Stalingrad, nor had it stopped him listening to banned broadcasts from Germany's enemies and even endorsing the views of President Roosevelt, one of Germany's key enemies. Freisler said that while Hans and Sophie had fully confessed their guilt, Probst had sought to offer excuses for his actions, most notably the illness of his wife and a 'psychotic depression'. Freisler dismissed these as not valid excuses nor any mitigation for his 'seditious' actions. Christoph Probst sat down.

Freisler then explained to the court that the punishment for all three defendants had to be death, as any other sentence would erode public support for the war. The deaths of the accused would show that the People's Court was supporting soldiers fighting in the war for the plight of Germany. The costs of the trial, said Freisler, would be charged to the estates and families of the accused. Freisler then got up and left the court having not given any details as to when and how the executions would be carried

7. The famous Lichthof (atrium) of Munich University (© Weisse Rose Sitftung)

8. Kurt Huber

9. Willi Graf

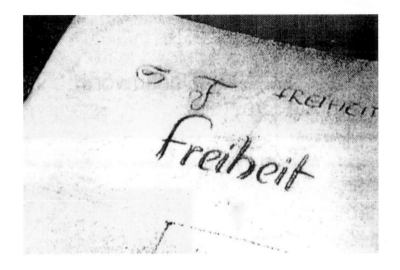

10. Sophie wrote the word *Freiheit* (freedom) on her indictment

11. Roland Freisler, the judge of the 'People's Court'

12. Traute Lafrenz (by permission of Traute Lafrenz-Page)

13. White Rose Memorial, Munich University. Christoph Probst can be seen smoking a pipe (*bottom right*) (© Weisse Rose Stiftung)

out.[17] This high-speed trial had lasted less than three hours. It sent out a chilling message: defy Hitler and pay with your life.

The announcement of the verdicts had been briefly interrupted by the belated arrival of Robert Scholl, who somehow managed to gatecrash the proceedings. He was accompanied by his wife, and his son Werner, on leave from his army duty and in uniform. Robert Scholl was extremely emotional and angry. Klein, the defence attorney, said to Freisler 'It's the father'; Freisler just angrily asked the guards to remove him from the courtroom.[18] With guards holding his arms, Robert Scholl shouted: 'There is a higher court [God's] before which we must all stand.' Magdalene Scholl nearly fainted when she was told her young children had been sentenced to death. At the end of the announcement of the verdict, the parents were not allowed back in the courtroom, but Werner Scholl did manage to sneak in. He shook hands with Hans and Sophie, then hugged them with tears in his eyes. 'Be strong', Hans told his young brother, 'Admit nothing.'[19]

The three condemned prisoners were then led handcuffed out of the courtroom to the exit of the vast Palace of Justice, where Hans and Christoph were bundled into a waiting police car. Sophie was escorted into a separate vehicle. Sophie travelled along cobbled streets to Munich's largest prison, located in the Giesing district of the city. Her one consolation on this dreadful day was that she could see the bright blue sky she loved out of the window.

FOURTEEN

'LONG LIVE FREEDOM'

The police car carrying Sophie Scholl soon reached the gates of Stadelheim prison.[1] It had held some notorious prisoners. Adolf Hitler served a four-week sentence in cell 70 in the summer of 1922 for breaking up a public meeting. In 1934, Ernst Röhm, the leader of the Nazi storm troopers (SA), was shot dead by a makeshift SS firing squad in the same cell. Between 1933 and 1945 1,035 executions were carried at the prison.

Sophie was met by prison guards and led into the dimly lit reception area. She was searched, handed over her possessions and was then escorted to a single cell.[2] Some members of the resistance remained on death row for several agonising months. The usual period before execution – even in the Nazi era – was ninety-nine days. But this was not a normal case. It had already been decided Sophie, Hans and Christoph would die before the sun set.

Paul Giesler, the Nazi *Gauleiter*, had wanted the three students to be hanged on Marienplatz, the central boulevard of the city. But Heinrich Himmler, the SS leader, rejected the idea of a public execution as it ran the risk of an embarrassing demonstration. It was finally decided to execute the group at 5 p.m., then make a public announcement of the executions on radio and give the local press enough time to print details on the following day.[3]

Meanwhile, back at the Palace of Justice, a shocked and emotional Robert Scholl waited in the corridor when the doors finally opened and spectators came flooding out. Sophie and Hans' lawyer made a point of walking straight up to Robert and Magdalene Scholl, not to offer sympathy, but to make a point of telling them, in a heartless manner, they 'should be ashamed' for bringing up their children so badly.

Leo Samberger, totally unaware of the pre-determined time of the execution, politely introduced himself to Robert Scholl and helped him to lodge a hopeless plea for clemency in the administrative office of the attorney general. A secretary diligently scribbled down the appeal. Robert Scholl asked if he could speak to the national prosecutor, but his request was turned down. The secretary urged Robert Scholl and his wife to go 'hurry along' as quickly as they could to Stadelheim prison to visit their children.[4] They soon arrived at Stadelheim and were allowed a final interview with Hans and Sophie. This was a most exceptional occurrence for prisoners condemned to death on charges of high treason in Nazi Germany.

The Scholl parents were taken to a small visiting room. Hans was brought in first, dressed in a striped prison uniform and his face – according to Robert Scholl – showed 'the strain of battle'. Hans did not dwell on his awful predicament, but used the time to thank his parents warmly for all the love, support and affection they had shown him throughout his life. 'I have no hate for anyone any more. I have put all that behind me', he told his parents.

'You will go down in history', his father replied fighting back the tears, 'I'm proud of you both.'

Hans then asked his parents to send his love to his friends and when he reached the last name in his litany, tears finally rolled down his cheeks.[5] But he quickly composed himself, shaking his mother and father warmly by the hand.

Hans was then led out of the visitor's room. In the corridor was Robert Mohr, the Gestapo agent. Hans thanked him for treating his sister with such consideration during her interrogation.[6] Mohr offered an empathetic nod.

Sophie, afforded the special privilege of remaining in her own clothes, minus her overcoat, was next led into the visiting room. She smiled at her parents.

'Do you want some sweets?' her mother said touchingly and reassuringly.

'Gladly. I've not eaten any lunch', Sophie replied.

Her mother held both her daughter's hands, looked her in the eye and said: 'Sophie, Sophie. To think you will never come through the door again.'

'Ah mother', Sophie sighed.

'We took everything upon ourselves. What will happen will cause waves.'

'Remember Jesus', Magdalene Scholl replied.

'Yes. But you [remember him] too', were the final words Sophie uttered to her parents.[7]

Sophie was escorted back to her cell. As Robert Mohr entered the cell, he could see Sophie sobbing. 'I've just said goodbye to my parents', she said, with tears rolling down her cheeks, 'I'm sure you understand.' Mohr offered a few more brief words of comfort. He left her, deeply impressed with her incredible strength of character and her rare faith in God.[8]

At 4 p.m. Sophie Scholl was escorted from her cell to a prison office. The chief prosecutor, Herr Weyersberg, seated at a large table, told her there would be no act of clemency and so 'Justice would take its course.' The death sentence against her would be carried out at 5 p.m.[9] This is the first time Sophie knew how soon she would die. Shortly afterwards, Hans Scholl and Christoph Probst were read similar declarations and told the same grim news.

Karl Alt, the prison chaplain, now came in to Sophie's cell. Alt was born in Nuremburg in 1897 and had visited thousands of condemned prisoners waiting on death row. He was a Lutheran pastor and a distinguished author on religious matters. He later recalled that Sophie remained totally calm and composed as she waited for the end to come. She discussed her strong belief in God. Alt tried to comfort her by getting her to read aloud from the Bible. The first passage Sophie read out loud in her quiet reassuring voice came from Corinthians 13:[10]

Love never faileth, but where there be prophecies, they shall fail, whether there be tongues, they shall cease: whether there be knowledge, it shall vanish away. For we know in part and we prophesy in part. But when that which is perfect has come then that which is part shall be done away. When I was a child I spake as a child, I understood as a child, I thought as a child, but when I became a man I put away childish things. For now we see through a glass darkly, but then face to face. Now I know in part, but then shall I know even as I am known. And now abideth faith, hope, love, these three, but the greatest of these is love.[11]

Alt then asked Sophie to read from Psalm 90, which Hans Scholl had requested in his earlier visitation with him. Alt once again urged Sophie to read the words out loud. She knew them by heart, but they had a special and deep religious meaning to her at this moment:

Lord, you have been our dwelling place throughout all generations; Before the mountains were born or you brought forth the earth and the world from everything everlasting you are God. You return men back to dust, saying 'Return to dust, O sons of men'. For a thousand years in your sight are like a day that has just gone by, like a watch in the night. You sweep men away in the sleep of death: they are like the new grass of the morning … satisfy us in the morning with your unfailing love, that we may sing for joy and be glad all our days … Teach us to consider that we must die, so that we may be wise.[12]

Finally, Alt offered Sophie a brief sermon, ending with the famous lines of John's gospel. 'Greater love hath no man than this, that a man lay down his life for his friends'.[13] Alt gave Sophie final communion and administered the last rites. A prison guard arrived at the door. The executioner was ready.[14]

Sophie was escorted to an anteroom. The representatives of the Nazi state were seated at a small table. The official asked her to confirm her identity. 'Sophie Magdalena Scholl', she replied. The death sentence was announced in cold mechanical bureaucratic language: 'For high treason and aiding and abetting the enemy' followed by the declaration: 'The court has sentenced you to death by guillotine.'[15]

The guillotine consisted of a tall upright wooden frame from which a razor-sharp blade was suspended and then released. It became a notorious execution method during the French Revolution. But the guillotine was used throughout Germany even before Hitler came to power. Nazi records show that 16,500 people were executed by this method between 1933 and 1945. Hanging – the British form of execution at this time – was viewed as a much less dignified and brutal method of execution. It was reserved in the Nazi era for members of the resistance, mostly communists, Jews and foreign workers. It was usual practice for soldiers to face a firing squad, but this had already been denied to Hans Scholl and Christoph Probst. The French Justice Ministry claimed the guillotine was 'the most humane form of execution', as death came almost instantaneously.[16]

Sophie remained 'calm and collected'. Standing near the guillotine was a man wearing a long black coat, pristine white gloves, a white shirt, black bow tie and a jet black tall top hat. His name was Johann Reichart, the most famous German executioner of the Nazi era. He kept detailed records of the 3,165 executions he personally carried out between 1933 and 1945. Reichart used two guards to hold a prisoner in place before the execution – rather than strap them down – as was usual practice by other executioners using the guillotine method. By this method he reduced the time from entry into the execution chamber to death to an average of less than 5 seconds.[17]

In less than 6 seconds from the moment Sophie Scholl entered the execution chamber, the blade was released by the executioner and a 21-year-old student, so full of life-affirming spirit, was dead. The whole execution from the time she left her cell to the pronouncement of her death by the prison doctor was 48 seconds. The time of her death was noted methodically: 5.01 p.m. Monday 22 February 1943.[18]

Sophie's beloved brother Hans Scholl was next into the execution chamber. He was brought up with Sophie, loved her and would now die with her. His execution from cell to death took 52 seconds.[19] Hans Scholl was only 24 years old and extraordinarily brave; he lived life to the full – not at second hand.

Christoph Probst was now led to the execution chamber and said nothing before the blade fell. His execution from cell to death took just 42 seconds.[20] Christoph Probst was just 23 years old, a loving husband and the father of three small children.

But the cold, detached execution records of the officials at Stadelheim notes one last extraordinary detail. Before the blade fell, Hans Scholl shouted in a defiant voice:

'Long live Freedom!'[21]

FIFTEEN

THE LEGACY

Sophie Scholl is now a legend in Germany, an iconic symbol of youthful defiance against a monstrous dictatorship. A very special German in the Nazi era who stood up for her beliefs while nearly everyone else joined in or looked the other way. There are over 190 schools in Germany named in her honour, she has been voted 'woman of the twentieth century' and in November 2003 the German TV channel ZDF conducted a nationwide poll of viewers in a series called *Greatest Germans*.[1] The winner was Konrad Adenauer, the first democratic leader of West Germany after the Second World War, but Hans and Sophie Scholl (the siblings were bracketed together in the voting) came fourth, ahead of Bach, Goethe and even Albert Einstein. Sophie Scholl was the highest-placed German woman of all. In February 2005, the German film *Sophie Scholl: The Final Days* was nominated for 'Best Foreign Film' at the 2006 Academy Awards. Julia Jentsch gave a gripping performance in the title role, winning best actress awards at the Berlin Film Festival and the European Film Awards. 'I admire her courage', Jentsch said; 'I tried to portray her as a person, with a great sense of compassion and strong religious beliefs.'[2]

To end my own search for the liberating spirit of Sophie Scholl, I put away the books, the articles, the letters, the diaries, the memoirs, the grim Gestapo files and the awful final execution records. I could not end my long journey frozen by the coldness and despair of her death. I decided to visit some of the important places and people in Sophie's life to find some meaning in this incredible story.

I decided to start my final journey at Franz Joseph Strasse, the last place Sophie lived with Hans. There is now a simple plaque in the street dedicated to them. I walked to the main building of Munich University. As I got closer towards the imposing building, I noticed the street sign said 'Geschwister-Scholl-Platz' (Scholl Sibling Square), and there were streets named after the other members of the White Rose nearby. There is a simple and dignified memorial outside the university. It displays copies of the leaflets embedded into the cobbled street.

I walked through the main entrance of Munich University, up a single flight of stairs. This was the famous Lichthof – so central to the end of the story. It is a quite eerie feeling standing on the marble ground floor of this huge entrance hall, with light shining down through the vast domed ceiling. I walked up the stone staircase and past the statues of two men in academic-looking robes.

As I got to the top of the first flight of stairs, I ambled along a corridor, walking past the large thick wooden doors of the lecture theatres. The Lichthof was completely empty and everything was quiet. I can now see why Hans and Sophie felt they could distribute the leaflets here and get away with it. I could have already scattered a briefcase full of leaflets.

I finally arrived on the third floor – just underneath a clock – and although the building was rebuilt following a bombing raid during the war, the atrium is the same as it was on 18 February 1943. I looked over the marble balustrade, standing in the exact place where Sophie threw a pile of leaflets over. I was in the place where it all happened. As I walked back down the stairs, I could hear in my head Schmid's bellowing voice echoing around the Lichthof – 'Stop! You're under arrest.'

There is a bust of Sophie Scholl by the sculptor Nicolai Tregor in a corridor, adjacent to the Lichthof. Nearby is the White Rose Museum, staffed by volunteers of the White Rose Foundation. The museum was opened in 1987 at the instigation of surviving members and close relatives of the White Rose resistance group. It is a non-party and non-profit-making association which aims to maintain 'the memory of the courageous members of the White Rose who stood up for human rights and moral courage'. It seeks to support research and publications about the White Rose and to cooperate with groups opposed to racism and all forms of intolerance.[3]

The museum tells the story of the resistance of the White Rose through photographs, quotations, and the stories and relics of all the individual members. There is the typewriter, the briefcase, diaries, letters, photographs and even personal clothing. It is a small, intimate, but welcoming and friendly place. Visitors come here from all over the world. I spoke briefly with one of the volunteer assistants, Horst Plôtski, who tells me. 'The basis of White Rose philosophy is freedom of the individual. They were visionaries. They showed what Germans should have done in Hitler's time.'[4]

My next destination was Ulm. The city is 90 miles north of Munich. My ultra-modern German ICE train was warm, fast and comfortable. Sophie made this journey many times. From my window – on a cold, but bright and sunny winter's day – I could see the Bavarian hills and even the Alps in the far distance. I was reminded of how important nature was to Sophie. The train made just one stop on the way: Augsburg. Sophie got off there in the dead of night – and risked her life – delivering White Rose leaflets.

As the train approached Ulm I could see the magnificent and unmistakably gothic Ulm Cathederal ('the Münster').[5] Ulm now has a population – when taking account of nearby 'New Ulm' – of 165,000. The beautiful Danube threads its way through the city. To get the best bird's eye view of the city, you have to climb the 768 steps of the Münster. My guide says the city motto is 'Tradition and risk.' The city is surrounded by countryside.

I first wanted to see Sophie's school: the Ulm Gymnasium. My taxi driver knew where it is. All the Scholl children went to this school. Back then, it was divided into separate schools for boys and girls, but now it's mixed. It was opened in 1897 and looks similar to many old English grammar schools. The name sign says 'The Hans and Sophie Scholl Gymnasium'.[6] When Sophie was here she was nicknamed *Buabamädle* (tomboy), because of her ability to climb the tallest trees and her short boyish haircut.[7]

Inside the school there is a small photographic exhibition dedicated to Hans and Sophie. It seems a very lively and diverse school, with 80 teachers and 932 students. The school motto is 'We stand up against injustice.' I noticed there is also a stress on free speech and student involvement in decision making. In the staff room I had a chat with two young teachers about the legacy of Sophie Scholl. Philipp Pielenz is a polite and charming English teacher, who takes time during his hectic lunch break to tell me:

Sophie and Hans Scholl are important to values of the school. The school is a UNESCO school: so pupils go on foreign exchange visits and they are encouraged to be tolerant of all people, be interested in environmental issues and to take an active role in the local community.

Christiane Weiger, a History tutor, takes a more jaundiced view of the Scholl legend:

A lot of tourists don't know about the Scholls. Sophie embodies a key image of the German resistance, but I feel Hans and Sophie were quite self-centred and they acted pretty recklessly in the Lichthof. I think the White Rose when compared to the other more political groups did not have a wider perspective.[8]

My next port of call was Münsterplatz, the ornate square where the Scholl family lived from the summer of 1939 onwards. In the square is a memorial to Hans and Sophie Scholl, designed by their friend Otl Aicher who married Inge Scholl in 1952 and became a designer of world renown. Unfortunately, the Scholl family apartment was destroyed by Allied bombs.[9] On the site where it stood is the Ulm Tourist Information Office. As I enter, Albert Einstein's photo is everywhere. He was born in Ulm on 14 March 1879. During the Nazi era, Einstein fled to exile in the US, and when Ulm city council wanted to award Einstein 'Freedom of the City' in 1949, he said no, because of 'the crimes committed against Jews by the Nazi regime'. But when Inge Scholl asked Einstein if she could name the adult education centre she co-founded with Otl Aicher in his honour he was happy to oblige. Additionally, Otl Aicher, Inge Scholl and Max Bill set up the prestigious College of Design. These projects were made possible by a 1 million-mark grant by the US Allied Authorities to the 'Scholl-Foundation', also set up by Inge Scholl in 1950. The centre Inge set up is called *Einstein-Haus* (Einstein House). It runs adult education classes and there is a photographic exhibition dedicated to the White Rose. The current manager Klaus Schlaier acts as a tour guide, teaches workshops and produces theatrical productions about the White Rose and other resistance activities against the Nazi regime.

I was led by Klaus into his office on the ground floor of the building overlooking a pleasant square. Klaus is friendly, self-deprecating, but very passionate about his work. The focus of our conversation was Sophie, Hans and the White Rose group:

I would say Sophie was a very quiet, reserved person, but with tremendous underlying courage, integrity and moral strength. A very spiritual Christian. She wanted to live a normal free life. She hated the restrictions upon individual freedom in Nazi society. She believed it was a moral duty to resist and she accepted the possible consequences. It was not in Sophie's nature to want to lead the discussions in the group, but she was a central figure in every respect. In history projects on the White Rose, most students opt to write about Sophie Scholl. She is the iconic figure.

I asked Klaus about the role of Hans Scholl:

> He is a much more complex and controversial figure. He was charismatic,
> intellectual, courageous, full of energy, bristling with ideas. He did not just
> want to discuss resistance, he wanted to take some action. This was a tre-
> mendous asset and often helped to drive the group on. But this was also why
> some of the parents of other leading White Rose figures thought Hans was
> sometimes not careful enough about their activities.

I inquired what Klaus believed they were fighting for.

> In the short term they wanted to encourage resistance against the Nazi
> regime through the distribution of the leaflets. Such a stance demanded
> great courage. For the future, they wanted a liberal idea of parliamentary
> democracy, which upheld basic rights: free speech, democratic elections,
> freedom of religion, free trade, toleration, a united Europe within Federal
> states. They were very international in outlook. They wanted a peaceful
> world, but they were also prepared to oppose tyranny and fight for human
> rights[10]

Klaus also helped my final journey in another very important way. He gave
me the contact details of the one surviving member of the immediate
Scholl family still alive: Elisabeth Hartnagel. My final destination was
Stuttgart, just 60 miles north of Ulm, where Sophie Scholl's 88-year-old
sister now lives.

I got into a taxi from Stuttgart's bustling central railway station at 2.00
p.m. the following day. The bright yellow private hire car sped up a steep
incline, through a long road tunnel, emerging in the suburbs, into the hills
overlooking the city. Elisabeth lived in a road of large terraced houses.[11]
I rang the bell and the door was opened by a slim, diminutive women,
who greeted me in a very quiet, comforting voice. The family resem-
blance, it has to be said, is quite startling. 'Come in' she said calmly, 'I live
upstairs. It's very cold on the ground floor and pretty expensive to keep
warm in the winter.'

Her late husband was Fritz Hartnagel, Sophie's romantic friend. After
Sophie's death, Elisabeth and Fritz grieved together. This soon blossomed
into love and then marriage. During my interview, I found Elisabeth good
humoured, pragmatic, unfailingly polite and rarely melancholic. She had a
remarkably clear memory.

What was Sophie like as a person? I asked Elisabeth:

She was quiet and shy, but with a very good sense of humour. She had a distinctive personality; she had her own opinions and was very independently minded. She was very religious, read the Bible regularly and prayed to God each night.

What about her relationship with Hans? 'They were very close and she admired him a great deal.' What about the years that followed? 'It was very difficult to cope with all the tragedies during the war.' She then paused for a moment. 'It's very sad. She was so young.'

I asked how she would sum up Sophie's legacy:

Sophie tried to show another way to the German people – that they still had a choice. Sophie represents what the German people should have done. Young people in Germany can identify with her. The great plus for all the family is that Sophie is now regarded as an inspiration to people.

We walked downstairs into the large front lounge. It contained a wall of bookcases. Elisabeth showed me two thick photo albums of the Scholl family. The photos were taken by her brother Werner – a talented photographer – who was killed in the war. I felt incredibly moved looking at these pictures of happy times, holidays, parties, smiling faces. These people looked like they lived life to the full. I then pointed out how many books there were in the house. 'Most of the books', Elisabeth said, 'belonged to Hans and Sophie'. As I stood in front of the bookcase, Elisabeth handed me a book of poetry. I opened the front cover: inside, written in pen were two words: 'Sophie Scholl'.[12]

As I said goodbye to Elisabeth I thanked her warmly. I then walked away down the street. The light was starting to fade. I turned left and entered the busy main road. I needed to find somewhere to sit down and gather my thoughts. There was a small café nearby and it was empty apart from the friendly proprietor. I found a table and here is what I wrote:

Sophie's inspirational and life-affirming story is not just another story about the past. It is a story of vital importance in the present and for the future. It is a story of bravery, of personal conscience and of freedom of opinion. It is really a story of today, about you and me. We must never forget she was just 21 years old when she was killed by the Nazis, but she possessed a life-affirming personality no dictatorship could ever silence. Sophie chose the path of resistance when she could have just as easily have led a quiet life. This makes Sophie's decision to oppose the Nazis all the more remarkable.

Sophie's life was not lived with any desire to achieve greatness. She conducted a constant inward dialogue with the mind and soul, which is remarkable in a person so young. She was not prepared to be silenced by a criminal regime or to betray her friends or her principles. Her death in defence of basic human rights and the freedom of the individual is a great moral victory that will stand for all time.

We should never forget also she was a *woman* fighting against the extreme values of male domination embedded in Nazi ideology. Adolf Hitler believed that a 'woman's place is in the home'. For a women in such a society to even think of going to university was an act of supreme defiance in itself. Sophie was also a full participant in the political and propaganda activities of the White Rose from beginning to end. She was determined to be the author of HER STORY and to make HER HISTORY. A woman of her time yes, but also a woman before her time.

Sophie Scholl faced her own death with supreme fearlessness and a deep faith in her moral, political and religious convictions. She showed that brutal dictatorships can only be averted through the courage and resistance of all citizens. She walked towards the guillotine calmly and with no trace of fear, believing that what she had done was the right thing to do. There have been many brave individuals in history. Sophie Scholl walks alongside the very bravest of them all. A white rose that will never die – with a profound message:

FREEDOM

Please pass Sophie's message on.

NOTES

Chapter One

1 J.Fest, *Hitler*, London, 1974, p.78.

2 The Versailles Treaty was signed on 28 June 1919.

3 For the impact of Versailles see: A.Adamthwaite, *The Lost Peace, 1918–1939: International Relations in Europe,* London, 1980; R.Henig, *Versailles and After,* London, 1980.

4 *Daily Mail,* 29 July 1923.

5 Robert Scholl's official title was *Stadtsschultheiss* – a lower level of mayor to a *Bürgermeister* – who was responsible for areas with a much larger population.

6 Elisabeth Hartnagel (née Scholl) said her father remained a 'pacifist' all his life. Interview with Elisabeth Hartnagel, Stuttgart, 15 February 2008.

7 H.Vinke, *The Short Life of Sophie Scholl,* New York, 1980, p.13.

8 Ibid., pp.14–15.

9 Interview with Elisabeth Hartnagel, 15 February 2008.

10 Vinke, *The Short Life of Sophie Scholl,* p.10.

11 I. Scholl, *The White Rose,* Munich 1942–1943, US, 1970, pp.5–6.

12 Vinke, *The Short Life of Sophie Scholl,* pp.27–28.

13 Interview with Elisabeth Hartnagel, 15 February 2008.

14 R.Hanser, *A Noble Treason: The Revolt of the Munich Students against Hitler,* New York, 1979, p.39.

15 I. Jens (ed.), *At the Heart of the White Rose: Letters and Diaries of Hans and Sophie Scholl,* New York, 1987, p.xii (hereafter *Letters and Diaries*).

16 Ibid., p.20.

17 Bundesarchiv Berlin, ZC13267, Sophie Scholl, first interrogation, 18 February 1943 (hereafter BA).

18 For details see: A.Ziegler, *Geschwister Scholl*, Schönaich, 2001. Robert Scholl's 'love affair' in Forchtenberg is one of many incidents that might suggest the Scholl family was 'dysfunctional'. There are indications in the family correspondence of tensions within the Scholl marriage at times, and between Inge Scholl and Hans, and especially between Sophie and Inge. Sophie often did not see eye to eye with her 'big sister'. Robert Scholl was opinionated. This sometimes caused tension in his work relationships and within his family. Sophie and Hans had bouts of melancholy and depression which feature in their diaries and letters. Hans had difficulty coming to terms with his sexuality and his intimate relationships. But I doubt these problems were any different from most families. To paint the Scholls as 'dysfunctional' – as some historians have – is absurd, far-fetched and defamatory. The Scholls were a talented and intelligent family of likeable and outgoing individuals. They were not robots, but people who were willing to be different in a society that demanded obedience. This is why they did not want to live in Hitler's Germany and why, ultimately, they died fighting against Nazism.

19 A. Hahn, *Ludwigsburg*, Ludwigsburg, 2004.

20 Vinke, *The Short Life of Sophie Scholl*, p.15.

21 For details see: *Anton Bruckner School: 100 Years 1907–2007*, Ludwigsburg, 2007.

22 BA-ZC13267, Sophie Scholl, first interrogation, 18 February 1943.

23 Hanser, *A Noble Treason*, p.36.

Chapter Two

1 German National Radio, 30 January 1933.

2 There is a very illuminating newspaper report of the reaction to Hitler coming to power in Cologne, a city that had not been enthusiastic about the Nazi Party at all. See: *Westdeutscher Beobachter*, 30–31 January, 1933.

3 Scholl, *The White Rose*, p.5.

4 *Unter den Linden* means Under the Lime Trees.

5 *Berliner Illustrierte Nachausgabe*, 31 January 1933.

6 R. Evans, *The Coming of the Third Reich*, London, 2004, p.312.

7 For details see: Ingo Müller, *Hitler's Justice: The Courts of the Third Reich*, Cambridge, MA, 1991. The special courts were originally set up – after the Reichstag fire – just to deal with communist opposition, but their scope grew extensively during the Nazi era to deal with all kinds of opposition. They usually dealt with cases below the level of 'high treason'. The 'People's Court' concentrated on the most serious cases.

8 A typical example of the essential illegality of much Nazi political law – taken from a real Gestapo case file from July 1940 – shows how the Nazis turned harmless actions into criminal offences. The case in question concerns a day out

with a group of friends in Cologne. A young man, accompanied by three of his wife's friends, went out for an afternoon of drinking on a pleasant summer's day. They wound up in a local park, laughing and joking, and pretty tipsy. One of the women suddenly lifted her leg and broke wind ferociously – at which point her girl friends raised their arms in unison, shouting loudly 'Heil Hitler' – then burst out laughing hysterically. Amazingly, the husband reported this incident to the Gestapo the next day, and all four women – including his own wife – were arrested, interrogated, then charged with the 'criminal' offence of 'slandering the Führer', which carried a prison sentence. What happened in this case was outrageous and shows that much Nazi so-called 'law' was simply legalised injustice. See Haupstaatsarchiv Düsseldorf, RW-58-65449 (hereafter HD).

9 The classic study is R. Gellately, *The Gestapo and German Society: Enforcing Racial Policy, 1933–1945*, Oxford, 1990.

10 Hanser, *A Noble Treason*, p.39.

11 It was closed down in 1936.

12 Details on membership in: M.Kater, *The Nazi Party: A Social Profile of its Members and Leaders, 1919–1945*, Oxford, 1983.

13 A good contemporary account of Schirach's view on the Hitler youth is: B. von Schirach, *Die Hitlerjugend, Idee und Gestalt*, Berlin, 1934. In the end, being promoted at such a young age proved too much for Schirach, who became a hopeless alcoholic, seemingly brought on by the stress of his job.

14 M. Domarus (ed.), *Hitler's Speeches and Proclamations 1932–1945: The Chronicle of a Dictatorship*, vol. 2, London, 1962–1963, p.701.

15 Ibid., p.138.

16 Scholl, *White Rose*, pp.5–6.

17 Interview with Elisabeth Hartnagel, Stuttgart, 15 February 2008.

18 Ibid.

19 Ibid.

20 Hanser, *A Noble Treason*, p.42.

21 Vinke, *The Short Life of Sophie Scholl*, p.39.

22 English title: 'The Hitler Youth called Quex'.

23 M. Fitzgerald, *Hitler: A Portrait*, Stroud, 2001, p.143.

24 Vinke, *The Short Life of Sophie Scholl*, p.39.

25 K. Behnken (ed.), *Deutschland-Berichte der Sozialdemokratischen Partei Deutschland*, Frankfurt, 1980, vol. 3, (1936), nos 1,322–1,323 (hereafter Sopade Reports).

26 The date of March 1933 was given by Hans Scholl to his Gestapo interrogators in Munich in 1943. See BA- ZC13267, Statement of Hans Scholl to Gestapo, 18 February 1943. But in the report of a chief prosecutor in the *Bündische* Youth trials of 1938, it is claimed Hans Scholl joined the Hitler Youth on 1 May 1933. See HD-292-295, Report of Chief Prosecuting Officer, Special Court, Stuttgart, dated 7 May 1938, Dusseldorf.

27 Scholl, *White Rose*, p.6. The strongest supporters in rank order were Inge, Hans,

Sophie, Elisabeth and Werner. In fact, Werner was always the least keen in the family on the Hitler Youth and he left the organisation before he was eighteen.

28 For details see: R. Bessel (ed.), *Life in the Third Reich*, London, 1987. For the impact on women see: U. Frevert, *Women in German History: From Bourgeois Emancipation to Sexual Liberation*, New York, 1989.

29 A. Dumbach and J. Newborn, *Sophie Scholl and the White Rose*, Oxford, 2006, p.27.

30 Hanser, *A Noble Treason*, p.45.

31 A *Gruppenführein* was the leader of a group of BDM squads.

32 BA-ZC13267, Sophie Scholl, first interrogation, 18 February 1943.

33 Vinke, *The Short Life of Sophie Scholl*, p.42.

34 *Kinderland ist abgebrannt*, Ventura Films, (1997). Written by Ute Badura. Directed by Sibylle Tiedemann.

35 Vinke, *The Short Life of Sophie Scholl*, p.42.

36 Interview with Anneliese Wallersteiner, *Kinderland ist abgebrannt*.

37 For details see: M. Kaplan, *Between Dignity and Despair*, New York, 1998.

38 For details see: M. Kater, *Hitler Youth*, Cambridge, MA, 2004.

39 See P. Stachura, *The German Youth Movement 1900–1945: An Interpretation and Documentary History*, London, 1981.

40 R. Evans, *The Third Reich in Power*, London, 2005, p.274.

41 HD-17-292-295 Gestapo interrogation of Ulm member of d.j.1.11, Stuttgart, 21 December 1937.

42 HD-17-292-295, Report of Chief Prosecuting Officer, Special Court, Stuttgart, dated 7 May 1938.

43 The *Kohte* tent is shaped like a wigwam.

44 Hanser, *A Noble Treason*, p.70.

45 Vinke, *The Short Life of Sophie Scholl*, pp.46–48.

46 HD-17-292-295, Hans Scholl, Gestapo interrogation, Stuttgart, 21 December 1937.

47 HD-17-292-295, interrogation in Ulm of a member of d.j.1.11, Stuttgart, 21 December 1937.

48 T. Axelrod, *Hans and Sophie Scholl*, Irvine, CA, 2000, pp.33–34.

49 Inge Scholl thought it was the 1936 rally. This date is repeated in Hanser, *A Noble Treason*, p.49 and Dumbach and Newborn, *Sophie Scholl and the White Rose*, p.31. But there are no footnotes in either book and no way of establishing what the source was for this particular date. In a recent examination, based on evidence from German archives, Eckard Holler puts the date as 1935. Most White Rose scholarship – based on archival research – would suggest that 1935 is correct. Based on the surviving evidence and on the chronology of preceding and subsequent events, it appears to be the most likely.

50 Vinke, *The Short Life of Sophie Scholl*, p.45.

51 S. Hirzel, *Vom Ja zum Nein: Eine schwäbische Jugend, 1933–1945*, Tübingen, 1998, pp.43–44.

52 Hanser, *A Noble Treason*, p.53.

Chapter Three

1 Evans, *The Third Reich in Power*, p.634.

2 Inge Scholl, *The White Rose*, pp.11–13

3 About £80,000 per year: today's values.

4 For details see: E. Ehrenreich, *The Nazi Ancestral Proof: Racial Science and the Final Solution*, Indiana, US, 2007.

5 The exception here was Inge Scholl, who remained pretty committed to the Nazi cause.

6 Interview with Elisabeth Hartnagel, Stuttgart, 15 February 2008.

7 Axelrod, *Hans and Sophie Scholl*, p.32.

8 After March 1938, all German males had to serve two years military service – after six months of labour service.

9 HD-292-295, Trial Transcript, Special Court, Stuttgart, 2 June 1938.

10 Interview with Archivist, Institut für Zeitgeschichte Munich (who wished to remain anonymous), 12 February 2008 (hereafter IfZ).

11 HD-292-295, Hans Scholl statement, 21 December 1937 (microfilm copy in IfZ).

12 HD-292-295, Trial Transcript, Special Court, Stuttgart, 2 June 1938 (microfilm copy in IfZ).

13 Hanser, *A Noble Treason*, p.68.

14 HD-292-295, Gestapo interrogation of Hans Scholl, Stuttgart, 22 November 1937 (microfilm copy in IfZ).

15 HD-292-295, Gestapo record of Hans Scholl statement, 21 December 1937, Stuttgart (microfilm copy in IfZ).

16 Dumbach and Newborn, *Sophie Scholl and the White Rose*, p.34.

17 Hanser, *A Noble Treason*, pp.53–56.

18 Interview with Elisabeth Hartnagel, 15 February 2008.

19 Hanser, *A Noble Treason*, pp.55–59.

20 HD-292-295, Hans Scholl Statement, 21 December 1937, Stuttgart (microfilm copy in IfZ).

21 Ibid.

22 Ibid.

23 BA- ZC13267, Hans Scholl, first interrogation, 18 February 1943.

24 This was known as the *Volksgemeinschaft*: the folk or people's community. It was a term used to stress that the Nazi regime wanted to create a classless society. In reality, it was a myth. The class system remained pretty much unchanged in the Nazi era.

25 *Letters and Diaries*, pp.1–2.

26 Hans visited the exhibition with his sister Inge.

27 F. Kaiser, *Führer durch die Ausstellung Entartete Kunst*, Berlin, 1937, pp.34–38.

28 For details see: S. Barron (ed.), *'Degenerate Art': The Fate of the Avant Garde in Nazi Germany*, Los Angeles, CA, 1991.

29 Hanser, *A Noble Treason*, pp.57–58.

30 Dumbach and Newborn, *Sophie Scholl and the White Rose*, p.77.

31 Ibid., p.38.

32 Hanser, *A Noble Treason*, p.48.

33 Vinke, *The Short Life of Sophie Scholl*, pp.30–31. The Nazi regime called Geyer a 'degenerate artist' and a 'cultural Bolshevist'. Many of his paintings were on biblical themes and he painted many stained-glass windows in churches and cathedrals.

34 Ibid., pp.75–78.

35 IfZ–Sophie Scholl to Fritz Hartnagel, 21 April 1938.

Chapter Four

1 The only people named directly in this chapter on the *bündische* trial are Hans Scholl – as he is the centrally important historical figure – and Ernst Reden, as he faced the most serious charges. Only one figure involved is still alive, and he is named here as 'Teenager X'. The other two boys are similarly not named.

2 For details see: N. Wachsmann, *Hitler's Prisons: Legal Terror in Nazi Germany*, London, 2004.

3 R. Evans, *The Third Reich in Power*, p.277.

4 Ibid., p.51.

5 In a speech to SS officers on 'The Question of Homosexuality' on 18 February 1937, Himmler estimated that 2 million Germans were homosexuals. There were no Nazi plans to 'exterminate' all homosexuals, as is often supposed.

6 Gay people were criminalised and stigmatised everywhere at this time – not just in Nazi Germany.

7 For details see R. Plant, *The Pink Triangle: The War against Homosexuals*, Edinburgh, 1987; B. Jelloenek, *Homosexualle under dem Hakenkreuez: Die Verfolgung von Homosexuellen in Dritten Reich*, Paderborn, 1990.

8 The same was true in the UK before homosexuality was legalised in 1967. A good portrayal of the double life led by gay people in the UK – even in the early 1960s – is found in the film *Victim*.

9 H. Oosterhuis, 'Medicine, Male-Bonding and Homosexuality in Nazi Germany' in *Journal of Contemporary History*, vol. 32, 1987, pp.187–205.

10 Waschsmann, *Hitler's Prisons*, pp.144–149.

11 Ibid.

12 G. Giles, 'The Institutionalization of Homosexual panic in the Third Reich' in R. Gellately and N. Stoltzfus (ed.), *Social Outsiders in Nazi Germany*, Princeton, NJ, 2001, pp.233–255.

13 Evans, *The Third Reich in Power*, p.280.

14 B. Jellonek, *Homosexuelle unter dem Hakenkreuz: Die Verfolgung von Homosexuellen in Dritten Reich*, Paderborn, 1990, pp.95–110.

15 Vinke, *The Short Life of Sophie Scholl*, p.51.

16 IfZ-Sophie Scholl to Fritz Hartnagel, 29 November 1937.

17 HD-292-295, Gestapo Investigation document, dated 22 November 1937.

18 HD-292-295, Gestapo file on Ernst Reden, 15 November 1937.

19 HD-292-295, Statement of 'Teenager X', 15 November 1937.

20 IfZ-Hans Scholl to his mother, 27 November 1937.

21 HD-292-295, Trial Transcript of Special Court, Stuttgart, 2 June 1938, dated 28 June 1938. See also HD-292-295, Arrest Report on Hans Scholl, 14 December 1937, Stuttgart.

22 IfZ-Hans Scholl to his parents, 18 December 1937.

23 IfZ-Captain Scrupin to Robert Scholl, 20 December 1937.

24 IfZ-Captain Scrupin to Robert Scholl, 30 December 1937.

25 IfZ-Hans Scholl to Inge Scholl, 18 January 1938.

26 IfZ-Hans Scholl to his parents, 3 March 1938.

27 BA-ZC13267, Sophie Scholl, first interrogation, 18 February 1943.

28 IfZ-Sophie Scholl to Fritz Hartnagel, 26 February 1938.

29 For details see D.C. Watt, *How War Came: The Immediate Origins of the Second World War*, London, 1989.

30 IfZ-Hans Scholl to his parents, 14 March 1938.

31 IfZ-Hans Scholl to his parents, 28 March 1938.

32 IfZ-Hans Scholl to his parents, 25 April 1938.

33 For details see: R. Mann, *Protest und Kontrolle im Dritten Reich*, Frankfurt, 1987; H. Koch, *In the Name of the Volk: Political Justice in Hitler's Germany*, 1989; I. Muller, *Hitler's Justice: The Courts of the Third Reich*, Cambridge, MA, 1991.

34 Ibid.

35 Staatsarchiv Ludwigsburg – EL 902/20 AZ 37/41499, File on Hermann Cuhorst (hereafter SL).

36 S. Baur. 'Hermann Albert Cuhorst' in M. Kissener and J. Scholtyseck (eds), *Leaders of the Province – NS biographies of Baden Württemburg*, Constance, Germany, 1999, pp.116–132. See also J. Stephenson, *Hitler's Home Front: Württemburg under the Nazis*, London, 2005.

37 See International Military Tribunal (hereafter IMT), vol. 3, for a full transcript of the proceedings of the 'Judges Trial'.

38 The Trial was officially called The US v Josef Altstötter et al. The chief prosecuting counsel was Telford Taylor.

39 The transcript of this investigation only survived because copies were sent to Düsseldorf.

40 IMT, vol. 3, p.1158.

41 SL-EL 902/20 AZ 37/41499, File on Hermann Cuhorst.

42 IfZ-Hans Scholl to Inge Scholl, 11 June 1938.

43 HD-292-295, Rep. 17. Bd. 1, Trial transcript of *Bundische* Trial, Stuttgart, dated

28 June 1938. This is a written file record of the proceedings of 2 June 1938 held in the Superior State Court in Stuttgart. There are microfilm copies in many other archives, mostly notably, IfZ in Munich and SL in Ludwigsburg. For the record, the most serious charges Hans Scholl faced were under 175a, and 176 of the German Criminal Code – the two other charges related to the currency smuggling incident mentioned in chapter 3 – and membership of a *bündische* youth group.

44 Ibid.

45 IfZ–Hans Scholl to Inge Scholl, 27 June 1938.

46 S. Hirzel. *Vom Ja Zum Nein*, p.85.

47 Vinke, *The Short Life of Sophie Scholl*, p.53.

48 BA-ZC13267, Sophie Scholl, first interrogation, 18 February 1943.

49 Interview with Elisabeth Hartnagel, Stuttgart, 15 February 2008.

Chapter Five

1 IfZ–Sophie Scholl to Inge Scholl, 8 July 1938.

2 Herr Kammerer owned a photographic shop in Ulm, but because he refused to stop serving Jews, he was denounced by local Nazis as a 'Jewish lackey'.

3 IfZ–Sophie Scholl to Fritz Hartnagel, 28 August 1938.

4 For details of the Czech crisis see: R.A.C. Parker, *Chamberlain and Appeasement: British Policy and the Coming of the Second World War,* London, 1993; K. Robbins, *Munich 1938*, London, 1968.

5 *The Times*, 28 September 1938.

6 IfZ–Hans Scholl to Inge Scholl, 21 October 1938.

7 Hanser, *A Noble Treason*, p.88.

8 For details see: M. Grüttner, *Studenten im Dritten Reich*, Paderborn, 1995; G. Giles, *Students and National Socialism in Germany*, Princeton, NJ, 1985; G. Weber, *The German Student Corps in the Third Reich*, London, 1986.

9 IfZ–Hans Scholl to his parents, 18 December 1938.

10 Hanser, *A Noble Treason*, p.88.

11 IfZ–Hans Scholl to his parents, 8 November 1938.

12 IfZ–Sophie Scholl to Fritz Hartnagel, 28 August 1938.

13 Vinke, *The Short Life of Sophie Scholl*, p.64.

14 Hanser, *A Noble Treason*, p.81.

15 Vinke, *The Short Life of Sophie Scholl*, p.64.

16 BA-ZC13267, Sophie Scholl, first interrogation, 18 February 1943.

17 Vinke, *The Short life of Sophie Scholl*, p.55.

18 Hirzel, *Vom Ja Zum Nein*, pp.89–90.

19 Hanser, *A Noble Treason*, p.83.

20 Vinke, *The Short Life of Sophie Scholl*, p.32.

21 IfZ–Sophie Scholl to Fritz Hartnagel, 8 July 1938.

22 See H. Graml, *Anti Semitism in the Third Reich*, Cambridge, MA, 1992; Evans, *The Third Reich in Power,* pp.580–610.

23 Hanser, *A Noble Treason*, p.85.

24 Vinke, *The Short Life of Sophie Scholl*, p.77.

25 My examination of the letters and diaries of the Scholls during this period reveals that they simply did not put their views on *Kristallnacht* on paper. They were often silent on many other key political events.

26 Sopade Reports, vol. 5, 1938, no 1, no 191.

27 Evans, *The Third Reich in Power*, p.400.

28 Fritz Hartnagel to Sophie Scholl, 1 February 1939. Quoted in T. Hartnagel (ed.), *Sophie Scholl/Fritz Hartnagel, Damit wir uns nicht verkeren Briefweschel, 1937–1943*, Frankfurt, 2006 (hereafter Fritz Hartnagel/Sophie Scholl Letters), p.74.

29 Fritz Hartnagel to Sophie Scholl, 15 March 1939, Fritz Hartnagel/Sophie Scholl Letters, p.79.

30 Fritz Hartnagel to Sophie Scholl, 27 March 1939, Fritz Hartnagel/Sophie Scholl Letters, pp.81–82.

31 Interview with Elisabeth Hartnagel, 15 February, 2008. Elisabeth said that Werner did not reveal he had done this at the time, but confessed to the family later. See also: O. Aicher, *innenseiten des kriegs*, Frankfurt, 1985, pp.10–12.

32 The apartment block was bombed towards the end of the war and on the site today is the Ulm Tourist Information Centre. In her book, *The White Rose*, Inge Scholl gives the impression the family always lived in Münsterplatz. This impression is repeated in many other published English language books, notably Richard Hanser's *A Noble Treason*, 1979. For the record, the previous tenants of the Münsterplatz apartment were Jewish and left Germany after *Kristallnacht*.

33 IfZ-Sophie Scholl to Fritz Hartnagel, 28 July 1939.

34 IfZ-Sophie Scholl to Inge Scholl, 9 August 1939.

35 IfZ-Sophie Scholl to Elisabeth Scholl, 19 August 1939.

36 The Student Medical Units manned the Army Field Hospitals and did not undertake active combat.

37 IfZ-Sophie Scholl to Fritz Hartnagel, August 1939.

38 Fritz Hartnagel to Sophie Scholl, 3 September 1939, Fritz Hartnagel/Sophie Scholl Letters, p.101.

39 J. Toland, *Adolf Hitler*, New York, 1976, p.821.

40 W. Shirer, *Berlin Diary*, London, 1942, pp.158–160.

41 Fritz Hartnagel to Sophie Scholl, 3 September 1939, Fritz Hartnagel/Sophie Scholl Letters, p.101.

42 IfZ-Sophie Scholl to Fritz Hartnagel, 5 September 1939.

Chapter Six

1 IfZ-Sophie Scholl to Fritz Hartnagel, 19 September 1939.

2 IfZ-Hans Scholl Diary, 20 September 1939.

3 For details see: E. Turner, *The Phoney War on the Home Front*, London, 1961.

4 Joyce was born in the USA but lived in Ireland before moving to Germany. He was hanged for treason by the British at the end of the Second World War.

5 IfZ-Sophie Scholl to Fritz Hartnagel, 5 October 1939.

6 IfZ-Sophie Scholl to Fritz Hartnagel, 7 November 1939.

7 Ibid.

8 Fritz Hartnagel to Sophie Scholl, 20 December 1939, Fritz Hartnagel/Sophie Scholl Letters, pp.127–128.

9 IfZ-Sophie Scholl to Fritz Hartnagel, 12 January 1940.

10 The *Abitur* was the equivalent of UK 'A Levels' or the US High School Graduation Certificate. A pass entitled a student to university entrance.

11 IfZ-Sophie Scholl to Fritz Hartnagel, 12 January 1940.

12 IfZ-Sophie Scholl to Elisabeth Scholl, 8 March 1940.

13 IfZ-Sophie Scholl to Fritz Hartnagel, 3 April 1940.

14 IfZ-Sophie Scholl to Fritz Hartnagel, 9 April 1940.

15 IfZ-Sophie Scholl to Fritz Hartnagel, April 1940 (no exact date on letter).

16 Dumbach and Newborn, *Sophie Scholl and the White Rose*, pp.45–46.

17 R.A.C. Parker, *Struggle for Survival: The History of Second World War*, Oxford, 1989, p.45.

18 IfZ-Sophie Scholl to Fritz Hartnagel, 16 May 1940.

19 Fritz Hartnagel to Sophie Scholl, 16 May 1940, Fritz Hartnagel/Sophie Scholl Letters, p.165.

20 IfZ-Sophie Scholl to Fritz Hartnagel, 29 May 1940.

21 J. Toland, *Hitler,* London, 1976, p.836.

22 IfZ-Sophie Scholl to Fritz Hartnagel, 14 June 1940.

23 Hans Scholl served in a hospital in Paris in the summer of 1940.

24 R. Evans, *The Third Reich at War, 1939–1945*, London, 2008, p.133.

25 Fritz Hartnagel to Sophie Scholl, 26 June 1940, pp.187–188.

26 IfZ-Sophie Scholl to Fritz Hartnagel, 28 June 1940.

27 IfZ-Sophie Scholl to Fritz Hartnagel, 19 August 1940.

28 Vinke, *The Short Life of Sophie Scholl*, p.78.

29 IfZ-Susanne Hirzel to Inge Scholl, 27 August 1979.

30 IfZ-Sophie Scholl to Hans Scholl, 21 July 1940.

31 IfZ-Sophie Scholl to Fritz Hartnagel, 17 June 1940.

32 IfZ-Sophie Scholl to Fritz Hartnagel, 8 July 1940.

33 IfZ-Sophie Scholl to Fritz Hartnagel, 1 August 1940.

34 Axelrod, *Hans and Sophie Scholl,* p.33.

35 IfZ-Sophie Scholl to her parents, 12 August 1940.

36 IfZ-Sophie Scholl to Inge Scholl, 22 August 1940.

37 IfZ-Sophie Scholl to Fritz Hartnagel, 11 August 1940.

38 IfZ-Sophie Scholl to Fritz Hartnagel, 19 August 1940.

39 IfZ-Sophie Scholl to Inge Scholl, 22 August 1940.

40 IfZ-Sophie Scholl to Fritz Hartnagel, 15 August 1940.

41 IfZ-Sophie Scholl to Inge Scholl, 22 August 1940.

42 Fritz Hartnagel to Sophie Scholl, 21 August 1940, Fritz Hartnagel/Sophie Scholl Letters, pp.206–207.

43 IfZ-Sophie Scholl to Fritz Hartnagel, 3 September 1940.

44 IfZ-Sophie Scholl to Fritz Hartnagel, 12 September 1940.

45 IfZ-Susanne Hirzel to Inge Scholl, 27 August 1979.

46 For example, see: IfZ-Sophie Scholl to Fritz Hartnagel, 7 November 1940.

47 The exception is Robert Scholl, who was a Christian but less devout than his wife and children.

48 IfZ-Sophie Scholl to Fritz Hartnagel, 23 September 1940.

49 Vinke, *The Short Life of Sophie Scholl*, pp. 77–78.

50 Fritz Hartnagel to Sophie Scholl, 4 July 1940, Fritz Hartnagel/Sophie Scholl Letters, pp.190–191.

51 IfZ-Sophie Scholl to Fritz Hartnagel, 4 November 1940.

52 IfZ-Sophie Scholl to Fritz Hartnagel, 10 November 1940.

53 IfZ-Sophie Scholl to Fritz Hartnagel, 12 November 1940.

54 IfZ-Sophie Scholl to Fritz Hartnagel, 23 November 1940.

55 This comment was not really true. Sophie was always urging Fritz to write more often.

56 IfZ-Sophie Scholl to Fritz Hartnagel, 11 December 1940.

57 For details of specific battles and campaigns in the Second World War see: J. Keegan, *The Second World War*, London, 1989.

58 IfZ-Sophie Scholl Diary, 13 January 1941.

59 Hanser, *A Noble Treason*, p.103. See also: Dumbach and Newborn, *Sophie Scholl and the White Rose*, p.45.

60 IfZ-Sophie Scholl to Lisa Remppis, 13 April 1941.

61 IfZ-Sophie Scholl to Fritz Hartnagel, 21 February 1941.

62 IfZ-Sophie Scholl to Fritz Hartnagel, 28 February 1941.

63 Sophie wanted to become a full-time kindergarten teacher after she gained her degree.

64 IfZ-Sophie Scholl to Fritz Hartnagel, 22 March 1941.

Chapter Seven

1 For a brilliant, moving and masterly analysis see: Evans, *The Third Reich at War*, pp.217–318.

2 IfZ-Sophie Scholl to Elisabeth Scholl, 10 April 1941.

3 Vinke, *The Short Life of Sophie Scholl*, p.85.

4 IfZ-Sophie Scholl to Inge Scholl, 10 April 1941.

5 Fritz Hartnagel to Sophie Scholl, April 1941 (no date mentioned), Fritz Hartnagel/Sophie Scholl Letters, pp.296–297. Fritz also mentions in this letter that he is avidly reading *The Confessions of St Augustine*, but was still unclear about what conclusions to draw from his reading.

6. IfZ-Sophie Scholl to Inge Scholl, 10 April 1941.

7 IfZ-Sophie Scholl to Fritz Hartnagel, 10 April 1941.

8 IfZ-Sophie Scholl to Lisa Remppis, 13 April 1941.

9 Ibid.

10 Hanser, *A Noble Treason*, p.106.

11 IfZ-Sophie Scholl to Lisa Remppis, 13 April 1941.

12 IfZ-Sophie Scholl Diary, 14 April 1941.

13 IfZ-Sophie Scholl to Fritz Hartnagel, 20 April 1941.

14 IfZ-Sophie Scholl to her parents, 25 April 1941.

15 IfZ-Sophie Scholl to Lisa Remppis, 27 April 1941.

16 IfZ-Sophie Scholl Diary, 1 May 1941.

17 Fritz had obviously forgotten that Sophie had been a BDM member for many years and so wearing a uniform was not that unusual.

18 Fritz Hartnagel to Sophie Scholl, May 1941, Fritz Hartnagel/Sophie Scholl Letters, pp.306–307. It has recently been revealed by Thomas Hartnagel – in the edited edition of the Fritz/Sophie letters – that Fritz had a brief affair with a Yugoslavian woman during this period, because he felt that Sophie was pushing him away at this time.

19 IfZ-Sophie Scholl to Lisa Remppis, 5 June 1941.

20 Vinke, *The Short Life of Sophie Scholl*, p.90.

21 IfZ-Sophie Scholl to Hans Scholl, 23 June 1941.

22 IfZ-Sophie Scholl to Lisa Remppis, 11 August 1941.

23 Fritz Hartnagel to Sophie Scholl, June 1941, Fritz Hartnagel/Sophie Scholl Letters, pp.311–312.

24 IfZ-Sophie Scholl to Hans Scholl, 2 August 1941.

25 IfZ-Sophie Scholl to Lisa Remppis, 11 August 1941.

26 IfZ-Sophie Scholl to Hans Scholl, 16 August 1941.

27 IfZ-Sophie Scholl to Werner Scholl, 27 August 1941.

28 IfZ-Sophie Scholl to Lisa Remppis, 23 August 1941.

29 Hanser, *A Noble Treason*, pp.111–113.

30 Ibid., pp.133–135. Theodor Haecker (1879–1945) was a major German writer, translator and cultural critic. He translated works of the Protestant philosopher and theologian Søren Kierkegaard (1813–55) and of the English Catholic divine John Henry, Cardinal Newman (1801–90) into German. Having translated Newman's famous *Grammar of Assent*, Haecker converted to Roman Catholicism in April 1921. He is known for his consistent opposition to the Nazi regime, which took steps to silence him. Haecker's

theological influence on the White Rose was crucial, as German scholar and
Catholic theologian Jakob Knab has revealed in a comprehensive chapter on
the religious influences on Sophie Scholl. For details see: J. Knab, '"So ein
herrlicher sonniger Tag, und ich soll gehen": Sophie Scholl: Suche nach Sinn
und Bekenntnis zum Widerstand' in D. Bald (ed.), *Wider die Kriegsmaschinerie:
Kriegserfahrungen und Motive des Widerstandes der 'Weissen Rose'*, Essen, 2005,
pp.130–143 (hereafter Knab, *Sophie Scholl*).

31 Galen became known by opponents of Hitler as 'The Lion of Münster'.

32 I. Scholl, *The White Rose*, p.20.

33 Evans, *The Third Reich at War*, p.98.

34 Ibid., p.99.

35 For details see: F. McDonough, with J. Cochrane, *The Holocaust*, Basingstoke, 2008.

36 Hanser, *A Noble Treason*, p.138.

37 Vinke, *The Short Life of Sophie Scholl*, pp.93–94.

38 Ibid., p.96.

39 IfZ-Sophie Scholl Diary, Autumn 1941.

40 IfZ-Sophie Scholl Diary, 1 November 1941.

41 Ibid.

42 IfZ-Sophie Scholl to Professor Carl Muth, November 1941.

43 IfZ-Sophie Sholl Diary, 4 November 1941.

44 IfZ-Sophie Scholl Diary, 10 November 1941.

45 Vinke, *The Short Life of Sophie Scholl*, pp.93–94. Jakob Knab's detailed research on
the religious influences on Sophie Scholl has revealed many passages from her
letters in which she makes statements that show movement towards a conversion
to the Catholic faith. He dates the religious turning point in Sophie's life around
Good Friday 1941, because on 11 April 1941 she wrote in her diary about her
epiphany: 'This evening, as I glanced quickly out of the window of our cheerful,
bustling room, I saw the yellow skyline through the bare trees. It suddenly struck
me then that it was Good Friday. I was saddened by the strangely remote and
detached sky and by all the laughing people who were so divorced from the
sky.' ('*Himmel*' in German is ambiguous: either sky or heaven. So it is about all
the laughing people on Good Friday who are so divorced from heaven). *At
the Heart of the White Rose: Letters and Diaries of Hans and Sophie Scholl*, ed. Inge
Jens, New York, 1987, p.130; see also Knab, *Sophie Scholl*, pp.130–143. It is worth
adding that Sophie's sister Inge converted to Catholicism after Sophie's death.
She was baptised on 22 February 1944, exactly two years after Hans and Sophie
had been beheaded. Her spiritual guide had been Theodor Haecker. This makes
Knab's intriguing interpretation of where Sophie's search for the meaning of life
was leading one that commands attention.

46 IfZ-Sophie Scholl to Lisa Remppis, 10 October 1942.

47 IfZ-Sophie Scholl to Fritz Hartnagel, 18 November 1942.

48 Fritz Hartnagel to Sophie Scholl, June 1941 (no date recorded), Fritz
Hartnagel/Sophie Scholl Letters, pp.307–308. Fritz often admitted that Sophie's

method of intense concentrated reading made her more able to grasp some of the more complex religious and philosophical works they both read, as he could only read in short bursts, due to his responsibilities on military duty.

49 IfZ–Sophie Scholl to Otl Aicher, 10 December 1941.

50 IfZ–Sophie Scholl to Hans Scholl, 20 November 1941.

51 HD-11-1161, no 102, Justice Ministry Circular, 28 October, 1941.

52 O. Aicher, *Innenseiten des Kriegs*, Frankfurt, 1985, pp.62–70.

53 IfZ–Sophie Scholl Diary, 12 December 1941.

54 Vinke, *The Short Life of Sophie Scholl*, p.94.

55 Aicher, *innenstein des Kriegs*, p.140.

56 The tradition in Germany was/is to open presents on Christmas Eve.

57 IfZ–Sophie Scholl to Elisabeth Scholl, 6 January 1941.

58 Traute Lafrenz-Page to author, 9 November 2008 (hereafter Lafrenz Recollections).

59 IfZ–Sophie Scholl to Otl Aicher, undated, but probably January 1942, as it mentions the recent Coburg skiing trip.

60 IfZ–Hans Scholl to Elisabeth Scholl, 6 January 1942.

61 IfZ–Sophie Scholl to Lisa Remppis, 14 January 1942.

62 IfZ–Sophie Scholl Diary, 12 February 1942.

63 Hanser, *A Noble Treason*, p.197.

64 IfZ–Sophie Scholl to Lisa Remppis, (end) March 1942.

65 IfZ–Sophie Scholl to Lisa Remppis, 5 April 1942.

66 Quoted in Vinke, *The Short Life of Sophie Scholl*, p.97.

Chapter Eight

1 The exact date is very difficult to determine. Inge Scholl - not very reliable with dates at the best of times - thought Sophie left for Munich University on 9 May 1942, but other evidence from eyewitness accounts, university term dates and memoirs suggests this is incorrect. The available evidence would place the date on or near and most probably, 1 May 1942.

2 By 1942, domestic consumption in Germany was 25 per cent of the pre-1939 level and rationing was now a fact of life.

3 Now Traute Lafrenz-Page.

4 Evans, *The Coming of the Third Reich*, pp.176–194.

5 *White Rose Stiftung*, guide to White Rose, p.15.

6 For details see: M. Schreiber, *Walter Wüst: Dean and Rector of the University of Munich 1935–1945*, Munich, 2008.

7 For details see: M. Gruttner, *Studenten in Dritten Reich*, Paderborn, 1995.

8 R. Evans, *The Third Reich in Power*, pp.291-320.

9 Hanser, *A Noble Treason*, pp. 50–52.

10 Interview with Elisabeth Hartnagel, 15 February 2008.

11 IfZ-Sophie Scholl to parents, 6 June 1942.

12 Vinke, *The Short Life of Sophie Scholl*, p.101.

13 Lafrenz recollections.

14 Chistoph Probst mentions such a gathering in his Gestapo interrogations. See
   BA-ZC13267, Christoph Probst interrogation, 20 February 1943. There is no
   doubt Sophie met Alex, Christoph and most of Hans' other acquaintances
   in the first month and Willi Graf some time in June 1942, when he became
   friendly with the small circle of friends.

15 Axelrod, *Hans and Sophie Scholl*, p.52.

16 Ibid., p.46.

17 Interview with Elisabeth Hartnagel, 15 February 2008.

18 *White Rose Stiftung*, guide, p.31.

19 Vinke, *The Short Life of Sophie Scholl*, p.102.

20 Hanser, *A Noble Treason*, pp. 182–183.

21 Lafrenz-Page Recollections.

22 BA-NJ1704, Letter from Dr Kurt Port, in Kurt Huber's clemency petition, 4
   May 1943.

23 Ibid.

24 *White Rose Stitfung*, guide, p.25.

25 Axelrod, *Hans and Sophie Scholl*, p.60.

Chapter Nine

1 Lafrenz Recollections.

2 L. Furst-Ramdohr,*Freundschaften in der Weisse Rose*, Munich, 1995, pp.38–44.

3 BA-ZC13267, Sophie Scholl, second interrogation, 18–19 February 1943.

4 Axelrod, *Hans and Sophie Scholl*, pp.62–63.

5 *White Rose Stiftung*, guide, p.19.

6 Lafrenz Recollections.

7 Vinke,*The Short Life of Sophie Scholl*, p.108.

8 BA-NJ1704, Alexander Schmorell, interrogation, 26 February 1943.

9 Axelrod, *Hans and Sophie Scholl*, p.50.

10 Traven also wrote *The Treasure of the Sierra Madre*, which became a successful
   Hollywood film in the 1950s. He never revealed his identity and his real name
   has never been fully established. He could have been American or German.
   Some names have been advanced, such as Otto Fiege, Hermann Wienecke
   and most convincingly Hal Croves – his supposed literary agent – as his wife
   was shown to have owned the copyright in the works. It seems Crove's real
   identity was Traven Torsvan and he had lived in Germany before emigration
   to the USA via Mexico. See B.Traven, *Life and Work*, Penn State, 1987.

11 BA-ZC13267, Hans Scholl, third interrogation, 20 February 1943.

12 Ibid.

13 White Rose leaflet no 1. The most important aspect of Jakob Knab's research on the theological influences on Sophie Scholl is his view that both she and Fritz were increasingly drawing inspiration from the writings of Cardinal Newman in this crucial period. When Sophie met Fritz for the last time on 20 May 1942 she gave him a farewell present of, among other things, two volumes of sermons by Newman. In a letter from Fritz on 26 June 1942 he told Sophie that after reading these he too had discovered what he called the 'wonderful world' of John Henry Newman. Fritz said he had absorbed every line like 'drops of precious wine'. In a further letter at the beginning of July 1942 Fritz wrote that, after reading Newman while witnessing the anti-Jewish atrocities and views of many Wehrmacht officers, he could see more clearly that 'we stand in a relationship of moral obligation to our Creator. Conscience gives us the capacity to distinguish between Good and Evil.' Knab has found out, through detailed research, that it was during this period that Fritz read Newman's sermon *The Testimony of Conscience*. Here, Newman – using a passage from the Second Letter of St Paul to the Corinthians as his starting point – develops the central theme of his doctrine about conscience: 'We are by nature what we are: full of sin and corruption ... Man is capable of both good and evil ... If doing good be evidence of faith, then doing evil must be even more convincing proof that he lacks faith.' Fritz concluded his letter to Sophie with the precept: 'We must submit our reason to these mysteries and acknowledge our faith.' It seems that Sophie had been greatly inspired by these passages too, and they also offered Fritz a graphic illustration of what he found disturbing about the behaviour of the Wehrmacht in the Soviet Union, which led him to denounce the anti-Semitic doctrines that underpinned the Holocaust. After Fritz had seen the corpses of Soviet prisoners of war who had collapsed from exhaustion and had been shot by their German guards, and had heard of mass executions among the Jewish population, he wrote to Sophie: 'It's frightening, the cynical insensitivity with which my commanding officer describes the slaughter of all those Jews in occupied Russia, and the way he is totally convinced of the rightness of his course of action. I sat there, my heart pounding. How relieved I was to be back on my own, lying on my camp bed, where I could take refuge in prayer, and in thoughts of you.'

14 BA-ZC13267, Second Report on the White Rose Leaflets, Professor Harder, 18 February 1943.

15 Vinke, *The Short Life of Sophie Scholl*, p.119.

16 BA-ZC13267 Sophie Scholl, third interrogation, 20 February 1943.

17 Ibid.

18 Lafrenz Recollections.

19 Vinke, *The Short Life of Sophie Scholl*, p118.

20 Interview with Elisabeth Hartnagel, 15 February 2008.

21 Hanser, *A Noble Treason*, p.186.

22 White Rose leaflet no 2.

23 Hanser, *A Noble Treason*, pp.177–178.

24 White Rose leaflet no 3.

25 White Rose leaflet no 4.

26 BA-ZC13267, Sophie Scholl, third interrogation, 20 February 1942.

27 BA-ZC-13267, Hans Scholl, third interrogation, 20 February 1942.

28 BA-NJ1074, Kurt Huber interrogations, 27 February 1943, 8 and 19 March 1943.

29 Ibid.

30 BA-ZC13267, Katharina Schüddekopf interrogation, 24 March 1943.

31 BA-ZC14116, Hans Hirzel interrogation, 22 February 1943. The event is discussed in most books on the White Rose. See, for example: Dumbach and Newborn, pp.95–97.

32 IfZ-Sophie Scholl to Lisa Remppis, 27 July 1942.

33 E. Johnson, *The Nazi Terror: The Gestapo, Jews and Ordinary Germans*, London, 1999, pp.333–334.

34 Ibid. p.342.

35 IfZ-Trial and Verdict of Robert Scholl, August 1942. The trial transcript is also available in Staatsarchive Ludwigsburg- E3569. The proceedings also reveal that Robert Scholl was a member of three Nazi Associations: the Nazi Bar Association, Nazi Civil Defence League (German version of 'Dad's Army') and the Nazi Children's Welfare Service. It made sense for a local businessman to be seen as a 'national comrade', and to join these professional associations.

36 Vinke, *The Short Life of Sophie Scholl*, p.123.

37 Hanser, *A Noble Treason*. p.205.

38 IfZ-Sophie Scholl Diary, 10 October 1942.

39 Ibid., 9 August 1942.

40 Ibid.

41 IfZ-Sophie Scholl to Fritz Hartnagel, August 1942.

42 IfZ-Sophie Scholl to Lisa Remppis, 2 September 1942.

43 IfZ-Sophie Scholl to Otl Aicher, 5 September 1942.

44 BA-ZC14116, Hans Hirzel interrogations, 27 February 1943 and 3 March 1943.

45 IfZ-Sophie Scholl to Robert Scholl, 7 September 1942.

46 IfZ-Sophie Scholl to Robert Scholl, 22 September 1942.

47 IfZ-Sophie Scholl to Lisa Remppis, 10 October 1942.

48 Lafrenz Recollections.

49 Axelrod, *Hans and Sophie Scholl*, p.72.

50 IfZ-Sophie Scholl to Fritz Hartnagel, 7 November 1942. Munich University changed from a three-term system back to two-term format for the 1942–43 academic year, so the start date was pushed forward for the winter term to the first week in December.

Chapter Ten

1 The landlady was called Mrs Schmidt.

2 Schertling started a degree in Art.

3 BA-ZC13267 Sophie Scholl, first interrogation, 18 February 1943.

4 IfZ-Hans Scholl to Rose Nägele, 5 January 1943.

5 Mildred Harnack was the only US citizen executed in a German 'Special' or 'People's Court' by the Nazi regime.

6 This was in what used to be called the Sudeten German region of Czechoslovakia, but was now part of what was called in wartime 'The Greater German Reich'.

7 The Operation was called 'Valkyrie' and when it failed all of the leading conspirators were killed or executed.

8 BA-NJ1704, Willi Graf interrogation, 1 March 1943.

9 BA-NJ1704, Kurt Huber interrogation, 10 March 1943.

10 Hanser, *A Noble Treason*, pp. 216–217.

11 Fritz Hartnagel to Sophie Scholl, 18 October 1942 and 20 October 1942, Fritz Hartnagel/Sophie Scholl Letters, pp. 416–419.

12 IfZ-Sophie Scholl to Fritz Hartnagel, 30 December 1942.

13 IfZ-Sophie Scholl to Fritz Hartnagel, 1 January 1943.

14 IfZ-Sophie Scholl to Fritz Hartnagel, 3 January 1943.

15 IfZ-Hans Scholl to Rose Nägele, 5 January 1943.

16 IfZ-Hans Scholl to Otl Aicher, 12 January 1943.

17 IfZ-Sophie Scholl Diary, 13 January 1943.

18 Vinke, *The Short Life of Sophie Scholl*, p.142.

19 IfZ-Sophie Scholl to Otl Aicher, 19 January 1943.

20 BA-NJ1074, Kurt Huber interrogations, 27 February 1943 and 3 March 1943.

21 White Rose leaflet, No 5.

22 BA-ZC13267, Sophie Scholl, second interrogation, 19 February 1943.

23 In the Nazi Party it was much better to have a low membership number as this indicated membership in the very early years of the movement. Even so, a great many people who joined after 1933 still rose to very high positions, especially in the security forces.

24 IfZ-Robert Mohr memorandum, prepared for Robert Scholl, dated 19 February 1951 (hereafter Mohr Memorandum).

25 Ibid.

26 BA-ZC13267 Sophie Scholl, third interrogation, 20 February 1943.

27 BA-ZC13267 Hans Scholl, third interrogation, 20 February 1943.

28 Dunbach and Newborn, *Sophie Scholl and White Rose*, p.141.

29 BA- NJ1704, Kurt Huber interrogation, 2 March 1943.

30 IfZ-Sophie Scholl to Fritz Hartnagel, 7 February 1943.

31 BA-NJ1704, Alexander Schmorell interrogation, 25 February 1943.

32 The disagreement was discussed in the interrogations of Alexander Schmorell, Kurt Huber and Willi Graf.

33 For full accounts of the two meeting on 8–9 February see the
   interrogations of Harnack, Graf and Schmorell. See in particular,
   BA-NJ1704: Falk Harnack interrogations, 10 March 1943 and 11 March
   1943; Alexander Schmorell interrogation, 11 March 1943; Willi Graf
   interrogation, 1 March 1943.
34 IfZ-Sophie Scholl to Fritz Hartnagel, 10 February 1943.
35 IfZ-Sophie Scholl to Fritz Hartnagel, 13 February 1943.
36 IfZ-Sophie Scholl Diary, 13 February 1943.
37 BA-NJ1704 Alexander Schmorell interrogation, 30 March 1943.
38 BA-NJ1704 Kurt Huber's clemency petition written by A. Deppish, 21 March 1943.
39 Hanser, *A Noble Treason*, p. 247.
40 White Rose leaflet no 7 (hand-written draft by Christoph Probst).
41 BA-NJ1704 Willi Graf interrogation, 21 February 1943.
42 IfZ-Sophie Scholl to Fritz Hartnagel, 16 February 1943.
43 IfZ-Hans Scholl to Rose Nägele, 16 February 1943.
44 Staatsarchiv Munich, 12/530, Wilhelm Geyer interrogation, 24 February 1943.
45 IfZ-Josef Söhngen, 'Post War Memoir', pp.6–9.
46 Aicher, *Innenseiten des Kriegs*, Frankfurt, 1985, p.153.
47 BA-ZC14116, Hans Hirzel interrogation, 17 February 1943.
48 BA-ZC13267, Gisela Schertling interrogation, 1 April 1943.
49 A record player in 1943 was known in 1943 as a phonograph or gramophone.
50 IfZ-Sophie Scholl to Lisa Remppis, 17 February 1943.

Chapter Eleven

 1 BA-ZC13267, Sophie Scholl, first interrogation, 18 February 1943.
 2 Furst Ramdohr, *Freundshaften*, pp.120–122.
 3 Lafrenz Recollections.
 4 BA-ZC13267 Sophie Scholl, first interrogation, 18 February 1943 ('I entered
   the building at 10.50 a.m.' – Sophie Scholl).
 5 IfZ-Traute Lafrenz to Inge Scholl, 21 February 1946.
 6 In English 'Lichthof' would translate to 'Atrium'.
 7 BA-ZC13267, Jakob Schmid interrogation, 18 February 1943.
 8 Mohr Memorandum.
 9 Hanser, *A Noble Treason*, p.255.
10 Vinke, *The Short Life of Sophie Scholl*, p.160.
11 BA-ZC13267, Gestapo Arrest Report, 18 February 1943.
12 For details see: R. Garnett. *Lion, Eagle and Swastika: Bavarian Monarchism in
   Weimar Germany 1918–1933*, New York, 1991.
13 After Gisela Schertling was released from inside the locked university building,
   she went to Franz Joseph Strasse in the hope of finding Alex there. She

was met by Gestapo officers who arrested her. By this time, Otl Aicher had already been to the Scholl residence and was promptly arrested. 'I got a phone call from Ulm', recalls Aicher, 'I was told to inform Hans that the book *Power, State and Utopia* was out of print. I called Hans and said I had an important message for him. He made a date for the next morning. When I got there at eleven, I found the apartment locked. Half an hour later I returned and was received by the Gestapo. I was searched and for about an hour I witnessed the Gestapo seal the apartment. They took me and everybody they found relevant to Wittelsbach Palace.' The initial search of the Gestapo had turned up a portable typewriter in Sophie's room and a list of addresses for people living in Augsburg and Munich districts and it was concluded these addresses were a mailing list for the leaflet distribution. In the house, they also discovered a large quantity of bullets. Shortly after Aicher was taken away, more Gestapo officers went to the Scholl's apartment and conducted a more thorough second search.

Chapter Twelve

1 Evans, *The Third Reich at War*, pp.422–426.

2 Wachsmann, *Hitler's Prisons*, pp.118–125.

3 Fred Breinsdorfer, interview with Richard Phillips, 17 August 2006.

4 For example see: A. Gill, *An Honourable Defeat: A History of German Resistance to Hitler*, London, 1994, pp.191–194.

5 For details of how a 'special friend' was used during the 'Red Orchestra' interrogations see: S. Brysac, *Resisting Hitler: Mildred Harnack and the Red Orchestra*, Oxford, 2000, p.338. The tactic was also mentioned in many subsequent post-war Gestapo trials.

6 IfZ-Else Gebel to Inge Scholl, November 1946 (hereafter Gebel Memorandum). This is Gebel's account of Sophie's days in prison between February 18–22, 1943. See also: Inge Scholl, *The White Rose*, pp. 138–147.

7 Anton Mahler, who conducted Hans Scholl's harrowing four-day interrogation was later de-Nazified by the US authorities and given a job with the CIA. As Falk Harnack put it: 'The Americans employed all those National Socialist criminals in the CIA. They all worked for the CIA and defamed us (the resistance) after the war … A disgrace for the United States that it co-operated with these people, mass murderers. And the people who knew the truth, they were left on the outside' (See Brysac, *Mildred Harnack*, p.387).

8 G. Fieburg (ed.), *Namen des deutschen Volkes: Justiz und Nationalsozialismus: Katalog zur Ausstellung des Bundesministers der Justiz*, Cologne, 1989, pp.160–161.

9 They were known as *Verschärfte Vernehmung*. See: A. Sullivan, 'Vershärfte Vernehmung', *Atlantic Magazine*, 29 May 2007.

10 For details see: J. Delarue. *The Gestapo: A History of Horror*, London, 2008; R. Butler, *Gestapo: A History of Hitler's Secret Police 1933–1945*, London, 2003.

11 National Archives US (copy) HS 8/852, Report on Gestapo methods of interrogation, 17 March 1941.

12 See *Sophie Scholl: The Final Days*, 'Bonus Documentary'. German version, Blu-Ray/DVD, 2007.

13 These rumours probably emanated from Falk Harnack, as many of the members of the 'Red Orchestra' were tortured during their Gestapo interrogations, including his own brother Arvid.

14 Mohr Memorandum.

15 Sophie wrongly thought the arrests of the Scholl children took place in 1938.

16 BA-ZC13267, Sophie Scholl, first interrogation, 18 February 1943.

17 Mohr Memorandum.

18 Ibid.

19 BA-ZC13267, Gisela Schertling interrogation, 18 February 1943. Schertling also told the Gestapo that Hans was a drug addict and used morphine and amphetamines. These drugs were found in his apartment. Manfred Eickemeyer, in a later interrogation, claimed Hans used Pervertin ('speed') quite regularly to keep going during long bouts of work as a medical student. I feel the whole question of whether Hans was a drug user, or even a drug addict – as some historians have alleged – must be set in the context of the period. The terrible dangers associated with drug-taking were not as well established in the 1940s as they are today (nor were the dangers of smoking). Even in the 1960s a dangerous drug like LSD was perfectly legal. We must also remember that Hans was a medical student. He worked very long hours in field hospitals. He also had access to numerous drugs. The use of 'speed' was quite extensive among medical students in this period and many 'dabbled' with morphine too. At the same time, if Hans was a drug addict (and it is a big 'if', which cannot be proved either way) then that might have been a factor that led to the fatal decision to deliver the leaflets on campus. But we must remember that it was Sophie who pushed the leaflets over the balustrade and there is no evidence that she used drugs at all.

20 Gebel Memorandum.

21 BA-ZC13267, Gestapo Report, 18 February 1943.

22 In the course of the confession, Hans admitted that Christoph Probst had hand-written the seventh leaflet, but he tried to minimise Christoph's role by saying he had only asked him to write his 'views' and that he was not part of the group.

23 Mohr Memorandum.

24 BA-ZC13267, Sophie Scholl, second interrogation, 18–19 February 1943 (undated in file but other evidence suggests the night in question is the correct date).

25 BA-NJ1704, Willi Graf interrogation, 19 February 1943.

26 Mohr Memorandum.

27 Bormann made the Party Chancellery the centre of policy-making.
28 BA-ZC13267, Paul Giesler to Martin Bormann, 19 February 1943.
29 BA-ZC13267, Martin Bormann to Paul Giesler, 19 February 1943 (telex message).
30 BA-ZC13267, Note of trial details, 19 February 1943.
31 BA-NJ1704, Willi Graf interrogation, 19 February 1943.
32 Ibid.
33 BA-ZC13267, Sophie Scholl, third interrogation, 20 February 1943.
34 Mohr Memorandum.
35 BA-ZC13267, Robert Scholl interrogation, 13 March 1943.
36 BA-ZC13267, Magdelene Scholl interrogation, 13 March 1943.
37 Lafrenz Recollections.
38 Gebel letter.
39 BA-ZC13267, Christoph Probst interrogation, 20 February 1943.
40 BA-ZC13267, Indictment: Sophie Scholl, Hans Scholl, Christoph Probst, 21 February 1943.
41 Gebel letter.
42 BA-ZC13267, first White Rose trial, transcript, 22 February 1943.
43 BA-ZC13267, Munich University Report, 21 February 1943.
44 Gebel letter.
45 Mohr Memorandum.
46 Gebel letter.

Chapter Thirteen

1 I. Scholl, *White Rose*, pp. 56–58.
2 Ibid. The phrase was also used frequently by Robert Scholl.
3 Gebel letter.
4 I. Scholl, *White Rose*. p. 58
5 After 1945, most of the Nazi judges who played a central role in prosecuting and sentencing over 700,000 opponents of the regime were given a virtual amnesty by the Allied authorities. Only sixteen judges were tried as war criminals during the Nuremberg Trials in the late 1940s; only four of them received a life sentence. No other members of 'Hitler's judiciary' ever received a criminal conviction. Believe it or not, seventy-two former judges and prosecutors of the infamous 'People's Court' were re-employed by the Federal Republic of Germany. After 1950, the war trials were stopped altogether in the west. A mere 5,228 people were convicted of 'Nazi crimes' between 1945 and 1950 by German courts. Similar leniency was applied to Gestapo officers, the police force and members of the prison systems. By contrast, the sentences handed down against the members of the White Rose were not officially pardoned until the 1980s and not quashed until the 1990s.

6 For details see: 'The Hanging Judge' in G. Knopp, *Hitler's Hitmen*, Stroud, 2008, pp.213–251; H. Koch, *In the Name of the Volk: Political Justice in Hitler's Germany*, London, 1999.

7 Evans, *The Third Reich at War, 1939–1945*, London, 2008, pp.643–645.

8 See: R.J. Evans, *Rituals of Retribution: Capital Punishment in Germany 1600–1987*, Oxford, 1996; I. Müller, *Hitler's Justice: The Courts of the Third Reich*, Cambridge, MA, 1991.

9 Mohr Memorandum.

10 IfZ, ED474, Eye-Witness Report of first White Rose trial, Leo Samberger, February 1968 (hereafter Samberger Report).

11 In the official transcript it simply says 'the accused gave their evidence'. In similar trials, it was usual for defendants to offer a brief summary of their Gestapo confessions.

12 Samberger Report.

13 Hans' last words are mentioned in Mohr's memorandum. It is possible Robert Scholl heard this in the corridor outside the court or Samberger told him.

14 BA-ZC13267, first White Rose trial, Transcript of Proceedings, 22 February 1943.

15 Samberger Report.

16 Mohr Memorandum. Interestingly, Hans Scholl's final words were mentioned by Thomas Mann on BBC radio a few months later. See transcript of 'German Listeners'. BBC foreign radio broadcast by Thomas Mann, 27 June 1943.

17 BA-ZC1327, Verdict – with reasons – in case of Hans Scholl, Sophie Scholl, Christoph Probst, 22 February 1943.

18 Samberger Report.

19 Inge Scholl, *White Rose*, pp.59–60.

Chapter Fourteen

1 It was opened in 1894 and is located in the south of Munich.

2 Vinke, *The Short Life of Sophie Scholl*, p.156.

3 Dumbach and Newborn, *Sophie Scholl and the White Rose*, pp.155–156.

4 Samberger Report.

5 The final name was Josef Söhngen, the Munich bookshop owner.

6 Mohr Memorandum.

7 Hanser *A Noble Treason*. p.279.

8 Mohr Memorandum.

9 BA-ZC13267, Official notes on Sophie Scholl execution, 22 February 1943.

10 See K.Alt, *Death Candidates*, Munich, 1946. See also W. Reuter (ed.), *Crossing Boundaries*, Munich, 1994, which contains details of candidates Alt led to execution, including Hans and Sophie Scholl and Christoph Probst. There

remains an unresolved mystery about the last minutes of Sophie's life. This revolves around whether she wanted (like Probst) to convert to Catholicism. Susanne Hirzel claimed in her memoirs that she met Karl Alt a few days after the execution, while she was in Stadelheim, and that he told her that Sophie considered being baptised into the Catholic faith, but decided against it only because 'she did not want to cause any more pain to her mother'. See Hirzel, *Vom Ja zum Nein*, p.214. Jakob Knab writes: 'I know there's an intellectual tugging about Hans and Sophie Scholl whether they had died as Protestants or Catholics. My point of view: They died as true Christians; the breaking of the bread was their *viaticum*, their medicine of immortality.'

11 Bible, 1 Corinthians 13. In German this is called the 'High Song of Christian Love'.

12 Bible, Psalm 90.

13 Bible, Gospel of John 15:13.

14 According to a report by a warder, 'They were incredibly brave. The entire prison was impressed. That was why we took the risk, had we been found out there would have been grave consequences, of bringing the three together, right before the execution. We wanted them to be able to have a last cigarette together. It was only a few minutes, but I believe it meant a great deal to them.' Quoted in Vinke, *The Short Life of Sophie Scholl*, p.188. Unfortunately, Nazi executions were carried out with exact precision. The idea of putting three condemned prisoners in one room before an execution could not – in my view – have happened. The execution record states each prisoner was escorted individually. Alt also said later he was present when the guard arrived for Sophie. There was simply no 'window of opportunity' just before the execution for this to have happened. A nice story, but probably fiction.

15 BA-ZC13267, Execution Report for Sophie Scholl, 22 February 1943.

16 For details see: G. Daniel, *Guillotine: Its Legend and More*, London, 1992.

17 For details see: J. Dachs, *Tod durch das Fall Beil: Der Deutsche Scharfrichter Johnan Reichhart*, Ullstein, 2001. After the war Reichhart became a sad and lonely figure. His son committed suicide in 1951 – ashamed of his father's grisly role in the history of the Third Reich.

18 BA-ZC13275, Execution Record, Sophie Scholl, 22 February 1943.

19 BA-ZC13267, Execution Record, Hans Scholl, 22 February 1943.

20 BA-ZC13267, Execution Record, Christoph Probst, 22 February 1943.

21 BA-ZC13267, Execution Record, Hans Scholl, 22 February 1943.

Chapter Fifteen

1 It was a similar format to a BBC series called *Greatest Britons* that was won by Sir Winston Churchill, with Princess Diana voted the highest British female.

2 Julia Jentsch Interview, Berlin Film Festival, 2006, report on ZDF.

3 *The White Rose,* guide produced by the White Rose Stiftung, p.86.

4 Interview with Horst Plötski, White Rose Stiftung, 12 February 2008.

5 Ulm Tourist Guide, p.11.

6 The school was named in honour of Hans and Sophie Scholl in 1962, but there was some notable opposition to the move in debates in the local parliament and letters in local newspapers.

7 Stadt Ulm Information Leaflet, Hans and Sophie Scholl.

8 Interviews with Philipp Pielenz and Christiane Weiger, Hans and Sophie Scholl Gymasium, 14 February 2008.

9 The other Scholl residences in Ulm are: 29 Kernerstrasse (1932) and 81 Olgastrasse (renamed Adolf Hitler Ring in the Nazi era), where they lived from 1932 to 1939. Neither residence survives today.

10 Interview with Klaus Schlaier, Einstein House, Ulm, 14 February 2008.

11 Elisabeth's house looked like a British Edwardian terraced house in a quiet suburban area.

12 Interview with Elisabeth Hartnagel, 15 February 2008, Stuttgart.

APPENDIX ONE

THE WHITE ROSE LEAFLETS

Leaflet 1

Nothing is so unworthy of a civilized nation as allowing itself to be governed without opposition by an irresponsible clique that has yielded to base instinct. It is certain that today every honest German is ashamed of his government. Who among us has any conception of the shame that will befall us and our children when one day the veil has fallen from our eyes and the most horrible of crimes – crimes that infinitely outdistance every human measure – reach the light of day? If the German people are already so corrupted and spiritually crushed that they do not raise a hand, frivolously trusting in a questionable faith in lawful order of history; if they surrender man's highest principle, that which raises him above all other God's creatures, his free will; if they abandon the will to take decisive action and turn the wheel of history and thus subject it to their own rational decision; if they are so devoid of all individuality, have already gone so far along the road toward turning into a spiritless and cowardly mass – then, yes, they deserve their downfall. Goethe speaks of the Germans as a tragic people, like the Jews and the Greeks, but today it would appear rather that they are a spineless, will-less herd of hangers-on, who now – the marrow sucked out of their bones, robbed of their centre of stability – are waiting to be hounded to their destruction. So it seems – but it is not so. Rather, by means of gradual, treacherous, systematic abuse, the system has put every man into a spiritual prison. Only now, finding himself lying in fetters, has he become aware of his fate. Only a few recognised the threat of ruin, and the reward for their heroic warning was death. We will have more to say about the fate of these persons. If everyone waits until the other man makes a start, the messengers of avenging Nemesis will come steadily closer; then even the last victim will have been cast senselessly into the marrow of the insatiable demon. Therefore every individual, conscious of his responsibility as a member of Christian and Western civilization, must defend himself as best he can at this late hour, he must work against the scourges of mankind, against fascism and any similar system of totalitarianism. Offer passive resistance – resistance – wherever you may be, forestall the spread of this atheistic war machine before it is too late, before the last cities, like Cologne, have been reduced to rubble, and before the nation's last young man has given his blood on some battlefield for the hubris of a sub-human. Do not forget that every people deserves the regime it is willing to endure!

From Freidrich Schiller's The Lawgiving of Lycurgus and Solon:
Viewed in relation to its purposes, the law code of Lycurgus is a masterpiece of political science and knowledge of human nature. He desired a powerful, unassailable start, firmly established on its own principles. Political effectiveness and permanence were the goal toward which he strove, and he attained this goal to the full extent possible under the circumstances. But if one compares the purpose Lycurgus had in view with the purposes of mankind, then a deep abhorrence takes the place of the approbation which we felt at first glance. Anything may be sacrificed to the good of the state except that end for which the State serves as a means. The state is never an end in itself; it is important only as a condition under which the purpose of mankind can be attained, and this purpose is none other than the development of all man's power, his progress and improvement. If a state prevents the development of the capacities which reside in man, if it interferes with the progress of the human spirit, then it is reprehensible and injurious, no matter how excellently devised, how perfect in its own way. Its very permanence in that case amounts more to a reproach than to a basis for fame; it becomes a prolonged evil, and the longer it endures, the more harmful it is …

At the price of all moral feeling a political system was set up, and the resources of the state were mobilised to that end. In Sparta there was no conjugal love, no mother love, no filial devotion, no friendship; all men were citizens only, and all virtue was civic virtue.

A law of the state made it the duty of Spartans to be inhumane to their slaves; in these unhappy victims of war humanity itself was insulted and mistreated. In the Spartan code of law the dangerous principle was promulgated that men are to be looked upon as means and not as ends – and the foundation of natural law and of morality were destroyed by that law....

What an admirable sight is afforded, by contrast, by the rough soldier Gaius Marcius in his camp before Rome, when he renounced vengeance and victory because he could not endure to see a mother's tears! …

The state (of Lycurgus) could endure only under the one condition: that the spirit of the people remained quiescent. Hence it could be maintained only if it failed to achieve the highest, the sole purpose of a state.

From Goethe's The Awakening of Epimenides, Act II, Scene 4:

SPIRITS:
Though he who has boldly risen from the abyss
Through an iron will and cunning
May conquer half the world,
yet to the abyss he must return.
Already a terrible fear has seized him;
In vain he will resist!
And all who still stand with him
Must perish in his fall.
HOPE:
Now I find my good men
Are gathered in the night,
To wait in silence, not to sleep.
And the glorious word of liberty
They whisper and murmur,
Till in unaccustomed strangeness,
On the steps of our temple
Once again in delight they cry:
Freedom! Freedom!

Please make as many copies of this leaflet as you can and distribute them.

Leaflet 2

It is impossible to engage in intellectual discourse with National Socialist Philosophy, for if there were such an entity, one would have to try by means of analysis and discussion either to prove its validity or to combat it. In actuality, however, we face a totally different situation. At its very inception this movement depended on the deception and betrayal of one's fellow man; even at that time it was inwardly corrupt and could support itself only by constant lies.

After all, Hitler states in an early edition of 'his' book (a book written in the worst German I have ever read, in spite of the fact that it has been elevated to the position of the Bible in this nation of poets and thinkers): 'It is unbelievable, to what extent one must betray a people in order to rule it.' If at the start this cancerous growth in the nation was not particularly noticeable, it was only because there were still enough forces at work that operated for the good, so that it was kept under control. As it grew larger, however, and finally in an ultimate spurt of growth attained ruling power, the tumour broke open, as it were, and infected the whole body. The greater part of its former opponents went into hiding. The German intellectuals fled to their cellars, there, like plants struggling in the dark, away from light and sun, gradually to choke to death. Now the end is at hand. Now it is our task to find one another again, to spread information from person to person, to keep a steady purpose, and to allow ourselves no rest until the last man is persuaded of the urgent need of his struggle against this system. When thus a wave of unrest goes through the land, when 'it is in the air', when many join the cause, then in a great final effort this system can be shaken off. After all, an end in terror is preferable to terror without end.

We are not in a position to draw up a final judgment about the meaning of our history. But if this catastrophe can be used to further the public welfare, it will be only by virtue of the fact that we are cleansed by suffering; that we yearn for the light in the midst of deepest night, summon our strength, and finally help in shaking off the yoke which weighs on our world.

We do not want to discuss here the question of the Jews, nor do we want in this leaflet to compose a defence or apology. No, only by way of example do we want to cite the fact that since the conquest of Poland three hundred thousand Jews have been murdered in this country in the most bestial way. Here we see the most frightful crime against human dignity, a crime that is unparalleled in the whole of history. For Jews, too, are human beings – no matter what position we take with respect to the Jewish question – and a crime of this dimension has been perpetrated against human beings. Someone may say that the Jews deserve their fate. This assertion would be a monstrous impertinence; but let us assume that someone said this – what position has he then taken toward the fact that the entire Polish aristocratic youth is being annihilated? (May God grant that this programme has not yet fully achieved its aim as yet!) All male offspring of the houses of the nobility between the ages of fifteen and twenty were transported to concentration camps in Germany and sentenced to forced labour, and all the girls of this age group were sent to Norway, into the bordellos of the SS! Why tell you these things, since you are fully aware of them – or if not of these, then of other equally grave crimes committed by this frightful sub-humanity? Because here we touch on a problem which involves us deeply and forces us all to take thought. Why do German people behave so apathetically in the face of all these abominable crimes, crimes so unworthy of the human race? Hardly anyone thinks about that. It is accepted as fact and put out of mind. The German people slumber on in their dull, stupid sleep and encourage these fascist criminals; they give them the opportunity to carry on their atrocities; and of course they do so. Is this a sign that the Germans are brutalised in their simplest human feelings, that no chord within them cries out at the sight of such deeds, that they have sunk into a fatal unconsciousness from which they will never, never awake? It seems to be so, and will certainly be so, if the German does not at last start up out of his stupor, if he does not protest wherever and whenever he can against this clique of criminals, if he shows no sympathy for these hundreds of thousands of victims. He must evidence not only sympathy; no, much more: a sense of complicity in guilt. For through his apathetic behaviour he gives these evil men the opportunity to act as they do; he tolerates this 'government' which has taken upon itself such an infinitely great burden of guilt; indeed, he himself is to blame for the fact that it came about at all! Each man wants to be exonerated of a guilt of this kind, each one continues on his way with the most placid, the calmest conscience. But he cannot be exonerated; he is guilty, guilty, guilty! It is not too late, however, to do away with this most reprehensible of all miscarriages of government, so as to avoid being burdened with even greater guilt. Now, when in recent years our eyes have been opened, when we know exactly who our adversary is, it is high time to root out this brown horde. Up until the outbreak of the war the larger part of the German people was blinded; the Nazis did not show themselves in their true aspect. But now that we have recognised them for what they are, it must be the sole and first duty, the holiest duty of every German to destroy these beasts.

If the people are barely aware that the government exists, they are happy. When the government is felt to be oppressive they are broken.

Good fortune, alas! builds itself upon misery. Good fortune, alas! is the mask of misery. What will come of this? We cannot foresee the end. Order is upset and turns to disorder, good becomes evil. The people are confused. Is it not so, day in, day out, from the beginning? -

The wise man is therefore angular, though he does not injure others; he has sharp corners, though he does not harm; he is upright but not gruff. He is clear minded, but he does not try to be brilliant.
Lao-Tzu

Whoever undertakes to rule the kingdom and to shape it according to his whim – I foresee that he will fail to reach his goal. That is all. The kingdom is a living being. It cannot be constructed, in truth! He who tries to manipulate it will spoil it, he who tries to put it under his power will lose it.
Therefore: Some creatures go out in front, others follow, some have warm breath, others cold, some are strong, some weak, some attain abundance, others succumb.
The wise man will accordingly forswear excess, he will avoid arrogance and not overreach.
Lao-Tzu

Please make as many copies as possible of this leaflet and distribute them.

Leaflet 3

Salus publica suprema lex

All ideal forms of government are utopias. A state cannot be constructed on a purely theoretical basis; rather, it must grow and ripen in the way an individual human being matures. But we must not forget that at the starting point of every civilisation the state was already there in rudimentary form. The family is as old as man himself, and out of this initial bond man, endowed with reason, created for himself a state founded on justice, whose highest law was the common good. The state should exist as a parallel to the divine order, and the highest of all utopias, the *civitas dei*, is the model which in the end it should approximate. Here we will not pass judgment on the many possible forms of the state – democracy, constitutional monarchy, and so on. But one matter needs to be brought out clearly and unambiguously. Every individual human being has a claim to a useful and just state, a state which secures freedom of the individual as well as the good of the whole. For, according to God's will, man is intended to pursue his natural goal, his earthly happiness, in self-reliance and self-chosen activity, freely and independently within the community of life and work of the nation.

But our present 'state' is the dictatorship of evil. 'Oh, we've known that for a long time', I hear you object, 'and it isn't necessary to bring that to our attention again'. But, I ask you, if you know that, why do you not bestir yourselves, why do you allow these men who are in power to rob you step by step, openly and in secret, of one domain of your rights after another, until one day nothing, nothing at all will be left but a mechanised state system presided over by criminals and drunks? Is your spirit already so crushed by abuse that you forget it is your right – or rather, your moral duty – to eliminate this system? But if a man no longer can summon the strength to demand his right, then it is absolutely certain that he will perish. We would deserve to be dispersed through the earth like dust before the wind if we do not muster our powers at this late hour and finally find the courage which up to now we have lacked. Do not hide your cowardice behind a cloak of expediency, for with every new day that you hesitate, failing to oppose this offspring of Hell, your guilt, as in a parabolic curve, grows higher and higher.

Many, perhaps most, of the readers of these leaflets do not see clearly how they can practice an effective opposition. They do not see any avenues open to them. We want to try to show them that everyone is in a position to contribute to the over-throw of this system. It is not possible through solitary withdrawal, in the manner of embittered hermits, to prepare the ground for the overturn of this 'government' or bring about the revolution at the earliest possible moment. No, it can be done only by the co-operation of many convinced, energetic people – people who are agreed as to the means they must use to attain their goal. We have no great number of choices as to these means. The only one available is passive resistance. The mean-ing and the goal of passive resistance is to topple National Socialism, and in this struggle we must not recoil from any course, any action, whatever its nature. At all points we must oppose National Socialism, wherever it is open to attack. We must soon bring this monster of a state to an end. A victory of fascist Germany in this war would have immeasurable, frightful consequences. The military victory over Bolshevism dare not become the primary concern of the Germans. The defeat of the Nazis must unconditionally be the first order of business; the greater necessity of this latter requirement will be discussed in one of our forthcoming leaflets.

And now every convinced opponent of National Socialism must ask himself how he can fight against the present 'state' in the most effective way, how he can strike it the most telling blows. Through passive resistance, without a doubt. We cannot provide each man with the blueprint for his acts, we can only suggest them in general terms, and he alone will find the way of achieving this end:

Sabotage in armament plants and war industries, sabotage at all gatherings, rallies, public ceremonies, and organisations of the National Socialist Party. Obstruct the smooth functioning of the war machine (a machine for war that goes on solely to shore up and perpetuate the National Socialist Party and its dictatorship). Sabotage in all the areas of science and scholarship which furthers the continuation of the war – whether in universities, technical schools, laboratories, research institutes, or technical bureaus. Sabotage in all cultural institutions which could potentially enhance the 'prestige' of the fascists among the people. Sabotage in all branches of the arts which have even the slightest dependence on National Socialism or render it service. Sabotage in all publications, all newspapers, that are in the pay of the 'government' and that defend its ideology and aid in disseminating the brown lie. Do not give a penny to public drives (even when they are conducted under the pretence of charity). For this is only a disguise. In reality the proceeds aid neither the Red Cross nor the needy. The government does not need this money; it is not financially interested in these money drives. After all, the presses run continuously to manufacture any desired amount of paper currency. But the populace must be kept constantly under tension; the pressure of the bit must not be allowed to slacken! Do not contribute to the collections of metal, textiles, and the like. Try to convince all your acquaintances, including those in the lower social classes, of the senselessness of continuing, of the hopelessness of this war; of our spiritual and economic enslavement at the hands of the National Socialists; of the destruction of all moral and religious values; and urge them to passive resistance!

Aristotle, Politics: '... and further, it is part (of the nature of tyranny) to strive to see to it that nothing is kept hidden of that which any subject says or does, but that everywhere he will be spied upon, ... and further, to set man against the privileged and the wealthy. Also it is part of these tyrannical measures, to keep the subjects poor, in order to pay the guards and soldiers, and so that they will be occupied with earning their livelihood and will have neither leisure nor opportunity to engage in conspiratorial acts.... Further, (to levy) such taxes on income as were imposed in Syracuse, for under Dionysius the citizens gladly paid out their whole fortunes in taxes within five years. Also, the tyrant is inclined constantly to foment wars'.

Please duplicate and distribute!

Leaflet 4

Though we know that National Socialist power must be broken by military means, we are trying to achieve a renewal from within of the severely wounded German spirit. This rebirth must be preceded, however, by the clear recognition of all the guilt with which the German people have burdened themselves, and by an uncompromising battle against Hitler and his all too many minions, party members, Quislings, and the like ...

There is an ancient maxim that we repeat to our children: 'He who won't listen will have to feel'. But a wise child will not burn his fingers the second time on a hot stove. In the past weeks Hitler has chalked up successes in Africa and in Russia. In consequence, optimism on the one hand and distress and pessimism on the other have grown within the German people with a rapidity quite inconsistent with traditional German apathy. On all sides one hears among Hitler's opponents – the better segments of the population – exclamations of despair, words of disappointment and discouragement, often ending with the question: 'Will Hitler now, after all ...?'

Meanwhile, the German offensive against Egypt has ground to a halt. Rommel has to bide his time in a dangerously exposed position. But the push into the East proceeds. This apparent success has been purchased at the most horrible expense of human life, and so it can no longer be counted an advantage. Therefore we must warn against all optimism.

Neither Hitler nor Goebbels can have counted the dead. In Russia thousands are lost daily. It is the time of the harvest, and the reaper cuts into the ripe grain with wide strokes. Mourning takes up her abode in the country cottages, and there is no one to dry the tears of the mothers. Yet Hitler feeds with lies those people whose most precious belongings he has stolen and whom he has driven to a meaningless death.

Every word that comes from Hitler's mouth is a lie. When he says peace, he means war, and when he blasphemously uses the name of the Almighty, he means the power of evil, the fallen angel, Satan. His mouth is the foul-smelling pit of Hell, and his might is at bottom accursed. True, we must conduct a struggle against the National Socialist terrorist state with rational means; but whoever today still doubts the reality, the existence of demonic powers, has failed by a wide margin to understand the metaphysical background of this war. Behind the concrete, the visible events, behind all objective, logical considerations, we find the irrational element: the struggle against the demon, against the servants of the Antichrist. Everywhere and at all times demons have been lurking in the dark, waiting for the moment when man is weak; when of his own volition he leaves his place in the order of Creation as founded for him by God in freedom; when he yields to the force of evil, separates himself from the powers of a higher order; and after voluntarily taking the first step, he is driven on to the next and the next at a furiously accelerating rate. Everywhere and at all times of greatest trial men have appeared, prophets and saints who cherished their freedom, who preached the One God and who His help brought the people to a reversal of their downward course. Man is free, to be sure, but without the true God he is defenceless against the principle of evil. He is a like rudderless ship, at the mercy of the storm, an infant without his mother, a cloud dissolving into thin air.

I ask you, you as a Christian wrestling for the preservation of your greatest treasure, whether you hesitate, whether you incline toward intrigue, calculation, or procrastination in the hope that someone else will raise his arm in your defence? Has God not given you the strength, the will to fight? We must attack evil where it is strongest, and it is strongest in the power of Hitler.

So I returned, and considered all the oppressions that are done under the sun: and behold the tears of such as were oppressed, and they had no comforter; and on the side of their oppressors there was power; but they had no comforter. Wherefore I praised the dead which are already dead than the living which are yet alive.

Ecclesiastes 4

True anarchy is the generative element of religion. Out of the annihilation of every positive element she lifts her gloriously radiant countenance as the founder of a new world ... If Europe were about to awaken again, if a state of states, a teaching of political science were at hand! Should hierarchy then ... be the principal of the union of states? Blood will stream over Europe until the nations become aware of the frightful madness which drives them in circles. And then, struck by celestial music and made gentle, they approach their former altars all together, hear about the works of peace, and hold a great celebration of peace with fervent tears before the smoking altars. Only religion can reawaken Europe, establish the rights of the peoples, and install Christianity in new splendour visibly on earth in its office as guarantor of peace.

– Novalis

We wish expressly to point out that the White Rose is not in the pay of any foreign power. Though we know that National Socialist power must be broken by military means, we are trying to achieve a renewal from within of the severely wounded German spirit. This rebirth must be preceded, however, by the clear recognition of all the guilt with which the German people have burdened themselves, and by an uncompromising battle against Hitler and his all too many minions, party members, Quislings, and the like. With total brutality the chasm that separates the better portion of the nation from everything that is opened wide. For Hitler and his followers there is no punishment on this Earth commensurate with their crimes. But out of love for coming generations we must make an example after the conclusion of the war, so that no one will ever again have the slightest urge to try a similar action. And do not forget the petty scoundrels in this regime; note their names, so that none will go free! They should not find it possible, having had their part in these abominable crimes, at the last minute to rally to another flag and then act as if nothing had happened! To set you at rest, we add that the addresses of the readers of the White Rose are not recorded in writing. They were picked at random from directories.

We will not be silent. We are your bad conscience. The White Rose will not leave you in peace!

Leaflet 5

A Call to All Germans!
The war is approaching its destined end. As in the year 1918, the German government is trying to focus attention exclusively on the growing threat of submarine warfare, while in the East the armies are constantly in retreat and invasion is imminent in the West. Mobilisation in the United States has not yet reached its climax, but already it exceeds anything that the world has ever seen. It has become a mathematical certainty that Hitler is leading the German people into the abyss. Hitler cannot win the war; he can only prolong it. The guilt of Hitler and his minions goes beyond all measure. Retribution comes closer and closer.

But what are the German people doing? They will not see and will not listen. Blindly they follow their seducers into ruin. Victory at any price! is inscribed on their banner. 'I will fight to the last man,' says Hitler – but in the mean time the war has already been lost.

Germans! Do you and your children want to suffer the same fate that befell the Jews? Do you want to be judged by the same standards as your traducers? Are we to be forever a nation which is hated and rejected by all mankind? No. Dissociate yourselves from National Socialist gangsterism. Prove by your deeds that you think otherwise. A new war of liberation is about to begin. The better part of the nation will fight on our side. Cast off the cloak of indifference you have wrapped around you. Make the decision before it is too late. Do not believe the National Socialist propaganda which has driven the fear of Bolshevism into your bones. Do not believe that Germany's welfare is linked to the victory of National Socialism for good or ill. A criminal regime cannot achieve a German victory. Separate yourselves in time from everything connected with National Socialism. In the aftermath a terrible but just judgment will be meted out to those who stayed in hiding, who were cowardly and hesitant.

What can we learn from the outcome of this war – this war that never was a national war?

The imperialist ideology of force, from whatever side it comes, must be shattered for all time. A one-sided Prussian militarism must never again be allowed to assume power. Only in large-scale co-operation among the nations of Europe can the ground be prepared for reconstruction. Centralised hegemony, such as the Prussian state has tried to exercise in Germany and in Europe, must be cut down at its inception. The Germany of the future must be a federal state. At this juncture only a sound federal system can imbue a weakened Europe with a new life. The workers must be liberated from their condition of down-trodden slavery under National Socialism. The illusory structure of autonomous national industry must disappear. Every nation and each man have a right to the goods of the whole world!

Freedom of speech, freedom of religion, the protection of individual citizens from the arbitrary will of criminal regimes of violence – these will be the bases of the New Europe.

Support the resistance. Distribute the leaflets!

Leaflet 6

Fellow Students!

Shaken and broken, our people behold the loss of the men of Stalingrad. Three hundred and thirty thousand German men have been senselessly and irresponsibly driven to death and destruction by the inspired strategy of our World War I Private First Class. Führer, we thank you!

The German people are in ferment. Will we continue to entrust the fate of our armies to a dilettante? Do we want to sacrifice the rest of German youth to the base ambitions of a Party clique? No, never! The day of reckoning has come – the reckoning of German youth with the most abominable tyrant our people have ever been forced to endure. In the name of German youth we demand restitution by Adolf Hitler's state of our personal freedom, the most precious treasure we have, out of which he has swindled us in the most miserable way.

We grew up in a state in which all free expression of opinion is unscrupulously suppressed. The Hitler Youth, the SA, the SS have tried to drug us, to revolutionise us, to regiment us in the most promising young years of our lives. 'Philosophical training' is the name given to the despicable method by which our budding intellectual development is muffled in a fog of empty phrases. A system of selection of leaders at once unimaginably devilish and narrow-minded trains up its future party bigwigs in the 'Castles of the Knightly Order' to become Godless, impudent, and conscienceless exploiters and executioners – blind, stupid hangers-on of the Führer. We 'Intellectual Workers' are the ones who should put obstacles in the path of this caste of overlords. Soldiers at the front are regimented like schoolboys by student leaders and trainees for the post of *Gauleiter*, and the lewd jokes of the *Gauleiters* insult the honour of the women students. German women students at the university in Munich have given a dignified reply to the besmirching of their honour, and German students have defended the women in the universities and have stood firm … That is a beginning of the struggle for our free self-determination – without which intellectual and spiritual values cannot be created. We thank the brave comrades, both men and women, who have set us brilliant examples.

For us there is but one slogan: fight against the party! Get out of the party organisations, which are used to keep our mouths sealed and hold us in political bondage! Get out of the lecture rooms of the SS corporals and sergeants and the party bootlickers! We want genuine learning and real freedom of opinion. No threat can terrorise us, not even the shutting down of the institutions of higher learning. This is the struggle of each and every one of us for our future, our freedom, and our honour under a regime conscious of its moral responsibility.

Freedom and honour! For ten long years Hitler and his comrades have manhandled, squeezed, twisted, and debased these two splendid German words to the point of nausea, as only dilettantes can, casting the highest values of a nation before swine. They have sufficiently demonstrated in the ten years of destruction of all material and intellectual freedom, of all moral substance among the German people, what they understand by freedom and honour. The frightful bloodbath has opened the eyes of even the stupidest German – it is a slaughter which they arranged in the name of 'freedom and honour of the German nation' throughout Europe, and which they daily start anew. The name of Germany is dishonoured for all time if German youth does not finally rise, take revenge, and atone, smash its tormentors, and set up a new Europe of the spirit. Students! The German people look to us. As in 1813 the people expected us to shake off the Napoleonic yoke, so in 1943 they look to us to break the National Socialist terror through the power of the spirit.

Beresina and Stalingrad are burning in the East. The dead of Stalingrad implore us to take action. 'Up, up, my people, let smoke and flame be our sign!'

Our people stand ready to rebel against the Nationals Socialist enslavement of Europe in a fervent new breakthrough of freedom and honour.

Leaflet 7 (Christoph Probst draft)

Stalingrad! 200,000 German comrades were sacrificed for the honour and glory of a military fraud. The surrender conditions set down by the Russians were not disclosed to the soldiers who were sacrificed. General Paulus received the Oak Leaves [military medal]. High-ranking officers escaped the slaughter at Stalingrad by airplane. Hitler refused to allow those who were trapped and surrounded to retreat behind the line. Now the blood of 200,000 soldiers who were condemned to death accuses the murderer named Hitler.

Tripoli! They surrendered unconditionally to the British Eight army. And what did the English do? They allowed the citizens to carry on living their lives as normal. They even let the police and public officials stay in office. Only one thing did they alter: they rid the great Italian colonial city of every barbaric leader. The annihilating, irresistable superpower is approaching on all sides with absolute certainty. Hitler is less likely than Paulus to surrender: there will be no escape for him. And will you be deceived like the 200,000 who defended Stalingrad in a hopeless cause to be massacred, sterilised or robbed of your children? Roosevelt, the most powerful man in the world said in Casablanca on 24 January 1943: 'Our war of extermination is not against the common people, but against political systems.' We will also fight for an unconditional surrender. More thought will be required before a decision can be made. This concerns the lives of millions of people. Should Germany meet the same fate as Tripoli?

Today Germany is completely encircled just like Stalingrad. Will all Germans be sacrificed to the man who persecuted the Jews, eradicated half the Poles and who wanted to annihilate Russia? Sacrificed to the man who took away your freedom, peace, happiness, hope and joy and instead gave you soaring inflation? This will not and must not happen! Hitler and his regime must fall so Germany may live. Make up your minds: Stalingrad and defeat or Tripoli and a future of hope? And once again you have decided: Act!

APPENDIX TWO

THE FATE OF KEY INDIVIDUALS

PROSECUTED BY THE NAZI REGIME FOR INVOLVEMENT AND ASSOCIATION WITH THE WHITE ROSE

The Scholl family

Sophie Scholl, executed 22 February 1943 at Stadelheim prison and buried in Perlach Cemetery, Munich, 24 February 1943.

Hans Scholl, Sophie's brother, executed on 22 February at Stadelheim prison. Buried at Perlach cemetery on 24 February 1943.

Robert Scholl, Sophie's father. He was arrested by the Gestapo under the Nazi kinship laws, which held families jointly responsible for acts of resistance. He was sentenced to two years imprisonment in the Scholl family trial in August 1943, but was released in 1945 after the German defeat in the Second World War. In the post-war era, Robert Scholl became the mayor of Ulm and he continued to work in the financial services industry. He died in 1973.

Magdalene Scholl, Sophie's mother. She spent some time in prison after the execution of her children, but she was acquitted at the Scholl family trial in August 1943. She never really recovered from the trauma of losing three children during the war and she died in 1945.

Elisabeth Scholl, Sophie's sister (now Elisabeth Hartnagel). She was arrested by the Gestapo in 1943, but was soon released, due to ill-health, then later acquitted in the Scholl family trial. She formed a close romantic relationship with Sophie's friend Fritz Hartnagel in the months after her execution and they were later married. After 1945, Fritz Hartnagel became a lawyer and rose to the position of presiding judge of the Stuttgart regional court in West Germany. He was a supporter of humanitarian causes and a key activist in the peace movement. He died in April 2001. Elisabeth lives in Stuttgart.

Inge Scholl, Sophie's sister. She was arrested then later acquitted in the Scholl family trial in August 1943. After 1945, Inge became 'the heiress' of the legacy of Hans and Sophie Scholl. In 1952, she married family friend and talented artist Otl Aicher and together they helped to found the Ulm Adult Education Centre – a sort of 'community university' – and she also helped to found the Ulm Academy of Design, but in 1968 the local state government cut its funding and it was forced to close. The Adult Education Centre (called the Einstein House) continues to this day. Inge also set up the White Rose Foundation which strives to uphold human rights and promote the principles of the group. Inge also wrote a number of books, most notably, *The White Rose: Munich 1942-1943*, which has sold over 500,000 copies. She became a leading figure in the peace movement for the remainder of her life. In spite of her notable achievements, a few historians have offered critical assessments of Inge's role and have stressed she endorsed primarily 'saint-like' presentations of Hans and Sophie Scholl. In her defence, other historians have suggested that she has allowed scholars access to the extensive Scholl family archive (Aicher-Scholl Archive) at the Institute of Contemporary History (IfZ) in Munich. This invaluable archive collection is a key source of documentary evidence on Hans and Sophie Scholl's lives and White Rose history. Inge Scholl died in 1998.

Werner Scholl, Sophie's younger brother, was sent back to fight in the hopeless war on the Eastern Front after the executions. It could be said this was a death sentence in itself. Werner was killed in action in 1944. All the most memorable photos of Sophie Scholl – including the memorable cover photo of this book – were taken by Werner Scholl, a brilliant photographer and a true independent spirit.

The fate of the leading individuals in the White Rose group in Munich

Christoph Probst was executed at Stadelheim Prison on 22 February 1943 and buried in Perlach cemetery.

Alexander Schmorell was arrested on 24 February 1943 after being spotted in a Munich air-raid shelter by a local woman who called the Gestapo. Alex never knew or was told that Hans, Sophie and Christoph were already dead during his lengthy and brutal Gestapo interrogations and he bravely took full responsibility. Alex was charged with high treason and sentenced to death by guillotine at the second White

Rose trial on 19 April 1943. Freisler viewed Alex as the co-leader with Hans Scholl of the Munich group and he said they devised, discussed and participated in every activity of the group. In his final letters to his parents, Alex told them that he did not regret opposing Hitler and he assured them that he was at peace with his fate and did not fear death. On 13 July 1943, he was executed at Stadelheim prison and buried in Perlach cemetery.

Willi Graf refused to confess or incriminate his friends, but he was still charged with high treason and sentenced to death by guillotine in the second White Rose trial in April 1943. Freisler was impressed enough by Willi Graf not to engage in his usual verbal attacks and even offered a backhanded compliment by saying 'You almost got away with it.' The Gestapo played a very cynical cat and mouse game with Willi after he was condemned to death. They promised him the possibility of having his death sentence turned into a life sentence if he co-operated fully, but he refused to give names. Throughout this harrowing ordeal, Willi displayed enormous courage and remarkable strength of character by continually stonewalling questions and refusing to betray his friends. His strong Catholic faith provided great solace in his final days. He never once regretted opposing Hitler and he never blamed anyone for his predicament. In a deeply moving final letter to his parents Willi wrote: 'I could never say to you while I was alive how much I loved you, but now in these last hours I want to tell you … that I love you all deeply and that I have respected you.' On 12 October 1943, Willi Graf, a deeply humane and brave soul, was executed at Stadelheim prison. Willi's grave is in the St Johann cemetery in Saarbrücken – his home town. A number of German schools are named in his honour, including, the Willi Graf Gymnasium in Munich.

Kurt Huber was arrested in February 1943. After he confessed, he was stripped of his doctorate, dismissed from his university post and lost his pension rights. At the second White Rose trial, on 19 April 1943, he faced a number of charges, including treason and sabotaging the war effort. In an emotional and brilliantly argued final speech, in front of Freisler, Huber claimed he had wanted to arouse students to oppose the Nazi regime, not through acts of violence, but the written word. He said he was no revolutionary figure, but a German patriot who wanted to return 'the rule of law' to Germnay. He was found guilty of high treason and executed by guillotine on 13 July 1943 at Stadelheim prison and buried at Waldfriedhof cemetery in Munich. He went to his execution convinced that his death was not in vain. After the war the square opposite the main university building was renamed Professor Huber Platz in his honour and his biography of Gottfried Wilhelm Leibniz, which he tried to complete before his execution, became the standard work on the subject.

Traute Lafrenz (now Traute Lafrenz-Page) was a key figure in the Munich White Rose group and a figure of central importance in any study of female resistance to Hitler's regime. She was arrested by the Gestapo and charged with having 'knowledge of the leafleting campaign'. She cleverly managed to conceal her important role in the White Rose group and was sentenced to one year in prison on 19 April 1943 at the second White Rose trial. But when the Gestapo investigated the Hamburg branch – which she played an important role in establishing – Traute was taken back into custody and was only released in 1945. In 1947, she moved to the US and completed her medical studies at the University of California, Berkeley. She went on to work successfully in the treatment of handicapped children and lives today in South Carolina.

The fate of individuals associated with leading White Rose figures or involved with White Rose resistance activities in Munich

Josef Söhngen, the owner of a bookshop on Marienplatz, Munich, was arrested by the Gestapo in March 1943 and questioned extensively about his 'relationship' with Hans Scholl. Söhngen claimed his friendship with Hans was 'purely personal' and based on mutual interests in music, religious philosophy and literature. He was charged with the minor offence of 'failing to report' seditious activity and sentenced to six months in prison at the third White Rose trial in Munich on 13 July 1942. He lived in Munich after the war and died in 1972.

Falk Harnack was arrested by the Gestapo and charged with 'failing to report' the propaganda campaign at the second White Rose trial on 19 April 1943. Freisler described Harnack as 'highly talented' and said because many of his family had been executed during the 'Red Orchestra' trials, his situation was 'unique'. Freisler even said – unbelievably – that Harnack was 'a committed National Socialist', but it was enough for him to be the only person set free by Freisler in both trials. Harnack took part in resistance activities for the rest of the war. After 1945 he initially settled in East Germany, but then moved to West Germany and became a highly acclaimed TV producer, script writer and film director. In 1955, he produced a film called 'The 20th July' about the bomb plot against Hitler. Harnack never categorised himself as a member of the White Rose and he felt the communist resistance had played the most important role in the opposition to Hitler. He died on 3 September 1991, after a long illness.

Katharina Schüddekopf, Kurt Huber's doctoral student, friend of Sophie's at Munich University and an associate of the Munich White Rose group. White Rose scholars think her exact role in the group – like Geyer's – is difficult to determine conclusively. She was charged with distributing leaflets and sabotaging the war effort. She was sentenced to one year's imprisonment at the second White Rose trial on 19 April 1943. She died in 1992.

Gisela Schertling, a 'friend' of Hans and Sophie before their arrest. She was a loyal Nazi who did not approve of or support the resistance activities of the White

Rose. During her Gestapo interrogations she incriminated many members of the Munich circle. In the end, she was charged with distributing leaflets and weakening national security and sentenced to one year in prison at the second White Rose trial on 19 April 1943. Freisler said she had 'stumbled' into the White Rose circle due to her friendships with Sophie and Hans, but she had participated and had to be punished. After the war, Schertling was very remorseful, regretted her actions during her interrogations, and tried to atone by devoting her life to educational projects that warned of the dangers of Nazism.

Manfred Eickemeyer, the architect whose basement studio had been a key part of the White Rose leafleting and graffiti operations, was arrested, but was acquitted at the third White Rose trial in Munich on 13 July 1943, as the judge could not decide that he knew about the activities going on in his basement studio. Eickemeyer explained that he was working in Nazi-occupied Poland while the leafleting campaign was conducted and the judge accepted this story, even though it was not true. He died in 1978.

Wilhelm Geyer, the artist, close friend of Sophie, was renting Eickemeyer's studio at the time of Sophie and Hans' arrest. Geyer's role in the Munich group is difficult to determine. He certainly fits a description given by a member of the public to the Gestapo – just before the events in the Lichthof – of a person daubing anti-Nazi graffiti on a Munich building. He was arrested, interrogated and acquitted – due to lack of evidence – at the third White Rose trial on 13 July 1943. After 1945, Geyer's artistic reputation grew as a painter, graphic artist and designer. He is most well known as the artist of many stunning stained-glass windows in German churches and cathedrals, most notably the bride window in Ulm Münster. He also lectured at the design institute established by Inge Scholl and Otl Aicher in Ulm. He died on 5 October 1968.

Harald Dohrn, Christoph Probst's father in law, was a long-standing and outspoken critic of the Nazi regime. He was arrested after being remembered offering dissident views about the regime at the farewell party at Eickemeyer's studio in July 1942. He was a defendant at the Third White Rose trial on 13 July 1943, but was acquitted because there was no evidence that he even knew about the leafleting activities of the White Rose group. He continued to oppose the Nazi regime and was shot dead during a Gestapo sweep of resistance activists in 1945.

Individuals from Ulm/Stuttgart involved with White Rose resistance activities

Hans Hirzel, a friend of Hans and Sophie Scholl was arrested and sentenced to five years' imprisonment for spreading 'treasonous' propaganda at the second White Rose trial on 19 April 1943. Roland Freisler felt that Hans Hirzel, whom he described as 'an immature boy', had 'come under the influence' of Sophie Scholl. In reality, Hans Hirzel was in two minds about resisting Hitler at all, but he did engage in the leafleting operation and even bought a duplicating machine, with money supplied by Sophie, which he threw in the Danube and never delivered to her. After the war, he was a very successful newspaper journalist and editor. He became active in the Christian Democrat Party (CDU) and held many local government posts. He was a candidate for the German parliament in the 1994 national elections. He died in 2006.

Susanne Hirzel, a friend of Sophie Scholl, was arrested for taking part in the leafleting campaign. Her only 'crime' was delivering copies of the fifth leaflet in Stuttgart on one night in January 1943, at the request of her brother Hans. Roland Freisler felt Susanne – whom he described as 'a blond German maiden' – was essentially a loyal member of 'the national community' and was not aware of 'the treasonous nature' of the leaflet she was delivering. She received a sentence of six months' imprisonment. After the war, she spent thirteen years in Basel (Switzerland), then moved to Stuttgart. In October 2000 she published her memoirs, *Vom Ja zum Nein*.

Franz Josef Müller was recruited to the White Rose leafleting campaign by his friend Hans Hirzel. He was arrested, charged with distributing treasonous propaganda and sentenced to five years in prison in the second White Rose trial on 19 April 1943. Today, he still gives entertaining talks about his experiences in the White Rose and his memories of Hans and Sophie Scholl at the White Rose Foundation at Munich University.

Eugen Grimminger was a business associate of Robert Scholl and friend of the Scholl family. He was arrested by the Gestapo on 2 March 1943, interrogated over the funding of the leafleting operation and eventually sentenced to ten years in prison at the second White Rose trial on 19 April 1943 on a charge of 'rendering money' for treason. The Gestapo saw Grimminger – quite wrongly – as a sort of financial 'Mr Big' in the White Rose. It was only the clever defence case put forward by his female lawyer Tilly Hiles that convinced Freisler that he gave the money, but he did not know for what purpose it was going to be used. His Jewish wife – Jenny – whom he had protected before his arrest was later arrested while he was in prison, deported to Auschwitz and murdered. After the Second World War, Grimminger became President of the National Association of Co-operatives. He lived in a suburb of Stuttgart until his death in 1986.

Heinrich Guter, a classmate of Hans Hirzel at the Ulm Gymnasium, was sentenced to eighteen months in prison at the second White Rose trial on 19 April 1943 for failing to report knowledge of the leafleting operation.

Individuals associated engaged in White Rose activity in the Rhineland area

Heinz Bollinger, a friend of Willi Graf, was charged with distributing leaflets, sabotaging the war effort and listening to foreign radio broadcasts at the second White Rose trial on 19 April 1943. He was sentenced to seven years in prison. He died in Freiburg in 1990.

Willi Bollinger, the twin of Heinrich, was tried alone for his role in the White Rose activities in Saarbrücken on 3 April 1944. He was sentenced to three months for 'failing to report treasonous activity'. After the war he qualified as a chemist. He died in 1975.

Helmut Baur, recruited to support the White Rose by Willi Graf, was found guilty of treasonous activity and listening to foreign radio broadcasts at the second White Rose trial on 19 April 1943 and sentenced to seven years in prison. He was released in 1945, but died of tuberculosis in 1952.

The fate of the 'Hamburg Branch' of the White Rose

The Hamburg Branch had been established largely through the efforts of Traute Lafrenz. The group reprinted and circulated the leaflets of the White Rose. The group were arrested and tried at a number of trials in 1944 and 1945. The dead of the Hamburg group included Hans Leipelt, executed 29 January 1945; Katharina Leipelt, forced to take her own life, 9 January 1945; Elisabeth Lange, forced to take her own life, 28 January 1944; and Curt Leiden, hanged on 23 April 1945. Gretl Mrosek, Reinhold Meyer, Frederick Geussenhainer and Greta Roth all died in custody before the end of the Second World War.

The fate of leading Nazi figures who played a role of significance in White Rose history

Adolf Hitler, the Dictator of Germany, retreated to his underground bunker in Berlin as the Red Army reached the city in the spring of 1945. He refused to believe the inevitability of the German defeat and blamed the catastrophe on 'the Jews' and the German people, who had proved themselves not racially strong enough to bring about victory. On 30 April 1945 he married his partner Eva Braun and then committed suicide by simultaneously biting on a cyanide capsule and firing a single bullet through his head.

Roland Freisler, the ranting and raving judge at the first and second White Rose trials in Munich, continued ordering executions to the last day of his life. On

3 February 1945, he was sheltering in the cellar of the People's Court building in Berlin when an Allied bombing raid scored a direct hit. A wooden beam crashed through the floor into the cellar below and struck him on the head. He was killed instantly.

Paul Giesler, the Munich *Gauleiter*, committed suicide on 8 May 1945 on the same day the Nazi authorities signed the 'unconditional surrender' to the Allies that ended the Second World War in Europe.

The fate of the Gestapo officers/prison officials associated with the arrest, interrogation and execution of Sophie Scholl

Robert Mohr was arrested by the French occupation authorities in 1947 and placed in a transit camp, but he was released in 1948. He was never charged with any crime related his period as a Gestapo officer and he retained his pension rights under the de-Nazification laws. He died in 1977.

Else Gebel offered an explanation of Sophie's final days for Inge Scholl in 1946, but she rarely discussed her role afterwards and died in 1964.

Jakob Schmid, the university caretaker who arrested Sophie and Hans Scholl on 18 February 1943, was arrested by US authorities at the end of the war and served a prison sentence, but he complained that 'he was only doing his job' and felt his imprisonment was unfair. He died in 1964.

Karl Alt, the German pastor at Stadelheim prison who administered the last rites to Sophie Scholl before her execution, died in 1951, aged fifty-four.

Johann Reichhart, the executioner at Stadelheim prison, was a lonely and isolated figure in the post-war years and died in 1972.

GLOSSARY OF GERMAN TERMS AND ORGANISATIONS

Abitur	The school-leaving qualification which was required as acceptance for university entrance.
Autobahn	Superhighway or motorway
Blitzkrieg	Lightning war
Führer	Leader (Adolf Hitler)
Gauleiter	District Leader of the Nazi Party
Gestapo (*Geheime Staatspolizei*)	Secret State Police
Gleichschaltung	Co-ordination. The term used by Nazis to explain the process to make the population accept and support National Socialist rule.
Hitlerjugend (HJ)	Hitler Youth. The organisation set up for young boys–aged 14 to 18 years of age. Between 10 and 14 boys were member of the *Deutsches Jungvolk* (DJ).
KPD	Communist Party
Kripo	Krimalpolizei: Criminal Police. The criminal investigation branch of the German civilian police force.
Labour Service (RAD)	A compulsory state work scheme which every German aged 18 to 25 was required to complete. There were separate organisations for males and females.
League of German Girls	Bund Deutscher Mädel (BDM) was the female branch of the Hitler Youth movement and was for girls aged 14 to 18 years of age. Between 10 and 14 girls were members of the feeder organisation: The Young Girls League (*Jungmädel*).

Lebensraum	Living Space. The term used by Hitler to describe his territorial aims.
Luftwaffe	German Air Force
Mittelstand	Middle class
People's Court	Special Nazi court designed to carry out swift trials of the so-called 'enemies of the people'.
Putsch	Revolt or coup. Used to describe Hitler's failed attempt to seize power in Bavaria in 1923 ('Munich Beer Hall Putsch').
NSDAP	Nationalsozialistische Deutsche Arbeitpartei. The National Socialist German Workers Party, commonly known as the Nazi Party.
Orpo	Ordenpolizei, the uniformed German police force.
Panzer	The name given to German tanks and to tank units.
Reichstag	The German Parliament
SA (Sturmabteilungen)	The Nazi storm troopers or 'Brownshirts'. The paramilitary private army of the Nazi Party.
Schutzhaft	Protective Custody. This allowed the Gestapo to arrest people and hold them without trial or even transfer them to a concentration camp.
Sippenhaft	'Family Guilt'. This allowed the Gestapo to arrest and imprison family members connected to a criminal. It was used increasingly during the war against the families of resistance members.
SPD	Social Democratic Party of Germany.
Special Court	A local court used to try crimes of a mainly 'political nature'.
SS (Schutzstaffel)	Hitler's personal elite bodyguard, dressed in distinctive black uniform, which under the leadership of Heinrich Himmler became the most powerful Nazi organisation within the state.
Volk	Folk or Race
Völkischer	Racial or Ethnic
Völkische Beobachter	*Racial Observer*. The official Nazi daily national newspaper.
Volksgemeinschaft	The Folk or People's Community. The slogan used by the Nazis to stress a kind of classless national solidarity.
Wehrmacht	The German Armed Forces

SOURCES AND BIBLIOGRAPHY

Archive Sources

Institut für Zeitgeschichte (IfZ), Munich
Nachlass Inge Aicher-Scholl (Scholl family papers)
Fa. 215- ED474
Sophie Scholl correspondence/diaries
Hans Scholl correspondence/diaries
Robert Scholl correspondence
Inge Scholl correspondence
Interrogation/trial/verdict for August 1942 Robert Scholl Trial
Robert Mohr Memorandum
Else Gebel Letter
Joseph Söhngen Memoirs
Leo Samberger Report
Interrogation files/trial and verdict of Harald Dohrn, Wilhelm Geyer, Manfred
Eickemeyer and Josef Söhngen
White Rose interrogation files/trial documents (available on microfilm)

Stadtarchiv, Munich
Gestapo Files
Polizeidirektion file no. 10145 (Jakob Schmid)
Spka K1104 (Anton Mahler)
Spka K 1634 (Jakob Schmid)
Spka K 2015 (Walter Wüst)
Bayerisches Haupstaatsarchiv, Munich
MK 43791 (Kurt Huber file)

Stadtarchiv Ludwigsburg
Files related to Scholl family

Archive of Munich University
University Archive files
E-II-1534: Archiv der Ludwig-Maximilians-Universität, München

Bundesarchiv, Berlin (BA)
Gestapo interrogation files/ investigation files/ Trial Transcrips related to White Rose
ZC13267
Gestapo interrogation transcripts
White Rose investigation files
Trial Documents
Execution Records
Bd. 2: Hans Scholl
Bd.3: Sophie Scholl
Bd.4: Christoph Probst
Bd.6: Traute Lafrenz
Bd. 7: Eugene Grimminger
Bd. 15: Gisela Schertling and Katharina Schüddekopf
NJ1074
Bd. 7: Kurt Huber
Bd. 8: Wilhelm ('Willi') Graf
Bd. 9: Falk Harnack
ZC14116
Bd. 1: *Hans Hirzel*
Bd 2: Susanne Hirzel and Helmut Bauer
(Microfilm copies also in IfZ Munich)

Haupstaatsarchiv, Düsseldorf (HD)
Gestapo Case Files.
Bündische Investigation, 1937–1938
Rep. 17. Bd. 292–295: Bündische interrogations/Trial/Verdict, 1937–1938
(Microfilm copies of these files also consulted in *IfZ Munich*)

Museum of Resistance, Berlin
Material Related to White Rose

Interviews and Correspondence
Elisabeth Hartnagel
Traute Lafrenz-Page
Klaus Schlaier
Susanne Millet
Robert Bierschneider
Johannes Tuchel
Horst Plötzski
Christiane Weiger
Philipp Pielenz

Bibliography

Adam, Peter, *The Arts in the Third Reich*, London, 1992.

Aicher, Otl, *innenseiten des kriegs*, Frankfurt, 1985.

Aicher-Scholl, Inge, *Sippenschaft, Nachrichten und Botschaften der Familie in der Gestapo-Haft nach der Hinrichtung von Hans und Sophie Scholl*, Frankfurt, 1993.

Arendt, Hannah, *The Origins of Totalitarianism*, London, 1955.

Alexrod, Toby, *Hans and Sophie Scholl*, New York, 2001.

Bald, Detlef, *Die Weisse Rose: Von der Front in den Widerstand*, Berlin, 2003.

Baird, Jay W., 'From Berlin to Neubabelsberg: Nazi Film Propaganda and Hitler Youth Quex', *Journal of Contemporary History*, vol. 18, 1983, pp.495–515.

Balfour, Michael, *Withstanding Hitler in Germany, 1933–1945*, London, 1988

Bankier, David, *Germans and The Final Solution: Public Opinion under Nazism*, Oxford, 1992.

Barnett, Victoria, *For the Soul of the People: Protestant Protest against Hitler*, Oxford, 1992.

Barth, Karl, *The German Church Conflict*, London, 1965.

Bartov, Omer, *The Eastern Front, 1941-1945, German Troops and the Barbarisation of Warfare*, London, 1985.

Baxter, Richard, *Women of the Gestapo*, London, 1944.

Beevor, Anthony, *Stalingrad: The Fateful Siege, 1942–1943*, London, 1998.

Berenbaum, Michael, *A Mosaic of Victims: Non-Jews Persecuted and Murdered by the Nazis*, New York, 1990.

Bergen, Doris L., *Twisted Cross: The German Christian Movement in the Third Reich*, Chapel Hill, NC, 1996.

Bessel, Richard (ed.), *Life in the Third Reich*, London, 1987.

Best, Werner, *Die Deutsche Polizei*, Darmstadt, 1941.

Bielenberg, Christabel, *Ride out of the Dark: The Experiences of an Englishwoman in Wartime Germany*, New York, 1971.

Blackburn, Gilmer W., *Education in the Third Reich: A Study of Race and History in Nazi Textbooks*, Albany, NY, 1985.

Blaha, Tatjana, *Willi Graf und die Weisse Rose*, Munich, 2003.

Boehm, Eric (ed.), *We Survived: Fourteen Histories of the Hidden and the Hunted of Nazi Germany*, Santa Barbara, CA, 1985.

Bornscheuer, Karl-Dieter (ed.), *Justiz im Dritten Reich: NS-Sondergerichtsverfahren in Rheinland-Pfalz: Eine Dokumentation* (3 vols), Frankfurt am Main, 1994.

Bowder, George C., *Hitler's Enforcers: The Gestapo and SS Security Service in the Nazi Revolution*, New York, 1996.

Breinersdorfer, Fred (ed.), *Die Letzten Tage: Das Buch zum Film*, Frankfurt am Main, 2005.

Bridenthal, Renate, et al. (eds), *When Biology Became Destiny: Women in Weimar and Nazi Germany*, New York, 1984.

Brysac, Shareen Blair, *Resisting Hitler: Mildred Harnack and the Red Orchestra*, Oxford, 2000.

Burden, Hamilton, *The Nuremberg Party Rallies, 1932–1939*, New York, 1967.

Burleigh, Michael, *Death and Deliverance: 'Euthanasia' in Germany, 1900–1945*, Cambridge, 1994.

Burleigh, Michael, *The Third Reich: A New History*, London, 2000.

Buscher, Paulus, *Aus den Erfahrungren des Jugendwiderstandes: d.j.1.11, 1936–1945*, Nottingham, 1993.

Caplan, Jane, *Government without Administration: State and Civil Society in Weimar and Nazi Germany*, Oxford, 1988.

Cartarius, Ulrich, *Opposition gegen Hitler: Ein erzählender Bildband*, Berlin, 1984.

Chaussy, Ulrich, *Keine Stunde Null*, Munich, 2006.

Childers, Thomas, *The Nazi Voter: The Social Foundations of Fascism, 1919–1933*, Chapel Hill, NC, 1983.

Chramov, Igor (ed.), *Alexander Schmorell: Gestapo- Verhorprotokolle, Februar–Marz, 1943*, Orenburg, 2005.

Chroust, Peter, *Giessner Universität und Faschismus: Studenten und Hochsschullehrer, 1918–1945* (2 vols), Münster, 1994.

Delarue, Jacques, *The Gestapo: A History of Horror*, New York, 1987.

Düffler, Jost, *Nazi Germany, 1933–1945; Faith and Annihilation*, London, 1986.

Duhnke, Horst, *Die KPD von 1933 bis 1945*, Cologne, 1972.

Dumbach, Annete and Newborn, Jud, *Shattering the German Night: The Story of the White Rose,* Boston, 1996 (updated, revised and republished with new title: *Sophie Scholl and White Rose*, London, 2006).

Engelmann, Bernt, *In Hitler's Germany: Daily Life in The Third Reich*, New York, 1986.

Etlin, Richard (ed.), *Art, Culture and Media under the Third Reich,* Chicago, 2002.

Evans, Richard J., *The Third Reich*, 3 vols: Vol. 1: *The Coming of the Third Reich*; Vol. 2: *The Third Reich in Power*; Vol. 3: *The Third Reich At War*, London, 2003–2008.

Evans, Richard J., *The Feminist Movement in Germany, 1894–1933*, London, 1976.

Evans, Richard J., *Rituals of Retribution: Capital Punishment in Germany, 1600–1987*, Oxford, 1996.

Evans, Richard J., *In Hitler's Shadow: West German Historians and Attempt to Escape from the Nazi Past*, London, 1989.

Fest, Joachim, *Plotting Hitler's Death: The Story of the German Resistance*, London, 1979.

Finkelstein, Norman, G. and Birn, Ruth Bettina *A Nation on Trial: The Goldhagen Thesis and Historical Truth*, New York, 1998.

Fisher, Conan, *Stormptroopers: A Social, Economic and Ideological Analysis, 1929–1935*, London, 1983.

Frei, Norbert, *National Socialist Rule in Germany*, London, 1993.

Fröhlich, Elke (ed.), *Die Tagebücher von Joseph Goebbels* (Diaries of Joseph Goebbels), 24 vols, Munich, 1993–2000.

Fürst-Ramdohr, Lilo, *Freundschaften in der Weissen Rose*, Munich, 1995.

Gellately, Robert, *The Gestapo and German Society: Enforcing Racial Policy, 1933–1945*, Oxford, 1990.

Gellately, Robert and Stolfus, Nathan (eds), *Social Outsiders in Nazi Germany*, Princeton, NJ, 2001.

Gellately, Robert, 'Rethinking the Nazi Terror System: A Historiographical Analysis', *German Studies Review*, vol. 14, 1991, pp.23–38.

Geyer, Michael and Boyer John, (eds), *Resistance against the Third Reich, 1933–1990,* Chicago, 1992.

Giles, Geoffrey J., *Students and National Socialism in Germany*, Princeton, NJ, 1985.

Gill, Anton, *An Honourable Defeat: A History of German Resistance to Hitler*, London, 1994.

Glaser, Hermann and Silenius, Axel (eds), *Jugend im Dritten Reich*, Frankfurt, 1975.

Graf, Christoph, 'The Genesis of the Gestapo', *Journal of Contemporary History*, vol. 22, 1987, pp.419–435.

Grayling, Anthony C., *Among the Dead Cities: Was Allied Bombing of Civilians in World War 2 a Necessity or a Crime?*, London, 2006.

Grey, Helmut, *d.j.1.11*, Frankfurt am Main, 1976.

Griech-Polelle, Beth, A., *Bishop von Galen: German Catholicism and National Socialism,* New Haven, CT, 2002.

Gruchmann, Lothar, *Justiz im Dritten Reich*, Munich, 1988.

Grunberg, Richard, *Kurt Huber's Aesthetics of Music*, Cambridge, 1976.

Grüttner, Michael, *Studeten im Dritten Reich*, Paderborn, 1995.

Hanser, Richard, *A Noble Treason: The Revolt of the Munich Students against Hitler*, New York, 1979.

Hartnagel, Thomas (ed.), *Sophie Scholl/Fritz Hartnagel: Damit wir uns nicht verlieren Briefwechsel, 1937–1943* (Very important collection of the Fritz Hartnagel/Sophie Scholl Letters), Frankfurt am Main, 2005.

Hauner, Milan, 'Did Hitler want World Dominion', *Journal of Contemporary History*, vol.13, 1978, pp.15–32.

Hellfield, Matthias von., *Bündische Jugend and Hitlerjugend, Zur Geschichte von Annpassung und Widerstand, 1930–1939*, Cologne, 1987.

Henry, Francis, *Victims and Neighbours: A Small Town in Nazi Germany Remembered*, South Hadley, MA, 1984.

Herf, Jeffrey, *Divided Memory: The Nazi Past and the Two Germanys*, London, 1997.

Herzog, Dagmar (ed.), *Sexuality and German Fascism*, New York, 2005.

Hirzel, Hans, 'Flugblätter in Weissen Rose in Ulm and Stuttgart' in Rudolf Lil (ed.), *Hochverrat? Die Weisse Rose under ihr Umfeld*, Konstanz, 1993, pp.89–119.

Hirzel, Susanne, *Vom Ja zum Nein: Eine schwäbische Jugend, 1933–1945,* Tübingen, 1998.

Hoffmann, Peter, *The History of the German Resistance*, Cambridge, MA, 1977.

Hoffmann, Peter, *Stauffenberg: A family History*, 1905–1944, Cambridge, 1995.

Holler, Eckard (ed.), *Hans Scholl zwischen Hitlerjugend und d.j.1.11: Die Ulmer 'Trabanten'*, PULS 22 Stuttgart, 1999.

Höpfner, Hans-Paul, *Die Universität Bonn im Dritten* Reich, Bonn, 1999.

Horn, Daniel B., 'The Hitler Youth and Educational Decline in the Third Reich', *History of Education Quarterly*, vol.16, 1976, pp.425–447.

Huber, Kurt, *Leibniz Der Philosoph der universalen Harmonie*, Munich, 1951.

Jarausch, Konrad H., *Deutsche Studenten, 1811–1970*, Frankfurt am Main, 1984.

Jarausch, Konrad H., *The Unfree Professions: German Lawyers, Teachers and Engineers*, 1900–1950, New York, 1990.

Jenkins, Roy, *Churchill*, London, 2001.

Jens, Inge (ed.), *At the Heart of the White Rose: Letters and Diaries of Hans and Sophie Scholl*, New York, 1987.

Johnson, Eric A., 'German Women and Nazi Justice: Their Role in the Process from Denunciation to Death', *Historische Sozialforschung*, vol.22, 1997, pp.240–253.

Johnson, Eric A., *Nazi Terror: The Gestapo, Jews and Ordinary Germans*, London, 1999.

Kater, Michael, *The Nazi Party: A Social Profile of Members and Leaders*, 1919–1945, Cambridge, MA, 1983.

Kershaw, Ian, *Popular Opinion and Political Dissent in the Third Reich: Bavaria, 1933–1945*, Oxford, 1983.

Kershaw, Ian, 'Resistance without the People: Bavarian Attitudes to the Nazi Regime at the Time of the White Rose' in: Hinrich Siefken (ed.), *Die Wiesse Rose: Student Resistance to National Socialism, 1942–43*, Nottingham, 1991, pp.51–65.

Kershaw, Ian, *Hitler, 1889–1936*: vol 1: *Hubris*, London, 1998.

Kershaw, Ian, *Hitler, 1936–1945*: vol 2: *Nemesis*, London, 2000.

Kirkpatrick, Clifford, *Women in Nazi Germany*, London, 1939.

Kissener, Michael, 'Literatur zur Weissen Rose, 1971-1992' in Rudolf Lill (ed.), *Die 'Hitlerjugend' am Beispiel der region Ulm/Neu Ulm,* Ulm, 1993.

Klee, Ernst (ed.), *Dokumente zur 'Euthanasie'*, Frankfurt am Main, 1997.

Klemperer, Victor, *I Shall Bear Witness: The Diaries of Victor Klemperer, 1933-1941*, London, 1998.

Knab, Jacob, 'So ein herrlicher sonniger Tag, und ich soll gehen: Sophie Scholl: Suche nach Sinn und Bekenntnis zum Widerstand' in D. Bald (ed.), *Wider die Kriegsmaschinerie: Kriegserfahrungen und Motive des Widerstandes der 'Weissen Rose'*, Essen, 2005, pp.130–143.

Knab, Jakob, 'Wir schweigen nicht, wir sind Euer böses Gewissen …"Die Newman–Rezeption der Weißen Rose – und ihre Wirkungsgeschichte"' in Bernd Trocholepczy (ed.), *Wirklichkeit, Verwirklichung und Wirkungsgeschichte. John Henry Newmans 'Realizing' als Basis einer praktisch-theologischen Theorie, Newman Studien,* vol. XX, Frankfurt am Main, 2010.

Knab, Jakob, 'Fritz Hartnagel: vom Wehrmachtoffizier zum Ostermarschierer' in Detlef Bald and Wolfram Wette (eds), *Alternativen zur Wiederbewaffnung. Friedenskonzeptionen in Westdeutschland 1945–1955*, Essen, 2008, pp.123–137.

Knab, Jakob, '"Verhindert das Weiterlaufen dieser atheistischen Kriegsmaschine!" Religion als Leitlinie bei Hans Scholl' in Detlef Bald (ed.), *Wider die Kriegsmaschinerie. Kriegserfahrungen und Motive des Widerstandes der 'Weissen Rose'*, Essen, 2005, pp.34–56.

Knoop-Graf, Anneliese and Jens, Inge (eds), *Willi Graf und Aufzeichnungen*, Frankfurt, 1994.

Koch, H.W., *In the Name of the Volk: Political Justice in Hitler's Germany*, London, 1989.

Koonz, Claudia, *Mothers in the Fatherland: Women, The Family and Nazi Politics*, London, 1988.

Kraul, Margaret, *Das deutsche Gymnasium, 1870–1980*, Frankfurt am Main, 1984.

Leisner, Barbara, *Sophie Scholl: Ich würde es genauso wieder machen*, Munich, 2000.

Lill, Rudolf (ed.), *Hochverrat? Neue Forschungen zur Weissen Rose,* Konstanz, 1993.

Mann, Reinhard, *Protest und Kontrolle im Dritten Reich: Nationalsozialistische Herrschaft im Altag einer rheinischen Großstadt*, Frankfurt am Main, 1987.

McDonough, Frank, *Opposition and Resistance in Nazi Germany*, Cambridge, 2001.

McDonough, Frank, *Hitler and the Rise of Nazi Germany*, Harlow, 2003.

McDonough, Frank with Cochrane, John, *The Holocaust*, Basingstoke, 2008.

Merson, Alan, *Communist Resistance in Nazi Germany*, London, 1985.

Michalka, Wolfgang (ed.), *Das Dritte Reich*, (2 vols), Munich, 1985.

Michalczyk, John J. and Muller, Franz Josef, 'The White Rose Student Movement in Germany: Its History and Revelance Today' in John J.Michalczyk (ed.), *Confront!: Resistance in Nazi Party*, New York, 2004, pp.211–220.

Moll, Christiane, 'Acts of Resistance: The White Rose in the Light of New Archival Evidence' in Michael Geyer and John Boyer (eds), *Resistance against the Third Reich*, Chicago, 1992, pp.172–200.

Moll, Christiane, 'Alexander Schmorell im Spiegel unveröffentlichter Briefe', in Lill, Rudolf (ed.), *Hochverrat? Neue Forschungen zur Weissen Rose* Konstanz, 1993, pp.129–160.

Moorehouse, Roger, *Killing Hitler: The Third Reich and Plots against the Führer*, London, 2006.

Müller, Ingo, *Hitler's Justice: The Courts of the Third Reich*, Cambridge, MA, 1991.

Nicosia, Francis, R., and Lawrence Stokes (eds), *Germans against Nazism*, New York, 1990

Niven, Bill, *Facing the Nazi Past: United Germany and the Legacy of the Third Reich,* London, 2002.

Noakes, Jeremy and Pridham, Geoffrey, *Nazism, 1919–1945*, 4 vols, Exeter, 1983–1998.

Oosterhaus, Harry, 'Medicine, Male Bonding and Homosexuality in Nazi Germany', *Journal of Contemporary History*, vol.32, 1997, pp.187–205.

Overy, Richard, *The War Economy in the Third Reich*, Oxford, 1994.

Owings, Allison, *Frauen: German Woman Recall the Third Reich*, New Brunswick, NJ, 1993.

Petry, Christian, *Studenten aufs Schafott: Die Weisse Rose und ihr Scheitern,* Munich, 1968.

Peukert, Detlef J.K., *Inside Nazi Germany: Conformity, Opposition and Racism in Everyday Life,* New Haven, CT, 1987.

Plant, Richard, *The Pink Triangle: The Nazi War against Homosexuals,* New York, 1986.

Prittie, Terence, *Germans Against Hitler,* London, 1964.

Richter, Cornelia, *Sophie Scholl als Persönlichkeit,* Salem, 1994.

Rothfels, Hans, *The German Opposition to Hitler,* London, 1961.

Sachs, Ruth Hannah, *White Rose History,* 3 vols: vol. 1: *Coming Together;* vol. 2: *Journey to Freedom;* vol. 3: *Fighters to the Very End* (ring binding), Lehi, UT, 2002–2008.

Schmidt, Fritz, et al. (eds), *dj.1.11 Trilogy,* Edermünde, 2005.

Schmidt, Fritz, *Ein Mann zwischen zwei Welten: Eberhard Koebels politische: Entwicklung seine ersten Jahre in der Emigration und seine Wirkung auf illegale d.j.1.11,* Freudenstein, 1997.

Scholl, Hans, *Journal de Russie de Hans Scholl,* Paris, 1953.

Scholl, Inge, *The White Rose: Munich, 1942-1943,* Middletown, CT, 1993.

Scholl, Sophie, *Lettres de Sophie Scholl,* Paris, 1953.

Schönhagen, Benigna, 'Weinn keener etwas tut, dunner ändert sich nie etwas': Die Weisse Rose und Stuttgart', in Marlene P. Hiller (ed.), *Stuttgart im Zweitten Weltkreig,* Gerlingen, 1989, pp.247–254.

Schorocht, Claudia, *Philosophie an den Bayerischen Universitäten,* Erlangen, 1990.

Schüler, Barbara, *'Im Geiste der Gemordeten': Die Weisse Rose und ihre Wirking in der Nachkriegszeit,* Paderborn, 2000.

Shirer, William, *Berlin Diary: The journal of a Foreign Correspondent, 1934–1941,* New York, 1941.

Siefken, Hinrich (ed.), *Die Weisse Rose: Student Resistance to National Socialism,* Nottingham, 1991.

Siefken, Hinrich, *Die Weisse Rose und ihre Flugblätter: Dokumente, Text, Lebensbilder, Erläuterungen,* Manchester, 1994.

Steffahn, Harald, *Die Weisse Rose,* Hamburg, 1992.

Stephenson, Jill, *The Nazi Organisation of Women,* London, 1981.

Stephenson, Jill, 'Women's Labor Service in Nazi Germany', *Central European History,* vol.15, 1982, pp.241–265.

Stephenson, Jill, *Hitler's Home Front: Württemberg under the Nazis,* London, 2006.

Tuchel, Johannes, 'Von der Front in den Widerstand'?: Überlegungen zu Detlef Balds Neuerscheinung über die Weisse Rose' in Friedrich Veitl (ed.), *Zeitschrift fur Geschichtswissenschaft Heft 11',* Berlin, 2003, pp.1022–1045.

Tuchel, Johannes and Steinbach, Peter, *Widerstand in Deutschland, 1933–1945,* Munich, 1997.

Walker, Lawrence D., *Hitler Youth and Catholic Youth, 1933–1936: A Study of Totalitarian Conquest,* Washington, 1970.

Webster, Charles and Noble, Frankland, *The Strategic Air Offensive Against Germany, 1939–1945* (4 vols), 1961.

Sources and Bibliography

Welch, David, *The Third Reich: Politics and Propaganda*, London, 2002.

Welch, David, 'Propaganda and Indoctrination in the Third Reich: Success or Failure', *European History Quarterly*, vol.17, 1987, pp.403–422.

Vinke, Hermann, *The Short Life of Sophie Scholl*, New York, 1984.

Weyrauch, Walter Otto, 'Gestapo Informants: Fact and Theory of Undercover Operations', *Columbia Journal of Transnational Law*, vol 24, 1986, pp.554–596.

Zankel, Sönke, *Die Weisse Rose war nur der Anfang*, Cologne, 2006.

Zankel, Sönke, *Mit flugblättern gegen Hitler: der Widerstandskreis um Hans Scholl und Alexander Schmorell*, Cologne, 2008.

Ziegler, Armin, *Eugen Grimminger: Widerständler und Genossenschaftspionier*, Crailsheim, 2000.

ACKNOWLEDGEMENTS

Any book based on detailed archival research inevitably means a number of debts of gratitude have accumulated. I will now acknowledge them.

I am grateful to the following for allowing me full access to unpublished material in their possession or of which they own copyright, in particular the Insitüt fur Zeitgeschichte (IfZ), Munich, the depository of the Scholl-Aicher archive – the essential archive for any study of the White Rose. The copyright in the letters and diaries of Scholl family resides with Manuel Aicher and Elisabeth Hartnagel. I would additionally like to thank Manuel Aicher warmly for permission to use the wonderful photographs of Sophie and Hans Scholl in this volume. All photographs of Hans and Sophie Scholl © Manuel Aicher. The other archives consulted are all acknowledged in the bibliography and endnotes.

I would like to thank all those interviewed for this project, but especially Elisabeth Hartnagel and Traute Lafrenz-Page, whose input was enormously important. I would very much like to thank Klaus Schlaier, the manager of Einstein House in Ulm, who has been extraordinarily valuable in providing answers to my numerous questions. His knowledge of the subject is immense and has helped me in so many ways. Ursula Kaufmann of the White Rose Foundation, Munich, has been a tremendous help in supplying photographs and putting me in touch with the holders of copyrighted photographic material. All copyrights are fully acknowledged in the photo section.

I am extremely indebted to Marc Rothemund, the director of *Sophie Scholl: The Final Days*. I met him in 2005 while we were both being interviewed for 'Film 2005'. I found his film an inspiration for this biography. It made me want to find out how Sophie reached that dramatic ending to her life. I must also single out for a very special mention Tom Webber, the producer of the BBC 'Film' series. Tom was the source of the idea of the final 'Legacy' chapter and he also found the brilliant Churchill quotation at the beginning of the book. Thanks also to Cat Lewis of Nine Lives Media, who is developing a project based on my research into Sophie Scholl. The monumental scholarship of Professor Richard Evans has been a further inspiration during the completion of the project.

In preparing the paperback version of this biography I have benefited at every point in exchanging documents, ideas and criticism with the leading German scholar Jakob Knab, who has shared with me his crucial views on the religious influences on Sophie Scholl and the White Rose. Thanks to his valuable input I feel this version now gives proper emphasis to the religious nature of Sophie's journey. I have come to know Jakob very well in the past year, and his eye for detail and rigorous approach to scholarship and writing are truly remarkable, and his generosity of spirit is inspiring.

A number of people have offered enormously valuable assistance in the translation and interpretation of German documents and letters, most notably James West, Emily West, Milan Hauner and Klaus Schliair. Many of the issues in the life of Sophie and Hans Scholl impinge on legal history and I have benefited greatly in that regard from the expertise of Lori Charlesworth.

I would like to thank the following German experts for answering my detailed queries: Johannes Tuchel, the Director of the Museum of Resistance in Berlin; Dr Peter Kelpfish; Dr Rainer Stahlschmidt; and Dr Albrecht Ernst.

I would also like to thank: John Cochrane, Mike Benbough-Jackson, Tony Webster, David Clampin, Margaret Edwards, Tamsin Spargo, Rex Li, Lord David Alton, Andrew Roberts and Dermot Fenlon.

Simon Hamlet at The History Press has been a great supporter of the project and a very good person to work with.

Most of all I would like to thank Ann for her support throughout this project. She helped me enormously in reaching a very strict deadline. I have written many books, but this one has been an extraordinary experience and I will never forget it as long as I live.

The White Rose Foundation, Munich is committed to fighting human rights injustice all over the world and if you would like to find out details of how to become a member or to make a donation, contact info@weisse-rose-stiftung.de.

Thanks to the many kind readers who have sent such lovely letters to me saying they were deeply moved by the book.

INDEX